Gary L. Tandy
1995

*In recognition of their formative influence on our lives,*
*this book is gratefully dedicated to our parents,*
*Jack and Phyllis Middleton and Jean Marshall.*

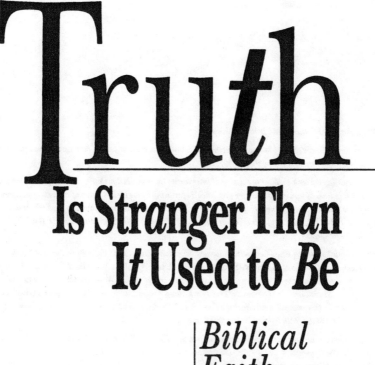

# Truth
## Is Stranger Than It Used to Be

*Biblical
Faith
in a
Postmodern
Age*

J. Richard Middleton & Brian J. Walsh

**InterVarsity Press**
Downers Grove, Illinois

InterVarsity Press® is the book-publishing division of InterVarsity Christian Fellowship®, a student movement active on campus at hundreds of universities, colleges and schools of nursing in the United States of America, and a member movement of the International Fellowship of Evangelical Students. For information about local and regional activities, write Public Relations Dept., InterVarsity Christian Fellowship, 6400 Schroeder Rd., P.O. Box 7895, Madison, WI 53707-7895.

Cover illustration: Roberta Polfus
ISBN 0-8308-1856-1

Printed in the United States of America ∞

**Library of Congress Cataloging-in-Publication Data**

Middleton, J. Richard, 1955-
   Truth is stranger than it used to be: biblical faith in a
postmodern age/J. Richard Middleton and Brian J. Walsh.
     p.   cm.
   Includes bibliographical references.
   ISBN 0-8308-1856-1
   1. Theology, Doctrinal—History—20th century.  2. Postmodernism—
Religious aspects—Christianity.  3. Evangelicalism.  I. Walsh,
Brian J., 1953-  . II. Title.
BT28.M494  1995
230'.09'04—dc20
                                95-5621
                                  CIP

| 19 | 18 | 17 | 16 | 15 | 14 | 13 | 12 | 11 | 10 | 9 | 8 | 7 | 6 | 5 | 4 | 3 | 2 | 1 |
|----|----|----|----|----|----|----|----|----|----|----|----|----|----|----|----|----|----|----|
| 11 | 10 | 09 | 08 | 07 | 06 | 05 | 04 | 03 | 02 | 01 | 00 | 99 | 98 | 97 | 96 | 95 | | |

# Preface

This book has its beginning in our desire to revise and thoroughly update our earlier book *The Transforming Vision*. We wanted to deepen our analysis of the decline of modernity in light of the cultural shift to what many have named "post-modernity." And we wanted to do so by means of a rearticulation of the biblical worldview that would attend to its narrative character and its rootedness in God's response to human suffering, communicated especially through the story of the exodus. Even apart from the issue of postmodernity, our inattention to these issues in *The Transforming Vision* led to a serious lacuna that we wanted to remedy.

Our publisher, however, wisely counseled against a revision and proposed instead that we write a totally new book specifically addressing the postmodern shift. *Truth Is Stranger Than It Used to Be* is the result. The title connects directly with the two main parts of the book. In part one, "The Postmodern Condition," we sketch our discernment of postmodernity via the four worldview questions we proposed in *The Transforming Vision*. Following a historical overview of the shift from modernity to postmodernity in chapter one, we inquire in chapters two through four concerning the main answers current in postmodern culture and among postmodern theorists concerning our sense of place or world (where are we?), identity or selfhood (who are we?) and the overall story we tell concerning good and evil (what's wrong? and what's the remedy?). Central to this part of the book is the dominant postmodern recognition that world, self and story are all human (social) constructs. Since all worldviews on a postmodern reading are merely human inventions, decisively conditioned by the social context in which they occur, and certainly not given to us by either nature or revelation, any "truth" we claim for our cherished positions must be kept strictly in quotation marks. This widespread constructivist epistemology is highlighted in the title, *Truth Is Stranger Than It Used to Be.*

But the title connects also to part two, "The Resources of Scripture," in which we bring the biblical worldview to bear on the postmodern condition. Having already suggested biblical answers to the four worldview questions in *The Transforming Vision,* here we attempt to nuance those answers by rereading the Bible in light of postmodern concerns (chapters five through seven), concluding the book with methodological reflections on how the Bible authorizes the church's praxis (chapter eight). The central question raised in part two is, Do the Scriptures have the resources to address the postmodern condition, speaking a redemptive word of healing for our times? We believe that they do, though our reading of the biblical text is not unaffected by postmodernity. We have found that our postmodern situation, although undoubtedly a time of crisis and tragedy, is also heuristic for a faithful reading of Scripture, pointing us to exciting dimensions of the biblical text of which we were previously unaware. Indeed, a faithful and sensitive submission to the biblical text as canonical discloses a coherent and empowering vision that stands in some tension with much popular Christian theology. It is not only postmodern constructivist epistemology but also the truth of the Bible that is stranger than it used to be.

As with *The Transforming Vision,* we have found coauthorship of this book to be an empowering experience. If there is something called truth—as strange as that truth may be—then it is never glimpsed or realized by solitary Cartesian knowers. Truth is sought and found only in community. Both the communal writing process and the cross-fertilization of ideas in coteaching and presenting this material to a variety of audiences over the last few years have produced a far better book than either of us could have written on our own. We therefore want to thank the audiences and students who have interacted with these ideas as they were aborning, for helping us clarify and work through the implications of our nascent reflections on postmodernity.

We are also mindful of the support and contributions of many other people without whom this book could not have been written. Foremost among the intellectual influences on our lives and writing are James Olthuis, our colleague and senior member in philosophical theology at the Institute for Christian Studies, Old Testament scholars Walter Brueggemann of Columbia Theological Seminary and Werner Lemke of Colgate Rochester Divinity School, New Testament scholar and dean of Lichfield Cathedral Tom Wright, and Canadian singer/songwriter Bruce

Cockburn. The marks of each of these "mentors" is evident throughout this book for those with eyes to see.

Profound thanks are also due to our parents, Jack and Phyllis Middleton and Jean Marshall; to our wives, Marcia Middleton and Sylvia Keesmaat; and to our children, Jubal Bartley-Walsh (fourteen years), Andrew Middleton (eight years), Kevin Middleton (one and a half years) and Madeleine Keesmaat Walsh, newly born at the time of this writing. The persistent love of our families, and even the expectation of the new arrival, has been a mark of grace in our lives.

We are also aware of God's guidance and empowerment through the support of two amazing church communities, Harbour Fellowship in St. Catharines and the Church of the Redeemer in Toronto. The many friendships, the opportunities for ministry and the energizing vision of these faithful local embodiments of Christ's love have been a deep source of healing and renewal for each of us. We especially want to thank Harbour Fellowship for the gracious donation of office space and secretarial support and St. Catharines for the use of photocopy and laser-printing services, which together with the office support of the Institute for Christian Studies in Toronto have greatly diminished the problems inherent in writing a book in cities some 120 kilometers apart.

Special mention must also be made of our student Mat Klemp for his painstaking work in putting together the index. His intimate knowledge of this manuscript (well beyond that needed for an index) has made him a creative dialogue partner in and out of class. Finally, a wise and supportive editor is a gift. Rodney Clapp believed in this project from the beginning, gave insightful editorial advice on the manuscript and showed tremendous patience when it became clear it was taking far longer than we had projected. For Rodney's constant encouragement, sparkling wit and growing friendship we are deeply grateful.

*St. Catherines*
*Easter 1995*

# Part I/The Postmodern Condition

# 1/The Crisis of Our Times

In one of the specialty coffee shops that we frequent in Toronto there has been an advertising campaign for a medium roast from Costa Rica. This coffee is called El Conquistador. Although we like medium roast coffees, we've resisted buying this one. The problem is not primarily a matter of economics and social justice. Although we know that workers in the coffee fields of most Latin American countries seldom get a fair return on their labor, this coffee is from Costa Rica, something of a model of democracy in Central America. No, the problem is deeper than concerns about economic justice; it is a problem of *image*. This coffee has a bad name. El Conquistador (the conqueror) isn't exactly what you could call a politically correct name. In fact, anyone aware of the Spanish (to say nothing of the French and English) conquest of the New World would be somewhat uneasy drinking a coffee that glories in the memory of the conquerors.

## Columbus and the Postmodern Turn
This conquest was very much on our minds during 1992. That was the year we

"celebrated" the 500th anniversary of the "discovery" of America by Christopher
Columbus. But not everyone believed there was cause for celebration. Parades,
worship services and other festivities throughout the Western hemisphere were
disrupted by people who thought that Columbus and the period of history he
inaugurated ought not be valorized. *1492: The Conquest of Paradise:* the title of the
blockbuster film that marks the anniversary gets it right, say the aboriginal peoples
of the Americas. What it has been all about is conquest.[1] The native peoples of the
Americas insist that 1992 marks the anniversary of 500 years not of glorious discovery but of cruelty, lies, oppression, genocide and the wanton rape of what was truly
a paradise.[2]

We are not going to attempt to adjudicate the debate concerning Columbus.[3] Our
concern in this book is the broader one of describing and evaluating the emerging
cultural phenomenon known as postmodernity and suggesting how Christians can
respond to this development with cultural integrity in a way that maintains a vibrant
fidelity to Scripture and brings personal and social healing. The significance of the
Columbus debate is that it illustrates the shift in worldview and cultural sensibility
from the modern to the postmodern world.

Not very long ago language about Columbus "discovering" America was essentially unproblematic. We all knew that he didn't really discover America and that
there were in fact inhabitants here thousands of years before who had developed
very sophisticated societies. Nevertheless, we still used the language of discovery and
this in at least two senses—geographical and historical.[4] In his "discovery" Columbus not only "ruptured the familiar and surveyable geography of the Middle Ages"[5]
but also opened up a new world of human possibility, the beginning of a new epoch
in human history. And every time we celebrated Columbus Day or learned about
Columbus in elementary school it was this new epoch that we commemorated.

But the five hundredth anniversary of this new epoch was disrupted by those who
told us that it wasn't all it was cracked up to be. They didn't celebrate; they mourned.
Instead of joy, their voices were raised in anger. They argued that our response to
the Columbus story should be shame, not pride. Why is it that we did not hear this
kind of critical questioning of Columbus when we were in elementary school? What
is the significance of this questioning? Could it be that such questioning is indicative
of an epochal shift in cultural sensibility? Philosopher Albert Borgmann suggests
that all shifts in historical periods in the Western world "have issued from a rising
sentiment of disaffinity, from a growing feeling that the kinship with what had gone
before was being attenuated and lost."[6] This certainly characterized the age of

Columbus in relation to the medieval period, and it seems to characterize our own. The fact that we now hear loud criticism of the Columbus era in Western history is one piece of evidence that a major cultural shift is afoot. "An epoch approaches its end," Borgmann goes on to say, "when its fundamental conviction begins to weaken and no longer inspires enthusiasm among its advocates."[7] The onset of postmodernity could be described as the loss of enthusiasm in the grounding convictions of modernity.

There are two reasons the Columbus controversy signals the end of modernity. The first is that the classical form of the Columbus story embodies the worldview that was once central and unproblematic in the West but is now rapidly losing its hold on the heart of our culture. The second reason is that an alternative version of the Columbus story, the version of the aboriginal peoples, is increasingly being told and *heard* when previously it had been effectively silenced.

We will return to this second point. But first, what is the worldview embodied in the Columbus story?

In *The Transforming Vision* we suggested that worldviews give faith answers to a set of ultimate and grounding questions. Those questions might be formulated as (1) *Where are we?* or What is the nature of the reality in which we find ourselves? (2) *Who are we?* or What is the nature and task of human beings? (3) *What's wrong?* or How do we understand and account for evil and brokenness? and (4) *What's the remedy?* or How do we find a path through our brokenness to wholeness?[8]

How does the Columbus story answer those questions? In a rough-and-ready way we might summarize the answers as follows:

1. *Where are we?* We are in the New World, the lost Eden which has now been found.[9] We are in a new world of wealth and promise that leaves behind the shackles of medieval Europe. We are in a world that is ripe for the taking and that offers up its riches to those who know how to exploit them.[10]

2. *Who are we?* We are the conquistadors. We are the conquerors who have taken this wild land inhabited by savages and tamed it. Those of us who are North Americans, especially, have reaped great blessings from this promised land.

3. *What's wrong?* Our progress has been impeded in the past by the static and hierarchical society of medieval Europe, and in the present it is further threatened by the primitiveness of the "Indians," combined with the wildness of these continents.

4. *What's the remedy?* We must release ourselves from the social, ecclesiastical and economic shackles of Europe and conquer the peoples and lands of the Americas

so we can build a progressive society. Only then will the nation of America be a city shining on a hill, and this continent the promised land.

This is what the Columbus story has taught us. Admittedly something of a caricature, this is nevertheless the basic shape of the worldview that the story embodies and communicates. The problem in the wake of the 500th anniversary of Columbus is that many of us don't believe it anymore. The story no longer rings true. Native peoples, of course, never did believe it. And this leads us to the second reason the Columbus controversy is indicative of a wide-ranging cultural shift.

The voice that is heard above all others in the Columbus controversy is that of the aboriginal peoples of the Americas. It is from their perspective, more than any other, that the Columbus story is being questioned. And it is from their angle that history is being rewritten.[11] This indicates, in our opinion, a profound cultural shift. It is not just that the Columbus story is being questioned or retold; more fundamental is the fact that aboriginal voices now have a significant hearing among us. Less than a generation ago few North Americans took seriously how native peoples might want to tell the story of the last 500 years. We simply did not think that they had anything to say to us that might be even remotely interesting. But now it is *their* voice that has set the definitive agenda for a culture-wide discussion. Why is this so? In a society that from its inception has honored "freedom of speech" and proudly espoused a liberal notion of tolerating people from different races and religions, why is it that only recently alternative voices have begun to be heard?

Of course, it is not just native peoples who are raising their voices in our society. The local news reports in any major American city will include items about prostitutes organizing to protest police harassment, black students complaining about insufficient funds for black cultural studies at high schools and colleges, and homosexuals campaigning for equal rights before the law. In our society gays are openly and militantly out of the closet, African-Americans are insisting that they have an ancient culture worthy of study and promotion, prostitutes demand the right to ply their trade with police protection, and native peoples are claiming that not only do they have a more honest way of telling the story of the last 500 years but they also have wisdom to impart to the dominant colonial culture. Claims such as these, whatever their relative merit, are causing deep divisions within our society, often within our churches and families.[12] And they can be overwhelming for those of us trying to find a redemptive Christian way in the midst of our cultural confusion. But beyond the question of the merits of these claims, it is culturally significant today that these groups have a voice *at all* in our society. Past "liberal" notions of tolerance and freedom of speech simply did not include views, traditions and practices of people as contrary to the mainstream as gays, African-Americans, prostitutes and Native Americans.

All of that has now changed. A characteristic feature of postmodern debates in a variety of cultural arenas is the insistence on the hearing of alternative voices. For example, debates about college curricula have been dominated by the question of the voice of "other cultures." What is the "canon" of literature with which all educated people should be familiar? Should it include the writings of previously marginalized groups which have not been widely read?[13] Similar debates have challenged the exhibition policies of art museums. Are these policies truly open to marginalized groups? Do the "masters" of the Western art tradition work from a perspective that is often racist and sexist?[14] And these debates extend to the very status of law in our judicial system. What are the foundational assumptions of our laws? Who benefits from the legal system, and why?[15]

What we are witnessing is nothing less than a challenge to the center of our society from the margins. In this critique of dominant cultural institutions such as universities, art galleries, museums and the legal system itself, we are now hearing from those previously voiceless, invisible and unrepresented. As psychologist Kenneth Gergen puts it, the postmodern condition "is marked by a plurality of voices vying for the right to reality."[16] Although this might at first appear to be a healthy opening up of our culture in such a way that the voiceless are finally heard, this opening up is something of a double-edged sword. When all those who were voiceless under modernity begin articulating their claims in a postmodern situation, the result is a bewildering cacophony. Psychologically, this cacophony can be confusing, disorienting and frightening. And it raises profound questions concerning the validity and limits of pluralism in a postmodern context.

But to understand this postmodern context in its depth (and certainly to answer normative questions about the validity of postmodern pluralism) we must first recount (and evaluate) the modernity that it supplants.

### A Spirit of Progress

The difficulty in providing a precise description of postmodernity is only increased by the difficulty in describing modernity itself. Even dating the *modern* period is a risky business. Although many postmodern writers treat modernity as synonymous with the Enlightenment, thus tracing its beginning to the eighteenth century, we have argued in *The Transforming Vision* that the basic impulses of the modern worldview are much earlier.[17] In our opinion, somewhere between 1470 (the beginning of the Italian Renaissance) and 1700 (the start of the Enlightenment) the modern world was born. Perhaps we could claim 1492 as the origin of the modern period, which would give us an epoch that was half a millennium long. As risky as dating modernity is, characterizing it is more so. Any characterization opens us up to charges of reducing the numerous intellectual and cultural movements during that period to one monolithic *essence*. Although this is a genuine danger, it is, nonetheless, appropriate to speak of the modern epoch as characterized by a dominant *spirit*.[18] Describing this spirit is a matter not simply of historical precision, but also of spiritual discernment. It is only by first discerning the spirit of modernity that we will then be able to understand and respond to the spirit (or spirits) of *post*modernity in an adequate manner.

Perhaps the most representative intellectual proponent of the spirit of modernity in the North American context was John Dewey, whose philosophy of education has permeated the public school system in North America. In *Reconstruction in Philosophy* Dewey described the spirit of modern life in terms of four changes from the premodern period in Western history. First of all, modernity is no longer preoccupied with the supernatural, but rather delights in the natural, the this-worldly and the secular. Secondly, instead of the medieval emphasis on submission to ecclesiastical authority, "there is a growing belief in the power of individual minds, guided by methods of observation, experience and reflection, to attain the truths needed for the guidance of life." In the third place, the modern period is characterized by belief in progress. Dewey puts it this way: "The future rather than the past dominates the imagination. The Golden Age lies ahead of us not behind us." Indeed, "Man is capable, if he will but exercise the required courage, intelligence and effort, of shaping his own fate." And fourthly, "the patient and experimental study of nature, bearing fruit in inventions which control nature and subdue her forces to social use, is the method by which progress is made."[19]

If we were to describe the overall cultural spirit or mood pervading Dewey's description of modernity, we would say that Dewey's modern "man" (the language is appropriately exclusivist[20]) is self-assured and in control of his own destiny. This man knows what he knows and he knows it with certainty because he knows it scientifically. He needs no authority outside of himself because he is autonomous, a law or authority unto himself. And he certainly needs no salvation outside of himself. Once he has liberated himself from past authorities and superstitions all he needs is the courage to follow his reason. With such courage and the employment of his rational abilities, he will, together with all other rational men, undoubtedly experience and enjoy the fruit of human progress.[21]

This is indeed a robust, confident worldview! Like our portrayal of the Columbus story, to which the modern worldview provides the backdrop, our description here is also something of a caricature. There are, of course, complexities that deserve further explication and critique. But the heart of the matter, and therefore our focus in this chapter, is that the spirit of modernity is a spirit of progress. Progress, which is what the Columbus story is fundamentally about, has long been recognized by historians as the "dominant motif in Western society,"[22] even as "the working faith of our civilization."[23] This recognition is strangely ironic, since modern people have characteristically claimed to have entered a new stage in cultural evolution that left the childishness of faith behind. Nevertheless, the progress ideal functions as an article of faith, the unifying commitment or civil religion of Western civilization.

The progress ideal is not just a faith; it tells a story. In this it bears striking resemblance to the role that "myths" (or founding stories) play in premodern societies. In the myth of progress, history begins with Egypt and Greece (*not* India and China, and *certainly not* sub-Saharan Africa!) and unfolds as a story of cumulative development leading up to modern times and to Western culture.[24]

### Modernity and the Tower of Babel

But the progress myth, although capable of bringing (some) classical civilizations under its purview, typically focuses on the epoch inaugurated by Columbus: the modern era. The myth of progress started with a grand dream or vision that began to emerge only in the fifteenth century. This cultural aspiration, symbolized by Columbus's quest for a new ocean route to Asia, looked not to the past and the known but to the future and the unknown. It was a bold and daring vision, one remarkably similar to that of the builders of the tower of Babel. Just as the story of Babel (recounted in Genesis 11:1-9) summarizes the primordial cultural aspirations of the human race in terms of the building of "a city with a tower reaching to the heavens," so we could characterize the modern Western dream of progress as the building of a vast, towering civilization, a social and cultural accomplishment of immense, even mythic proportions.[25]

People's dreams and aspirations have always been embodied in cities, buildings and especially towers. This is as true of the tower of Babel as it is of the cathedral at Chartres, the Eiffel Tower, the pyramids at Giza, the Toronto CN Tower or the World Trade Center in New York City. Such towering accomplishments do not happen by accident. They begin with a dream of what could be, which is then progressively embodied in the concrete, historical actions of vast numbers of people.

Like the architects of modernity, the builders of Babel had a grand aspiration: "Come, let us build ourselves a city, and a tower with its top in the heavens, and let us make a name for ourselves; otherwise we shall be scattered abroad upon the face of the whole earth" (Gen 11:4 NRSV). This twofold aspiration, on the surface, seems quite legitimate. It certainly is noncontroversial in terms of modernity.

On the one hand, these builders desired fame, distinction and glory. They dreamed of reaching heights no one had ever attained before and thus of making a name for themselves. These were no wimps, thinking timidly of constructing low-lying buildings. Their agenda did not include passive architecture, which blended naturally in with the lay of the land or the vegetation. On the contrary, these builders wanted to *stand out* and be noticed. For them, the sky was the limit. It is amazing how *modern* the tower of Babel sounds.

On the other hand, these builders desired cultural and social cohesion. Instead of scattering and fragmenting into small unproductive groups, they dreamed of the unity of the human race. In modern times this became the dream of a new society, where there would be social harmony, freedom from disease and prosperity for all.

In the fifteenth century this was a very daring and risky dream, since the dream was so new and the dreamers so few. But then the vision began to spread. In ever-increasing numbers people began to build that towering city which we have named modernity, the burgeoning culture of modern Western civilization. As the myth of progress tells it, that tower or building of modernity grew through three cumulative levels, three progressive floors or stories, as it rose boldly into the sky.

The first or ground floor of the building of modernity was science. Beginning with the scientific revolution in the sixteenth and seventeenth centuries in Europe and especially in England, right up to the present day, science has laid the foundation of modern progress. If only we could understand the world! If only we could learn the secrets of nature, said Francis Bacon, early in the seventeenth century. Then we could unlock so much benefit for human beings. Although Bacon was not himself a great scientist, he was a tremendous popularizer of science. And today it is Francis Bacon to whom we attribute the "scientific method," the whole notion of doing experiments, making inductive generalizations and testing them so they can be verified or falsified.[26] Science, says the modern myth of progress, is the ground floor in the towering dream of Western civilization.

After the seventeenth century, the age of the scientific revolution, came the eighteenth century, the age of "enlightenment," when we began, says the myth, to reap the fruits of scientific rationality and emerge from the darkness of superstition.[27] It was also the age of the industrial revolution: the age of the machine, of factories, of technology and of the beginnings of mass production. Scientific understanding of the way nature works (on the model of the machine) was applied in innovative ways to control and harness nature for our benefit. Technology thus constitutes the second floor in the Western building of progress. Of course, technology in one sense is conterminous with human beings. We've always had tools—we didn't have to wait for the eighteenth century for knives, hammers, levers and pulleys, or the wheel. But suddenly, beginning in the eighteenth century and continuing to the present day, we have the invention of complex machines—steam engines, internal combustion engines, jet engines, fusion drives and computers—in ever-increasing complexity and efficiency. Through our scientific understanding of nature and our insightful application of this understanding, we can control the very forces of nature. Through modern technology we can split the atom and store vast and complex information systems on microchips. If the first floor gave us insight and understanding, this second floor gives us power. It allows us mastery over our environment.[28]

But the building didn't stop there. What did we do with this insight and power we had acquired? According to our founding myth, we decided to use it for human benefit, to foster social well-being. Science and technology were harnessed to produce wealth, to raise the standard of living and better the human race. And so we have the origin of the market economy, which replaced the earlier feudal organization of society. By the start of the nineteenth century, the market, with its roots in the entrepreneurial spirit and the profit motive, had come into ascendancy in the West. So economic growth, seen as the purpose and raison d'être of industrial and scientific progress, became the third floor of the building of Western culture, the floor to which everything led, the floor which was to be the culmination of the whole enterprise.[29]

Imagine a building, a city, a society, an entire civilization in which ignorance was overcome, disease was cured, poverty was eradicated, war was rendered obsolete, there were no material or social needs and which continually improved itself! A civilization in which people would be genuinely happy and truly free—for the first time in history.

## A Culture of Confidence

To get a sense of how the dream of modernity inspired deep excitement in Western culture, consider the descriptions of the Crystal Palace Exhibition in Hyde Park, London, in the middle of the nineteenth century. This exhibition (a precursor of the world fairs of the late-nineteenth and twentieth centuries) was a celebration of the marvels of the modern age. After attending the opening of that exhilarating public event on May 1, 1851, even Queen Victoria wrote in her diary of being caught up in something of more significance than the royal office. From her initial glimpse of the transept, accompanied by the milling crowds and blast of trumpets, to her approach to the raised dais with its unoccupied chair (symbolizing the divine presence) in front of which was a crystal fountain (reminiscent of the "sea of glass, like crystal" in Rev 4:6), the British monarch was profoundly moved. It "was magical," she wrote, "so vast, so glorious, so touching. One felt—as so many did whom I have since spoken to—filled with devotion, more so than by any [religious] service I have ever heard." But this religious sense of awe was not vague or generalized. It was focused on the accomplishments of "this 'peace festival,'" which united the industry of all nations of the earth."

*The Times* (May 2, 1851) described the proceedings in, if anything, an even more awestruck tone. "There was yesterday witnessed a sight the like of which has never happened before and which in the nature of things can never be repeated." What was it that generated this incomparable sense of awe? Nothing less than the exhibition of "all that is useful or beautiful in nature or in art." Noting "the sense of wonder and even of mystery" which surged within the onlookers, the article went on to describe the glittering overhead arch as "far more lofty and spacious than the vaults of even our noblest cathedrals." But the devotional, religious imagery was heightened when the writer (alluding perhaps to 1 Cor 2:9) depicted the magnificence of the building, the art treasures on display and the solemn crowds as conspiring "to suggest something even more than sense could scan, or imagination attain." This eschatological allusion was then brought out into the open by the concluding comparison of the entire exhibition with "that day when all ages and climes shall be gathered round that Throne of their Maker." Thus human ingenuity ushers in the eschaton!

But both *The Times* and the Queen were only echoing the vision of Prince Albert himself (who had organized the exhibition) in his public speech on the opening day. "Nobody who has paid any attention to the peculiar features of our present era," he passionately asserted, "will doubt for a moment that we are living at a period of most wonderful transition, which tends rapidly to accomplish that great end to which indeed all history points—the realization of the unity of mankind." Not only do these words self-consciously place the achievements of the nineteenth century at the pinnacle of human progress, but they boldly confess that the aspiration of the builders of Babel was finally within reach.[30]

What was envisioned by increasing numbers of people, beginning in the fifteenth century, gaining momentum in the seventeenth century and culminating in the nineteenth century, was a veritable utopia of prosperity and progress in which the whole human race would be united. This vision, embodied in the progress myth, describes the essential contours of the cultural imagination and spiritual driving force of the West.[31] Human progress is not only possible but inevitable, we have come to believe, if only we allow autonomous reason the freedom to investigate our world scientifically. By this free and open investigation, we have confidently believed, humanity will be able to acquire the technological power necessary to control nature and bring about the ultimate human goal: increased economic consumption and affluence, with resulting peace, fulfillment and security.[32]

Until very recently this myth has been engraved in our grade-school textbooks, proclaimed in corporate advertising, phallically erected in towering office buildings, preached from both political and ecclesiastical pulpits and portrayed by the situation comedies, dramas and news broadcasts of the popular media.[33] This is a myth that has been woven into the fabric of our common Western existence. Langdon Gilkey summarizes well the role of the progress myth in our culture:

> It helps us determine what is creative and what is not in the world, and what our own priorities are or should be. It tells us what to defend and why we defend it. It gives meaning to our work, confidence in the midst of failure, and hope in the face of tragedy. . . . It helps us to distinguish good from evil forces in the world around us, and gives us confidence in the ultimate victory of good over evil in history. *Above all, it tells us who we are in history and why we are here.* It forms the ultimate set of presuppositions for most of our aims and so our patterns of education.[34]

Where are we? Who are we? What's wrong? What is the remedy? These are all worldview questions that the progress ideal could answer with confidence.

Modernity has answered the Where are we? question with a robust epistemological and technological self-confidence. We are in a world of natural resources that can be known objectively by means of the scientific method and controlled by technological power. Indeed, as Bacon said, "Knowledge *is* power." According to

the modern worldview we know what reality is, and we know how to investigate,
understand and control it.

This epistemological self-confidence is paralleled in an anthropological self-assuredness. Who are we? We are *homo autonomous.* Who is it that can know, investigate, understand and control reality so self-confidently? A self-secure, self-formed
and self-conscious subject. Autonomous human beings are the self-normed masters
not only of their own destiny but of the destiny of the world.

If this is where we are and who we are, then the answer to What's wrong? will
be discerned in anything that impedes our autonomy, inhibits our progress and
threatens our sense of world mastery. But the What's wrong? question also assumes
at least an implicit answer to its corollary, What's right? or What's the remedy? In
other words, to discern brokenness and evil we must have some implicit idea of
normativity or goodness and how this is to be achieved.

The modern worldview has provided a convincing and self-justifying answer to
this final question. Autonomous subjects, scientifically grasping and technologically
controlling and transforming the world, unimpeded by threats such as tradition,
ignorance and superstition, devise their own remedy. In the modern era we are our
own saviors. And we effect our salvation in secular redemptive history through the
ineluctable and inevitable march of progress. This is the heart of modernity's historical self-confidence.

### The Trouble with Modernity

Postmodernity, however, is no longer so self-confident. Although the progress myth
offered us, in the words of Christian songwriter Bruce Cockburn, a

> sweet fantasia of the safe home
>
> Where nobody has to scrape for honey at the bottom of the comb
>
> Where every actor understands the scene
>
> And nobody ever means to be mean,[35]

it has become ever more evident at the end of the twentieth century that this has
been a pipe dream. True, it is a story that many still (insistently) tell, but fewer are
able to believe it. The progress myth is losing its power. These days it sounds like
a fairy tale, too good to be true. It rings false to our ears. Its remaining proponents
sound like old-time street-corner evangelists, out of touch with reality, mouthing
timeworn phrases about "prosperity" and "economic recovery" while the passersby
cynically ignore them or look back nostalgically, dimly remembering the good old
days.

The trouble with the progress myth is that it doesn't tell the whole story. It is incomplete, and doubly so. It leaves out, first of all, the twentieth century. This account says nothing about the fourth floor of the building, the floor on which we are now standing. And second, what about the foundation? What is the edifice of Western progress built on?

An important clue to the nature of this foundation is found in the amazing self-confidence typical of the modern era. As John Dewey noted in his characterization of modernity, the modern eschatological vision of human betterment and progress is to be achieved solely by *human beings* (independent of divine help), as they attempt individually and collectively to understand and control nature. This is a fundamentally *humanistic* vision.

But, we may ask, what is wrong with that? Is there anything wrong with believing in ourselves? In our own abilities? Is there anything wrong with having an optimistic view of human nature? And of human history? Is there anything wrong with believing we can build a humane, peaceful, healthy, prosperous society? Not just sitting passively on our haunches and waiting for a miracle, but working our own miracles? Is there anything wrong with growing up as modern people and standing on our own feet? And putting behind us childish things, like fairy stories from the Bible about the new Jerusalem with streets of gold? Or, if not putting it behind us, at least separating that "religious" vision of heaven hereafter from what *we* can accomplish here on earth? Is there anything wrong with *surpassing* the biblical vision of "streets of gold"—if we can? When we will have finished building our city, "the streets will be platinum, never mind gold!"[36]

By now it has become evident what the foundation of this tower is. What is it that lies beneath the ground floor? Nothing but our own strong shoulders. We are carrying this building on our backs, like Atlas. Western culture is founded on human *autonomy*. This tower is built on a foundation of radical, self-determining freedom. But far from being a valid, life-enhancing freedom, this very closely resembles what is described in Genesis 3 as the primal human sin, which results in death. Autonomy, that is, declaring our moral independence from our Creator and setting ourselves up as the masters of our fate, is symbolized in Genesis 3 by the eating of "the tree of the knowledge of good and evil" (Gen 2:17). It means that we seek to transcend the norms offered by God and to define for ourselves, instead, the parameters or limits of right and wrong. We become quite literally autonomous: a law (*nomos*) unto ourself (*autos*).

The modern myth of progress, in other words, is rooted not simply in a faith, but in what must be judged from a biblical standpoint as a false, idolatrous faith. And if the foundation is false, then it may be that there is something false also in the account of the three floors in the building of modernity rising up as glorious human accomplishments. If the foundation of modernity is essentially idolatrous, perhaps the towering three-storied edifice constitutes an immense three-tiered idol erected in the service of an "unholy trinity."[37] In place of valuing science, technology and economic growth as the positive, though limited and relative, dimensions of God's good created world that they really are, modern Western people have historically absolutized these dimensions of life and elevated them into a triad of false gods, to which they have committed themselves for guidance and salvation. As absolutizations of that which is only relative, these false gods may be appropriately described as a triad of "isms."

*Scientism,* the first tier of the idol, corresponds to the modern belief that science functions as the omniscient source of revelation in our culture and provides us with authoritative knowledge of what is truly important. *Technicism,* the second tier, corresponds to the modern belief that the effective translation of scientific knowledge into power over and control of the creation provides us with technological omnipotence, enabling us to achieve any end we may desire. *Economism,* the golden, crowning head of the idol, corresponds to the modern belief that a rising standard of living (defined largely in economic terms) is the ultimate goal in human life and the only route to personal happiness and social harmony.

### From Autonomy to Anxiety

The trouble with idols, however, is that they are *false* gods and so cannot save us. Despite their promise of blessing, to follow them results in death. The biblical record abounds with prophetic warnings, often in highly ironic language, mocking the impotence and instability of idols. Psalm 115, for example, portrays idols as unable to speak, see, hear, smell, feel or walk and predicts that those who trust them will become like them (vv. 3-8), while Isaiah depicts idols as heavy burdens, which instead of delivering the oppressed, as the true God does, have to be carried on the shoulders of the weary (Is 46:1-7). And Jeremiah, in a particularly memorable passage, compares idols to scarecrows in a melon patch that have to be securely wired so they don't topple, presumably in a strong wind (Jer 10:3-5). Such is the shaky fate of that which is taken to be ultimate but is really the product of human hands. And woe to those who trust in such fragile "gods"!

Not only is the self-confidence of human autonomy no more stable than graven images constructed from blocks of wood or stone, but building on this foundation is a sure guarantee of crisis to come. Autonomy cannot possibly support the whole edifice of modernity. The building is rotten from the foundation up, and now, in the twentieth century, this is finally becoming manifest to its dwellers. As the engine of progress begins to run out of steam and Western self-confidence begins to wane, the building project of modernity has come to a grinding halt, prematurely, right in the middle of fourth-floor construction. But the entire fourth floor—the twentieth century—has in fact been plagued by shoddy workmanship. For those with eyes to see, the building never did match the romanticized blueprint.

It is well known, for example, that the naive optimism generated by the progress ideal of the nineteenth century was shattered first by the bombs, mustard gas and trench warfare of the Great War (1914-1918) and then by the Great Depression of the 1930s. Although committed believers in progress tried valiantly to interpret the horrendous devastation of World War I as "the war to end all wars," World War II less than twenty years later, with its twin horrors of the Holocaust and the nuclear devastation of Hiroshima and Nagasaki, seemed to put the definitive nails in the coffin of peace, if not economic progress (indeed, for a while the war stimulated the American economy).

But the crisis of modernity is perhaps best seen in the postwar existentialist movement in Europe (associated with names like Jean-Paul Sartre, Albert Camus and Karl Jaspers). Existentialist writers, whether Christian or atheist, articulated in novels, plays, essays and assorted philosophical writings a profound loss of hope and sense of angst (undefined anxiety or dread) about the meaning and purpose of life in modern times. In this they became precursors of our contemporary postmodern consciousness.[38]

And if the tortured despair of existentialism gave way to a resurgence of modern confidence in the "golden fifties" (at least in North America), the new horrors of a prolonged war in Vietnam and the student counterculture of protest in the 1960s served once more to undermine American confidence in the accomplishments of the West and to signal modernity's inevitable demise.

But these twentieth-century harbingers of impending crisis were prefigured even in the nineteenth century by the monumental pollution and the exploitation of child labor associated with the progressive and innovative English factory system, and even before that by the three hundred years of African slavery upon which European and American "progress" was built. And, for those with eyes to see, premonitions of modernity's crisis were evident as far back as Columbus's enslavement of the Indians at the very outset of the modern era.

Today postmodernity has set in with a vengeance. The dissolution of the Soviet Union, the rise of neo-Nazism in Germany, the so-called ethnic cleansing in the Balkans and the continuing recalcitrance of Saddam Hussein to the United States even after his decisive military defeat all testify not to the triumph of Western progress but to the postmodern fragmentation and tribalization of the globe.[39] Psychologist and feminist Jane Flax puts it this way:

> Western culture is in the middle of a fundamental transformation; a "shape of life" is growing old. The demise of the old is being hastened by the end of colonialism, the uprising of women, the revolt of other cultures against white Western hegemony, shifts in the balance of economic and political power within the world economy, and a growing awareness of the costs as well as the benefits of scientific and technological "progress."[40]

And alongside these social, economic and geopolitical shifts there is also a profound, underlying shift in what has been called "the structure of feeling."[41] That shift of feeling is well illustrated by an unforgettable viewing of the movie *Catch-22* in the mid-1980s.

The movie was being shown at Cornell University in Ithaca, New York. A nineteen-year-old American GI named Nately (played by Art Garfunkel) is a member of a bomber squadron stationed in the Mediterranean. The year is 1944, and Nately is on leave in Italy. In the living room of his Italian girlfriend sits a white-haired, wizened, 107-year-old man, possibly her great-grandfather (played by Marcel Dalio). The young American GI is talking animatedly about the war and about America, and he has a gleam in his eye. It is a gleam of freedom, of victory and progress. You can almost see the stars and stripes reflected there. "America is the strongest nation on earth," he pronounces with unflappable confidence. "The American fighting man is the best trained, the best equipped, the best fed."

The old man, however, interrupts him and explains that it is better to be weak and poor like Italy, which has not only survived so far but when the war is over will "still be in existence long after your country has been destroyed."

With incredulity, the GI responds: "What are you talking about? America is not going to be destroyed."

Then the old man, in a trembling, cracked voice, says, "Rome was destroyed. Greece was destroyed. Persia was destroyed. Spain was destroyed. All great countries are destroyed. Why not yours? How much longer do you think your country will last? Forever?"[42]

As that question hung in the air, there was dead silence in the auditorium. You could have heard a pin drop. The year was 1986. Only days before American jets had dropped bombs on Libya, and the Cornell campus had been alive with soapbox speeches pro and con the bombing. Most students were pro. America had strutted its stuff. It was standing tall again, showing the world (and especially Qaddafi) who was in charge. America was asserting its freedom and power, just like in the good old days—before Vietnam.

Then came *Catch-22*. And you could feel the angst, the existential anxiety, in that auditorium. It was so thick you could have cut it with a knife.

Today many of us feel the angst in late-twentieth-century Western culture. As theologian Langdon Gilkey puts it, "An autumnal chill is in the air; its similarity to the chill in other periods of cultural decline is undeniable."[43] It is the kind of chill you feel on the top floor of the tower of modern civilization, a tower reaching high above the clouds (who can doubt the skyrocketing achievements of modernity?). Yet we stand on a floor whose construction was never completed according to plan. Indeed, it is a floor with shattered walls, broken windows and the roof torn off by the postmodern winds of these icy heights. And as we look around us we see crowds of cowering people huddling in the corners, shivering in desperation, as a freezing wind chills their bones. Gilkey may have described the crisis of modernity as an "autumnal chill," but over a decade after he penned those words the chill no longer feels autumnal. It has gotten much colder. It feels as if we are in the depths of a cultural winter.[44]

As we approach the end of the twentieth century, modernity is in radical decline. Its legitimating myths are no longer believed with any conviction. The old "sacred canopy" of modern progress which had previously sheltered the inhabitants of modernity has blown off the fourth floor and the biting chill of anomie now settles on the "naked public square."[45] The result is that we are exposed to radical insecurity and to what anthropologist Clifford Geertz calls the "gravest sort of anxiety."[46] And anxiety is really the right word. It is not as if people fear clearly defined threats. Rather, it feels as if our whole culture has the willies. Intelligent, high-powered, well-educated people are worried about making what used to be ordinary life decisions like entering into committed relationships and having children. Susan Littwin, author of *The Postponed Generation: Why American Youth Are Growing Up Later*,[47] says the baby boomers have come of age in a land of lowered expectations and heightened anxiety that have contributed to their tendency to put off adulthood, with its assumed responsibilities and maturity, until they become thirtysomething.

Indeed, we could say that a psychology of fear has overwhelmed us—fear about the role of America in "the new world order," fear about environmental destruction, fear about economic security, fear about sexual morality, fear about different and odd ideas that we are constantly confronting.[48] Culturally, everything seems to be falling apart. Beliefs that were once certain and widely held—like the God-ordained right and responsibility of America to lead the world, the ability to solve all environmental problems by more Western technological ingenuity, the strength and durability of the capitalist market system, and the superiority of the Western intellectual tradition—are all being questioned on a daily basis.

In such a context the very normative ground on which one stands is shaken. The old answers and the old stories are no longer convincing, and ultimate worldview questions that once had some form of ultimate, faith-committed answers are reopened. Such reopening is usually experienced as terrifying. We are on the edge of an abyss. Again, Gilkey sums up our situation well: "Everything seems to slip: our landscape, our institutions, our values, our way of life—and so the security and meaning, the sense of being at home in a world we can understand and deal with that they brought."[49]

While such a slippage is evident in the growing cynicism we see in relation to political processes,[50] it is also something that many of us feel deep within our own experience. The postmodern condition could be described as being at once liberated from past distortions and lies, yet also "cast adrift—exposed, unprotected and above all frightened."[51] And with so much up for grabs, it is no wonder that *Time* magazine can run a cover story on "The Fraying of America."[52] Meanwhile, politicians are proclaiming with increasing volume and stridency that "America is *not* in decline."[53]

Many, of course, do not see the tragedy. Many successful, well-to-do, comfortable dwellers, especially in the Western regions of the top floor, simply pull their coats tighter around their bodies and deny that it is cold at all. (This is known as cocooning.) Meanwhile the wind howls around their ears. But they simply pluck up their courage and sing into the face of that chill wind, defiantly:

Oh sweet fantasia of the safe home
Where nobody has to scrape for honey at the bottom of the comb
Where every actor understands the scene
And nobody ever means to be mean

while the walls of modernity crumble and the ground opens beneath their feet. And the young man in the next room dies agonizingly of AIDS, while the woman in the corner sobs herself to sleep after her husband has again beaten and raped her, and "someone's on the bathroom floor doing her cocaine."[54] And the homeless are everywhere. Not to mention the populations decimated by famine and civil war in Bosnia, Somalia and Rwanda, and the emaciated, starving children staring at us from TV newsreels and documentaries.

But "Oh sweet fantasia of the safe home" is still the anthem of many. "Catch it in a dream," says Cockburn, "catch it in a song." But "seek it on the street," seek it on the roof, seek it on the fourth floor of the tower of modernity, on the real live streets of the twentieth century—"you find the candy man's gone." The modern dream of streets of "platinum, never mind gold" is a fantasy. As Cockburn insistently concludes: "Misplaced your faith and the candy man's gone."[55]

There never was any candy man, except as a figment of the modern imagination. It was all an illusion. The progress myth was a grand dream. And the dream has now become a tragic nightmare for millions of people on this globe. "Lord, spit on our eyes so we can see," sings Cockburn in another song, "how to wake up from this tragedy."[56] Those are lines Christians ought to pray in our time of cultural winter. Because if God doesn't graciously wake us up to this postmodern tragedy, one day we are going to have the sort of rude awakening the dreamers and builders of the tower of Babel got when, just as they thought they had accomplished their purpose and reached as high as heaven, God scattered and dispersed them in judgment. It is time for Christians to realize that we are living in a culture that is reaping the bitter fruits of its own distorted ideals.

What we need, however, is not an attitude of judgment, as if we stand over against our culture. Whatever claims to distinctiveness Christians like to make, we are all implicated in the crisis of modernity and we all need healing. But for healing, we need understanding. We need to listen sensitively and empathically to the cry of our age, especially for the resonance of that cry within ourselves. Only then will we be able to discern the contours of the emerging postmodern worldview. That listening and discernment is our task in the next three chapters.

# 2/Reality Isn't What It Used to Be

n this chapter and the two that follow, we will sketch in broad outline how contemporary Western culture is beginning to formulate distinctively new answers to the four worldview questions we discussed in chapter one. Paying close attention to these new answers permits us to discern the basic contours of the emerging postmodern worldview.

*Where are we?* Whereas the typically modern answer to the first worldview question exudes a naive confidence about what reality is, assuming that the real world is both knowable and manageable by human beings, in a postmodern situation this confidence has evaporated. Reality, says Walter Truett Anderson, isn't what it used to be.[1] It is not primarily that we have become convinced en masse by the arguments of philosophical relativism or French deconstructionism, although such arguments do crystallize the profound shift of feeling which has occurred. The shift, however, has taken place on a more visceral, less cerebral, level.

## From Confidence to Suspicion

It is as if we were parochial dwellers of some rural backwater that we took to be the center of the universe, never having visited (and never having cared to visit) anywhere else. Then, having for the first time traveled to other lands, we came to the painful and jarring realization that all the customs we had taken for granted as true and right were but local conventions, assumed to be natural, universal and inevitable by sheer force of habit.

In a similar manner, many citizens of late Western modernity, overwhelmed by the media-accelerated onrush of globalization, have come to the bewildering conclusion, or at least the troubling suspicion, that the sure, absolutist claims of modernity are nothing more than historically conditioned conventions, of no more intrinsic worth than the conventions of non-Western or premodern cultures. And this suspicion is bolstered by the growing awareness of the violence inflicted by the modern West over the past five centuries not only on colonized and marginalized peoples, including women, but also, increasingly, on the earth itself. It is not that non-Western nations are innocent of violence or environmental destruction, but that what we previously took for our higher moral status is now being unmasked as an ideological, self-justifying claim which blinded us to the inherent moral ambiguity in the modern project. Both epistemologically (in terms of what we can know) and morally (in terms of what is right), reality isn't what it used to be.

To get a sense of this shift—how our perceptions of reality have changed—consider these two vignettes, one from a Broadway play, the other from a dinner with some friends.

In Lily Tomlin's one-woman Broadway show, *The Search for Signs of Intelligent Life in the Universe*, the first character we meet is Trudy the bag lady. As our guide through the show, Trudy explains that she is helping some aliens from outer space to determine whether, in their search for intelligent life in the universe, the planet Earth might be a likely location. The prospects do not seem too promising!

Not only do we have the aliens' unusual perspective, but Trudy herself sees things aslant. Speaking of her own madness, Trudy exclaims:

I refuse to be intimidated by
reality anymore.
After all, what is reality anyway? Nothin' but a
collective hunch. My space chums think reality was once a
primitive method of
crowd control that got out of hand.
In my view, it's absurdity dressed up

in a three-piece business suit.

I made some studies, and
reality is the leading cause of stress among those in
touch with it. I can take it in small doses, but as a lifestyle
I found it too confining.[2]

Trudy figures that being "out of touch" with reality isn't such a bad idea. After all, it's less stressful. But what is reality anyway? Nothing but a collective hunch.

Consider a second vignette. We had finished a wonderful dinner with a couple of Christian friends. Over dessert and wine the topic turned theological. A question was put on the table by our hosts: "So, can we still believe that all the pagans who don't believe in Jesus (usually for good reason, considering the kind of Christians they've met) are destined for eternal damnation?" The stark way in which the question was posed indicated where our friends were likely to go on this one. *Of course* we can't believe that anymore!

Most sensitive Christians have raised this question at one time or another, at least to themselves, if not publicly. Christians (and others) who have raised this question have typically wondered how a just and loving God could damn people who had not heard the gospel or who had heard it under severely ambiguous circumstances. And for some people the question would also be colored by Western liberal notions of tolerance. Can we believe such an exclusivist, intolerant doctrine?

In the ensuing after-dinner discussion, however, things took a very different turn. The issue wasn't divine justice or even liberal tolerance. The issue was epistemological; it was a matter of what and how we *know*. How is it possible to judge the worldview of another person or group of people to be wrong when we realize that we have no privileged, universal access to truth and so can only pass judgment from the perspective of our own worldview? The epistemological issue here—and it is an issue that was burning in the hearts and minds of our dinner friends—is, How can we presume that our own worldview is so in touch with reality (to say nothing about being in touch with God!) that we can magisterially pronounce on the truth or falsity of any other worldview? To use Trudy the bag lady's terms, if reality is nothing more than a collective hunch (read: worldview), which is already too confining in itself, then why exclude one group's collective hunch as invalid? Isn't this the kind of pretense to certainty that leads one group to impose their collective hunch upon other groups?

Both Trudy's agnosticism about reality and our friends' way of asking the age-old question of divine retribution testify to a new postmodern sensitivity. If the Where are we? worldview question asks about the nature of reality, the typical postmodern answer is, "We are in a reality that we have constructed."

### The Social Construction of Reality

Walter Truett Anderson tells the joke of three umpires having a beer after a baseball game.[3] One says, "There's balls and there's strikes and I call 'em the way they are." Another responds, "There's balls and there's strikes and I call 'em the way I see 'em." The third says, "There's balls and there's strikes, and they ain't *nothin'* until I call 'em."

So what is reality? Are there balls and strikes objectively out there in the world as the first ump implies? Most baseball fans and hometown commentators insist that there are, though some might side with the second ump in his more honest appraisal of his own subjectivity. Many postmodern thinkers, however, wonder whether the third ump just might have the most honest position of the three. How do we know, after all, if there is anything "real" beyond our judgments?

At issue in the joke is not the particular *content* of the umps' judgment, whether they believe the pitch is a ball or a strike, but more fundamentally, the *status* of their judgments, what sort of calls they are making. "The new polarization," says Anderson, "is split between different *kinds* of belief, not between different beliefs."[4] The first ump and the third ump may agree that the pitch should be called a strike, but the belief functions differently for each (with the second ump occupying a position in the middle). The first ump is a *naive realist,* believing that human knowing is a matter of seeking direct correspondence between the external world and epistemological judgments. The second ump knows that access to the external world is always mediated by the perspective of the knower. He might be called a *perspectival realist* (or perhaps a critical realist), since he recognizes that the way he sees the world invariably affects his epistemological judgments. The third ump pushes this perspectivalism to its extreme. His perspective is all there is, or at least all that matters. This *radical perspectivalism* epitomizes the postmodern shift. It is, if you will, perspectivalism gone to seed![5]

While there is significant difference between the positions of the second and third umps (a difference which we will investigate further in chapter seven), it is fair to say that the current predominance of these positions (both in the academy and on the street) represents the demise of the naive realism of modernity.

Although modernity has never been simply an intellectual movement, the modern project was predicated on the assumption that the knowing autonomous subject arrived at truth by establishing a correspondence between objectively "given" reality and the thoughts or assertions of the knower. To the postmodern mind, such correspondence is impossible, for we simply have no access to something called "reality" apart from the way in which we represent that reality in our concepts, language and discourse. Since, as philosopher Richard Rorty puts it, we never encounter reality "except under a chosen description," we are denied the luxury or pretense of claiming naive, immediate access to the world.[6] We can never get outside our knowledge to check its accuracy against "objective" reality. Our access is always mediated by our own linguistic and conceptual constructions.

Another way to say this is that it is only in terms of some *worldview*, some over-arching, guiding and directing vision of life, that we experience the world. Everyone has a worldview. When we argued this in 1984 in *The Transforming Vision* (as we attempted to develop a distinctively Christian worldview), it was a potentially con-troversial point.[7] The fact that the term *worldview* is now common in Christian literature, general academic writing and the public press is an indication of how much things have changed in a rather short period of time.[8] One of the defining features of the emerging postmodern culture is our growing awareness, with the second ump, of the perspectival character of human life and knowing.[9]

But many postmodern thinkers would go much further than admitting that life is perspectival or that reality is mediated to us by our worldview. Since we have no way of checking to see if our constructions *correspond* to anything external, there is a growing postmodern tendency to side with the third ump in questioning wheth-er there is in fact any reality outside our constructions. While not exactly denying there is a "world" out there beyond our knowledge, postmodern thinkers typically deny that there are any features of this world which could function as independent-ly existing *norms* or *criteria* for truth and goodness to which we could appeal. Any criterion we might come up with, explains Rorty, is itself a human construction, and there is "no standard of rationality that is not an appeal to such a criterion, no rigorous argumentation that is not obedience to our own conventions."[10] We are caught, then, in a hermeneutical circle, impelled toward radical perspectivalism. While this does not mean, for Rorty, that each individual is trapped in her own private reality—since we can engage in conversation with each other—it does mean that rationality ceases to be a matter of universal truth. "The application of such honorifics as 'objective' and 'cognitive,' " he writes, "is never anything more than an expression of the presence of, and hope for, agreement among inquirers."[11] For either reason, then, whether reality is mediated to us by our perspective or is purely a human construct, the naive self-assured realism of modernity is impossible to the postmodern mind.

But not only is reality a human construct, it is more particularly a *social* construct. It is always *someone's* or *some group's* construction of reality that ends up being the dominant construction that guides social life. If what Rorty called our "chosen descriptions" of reality are, in the words of Trudy the bag lady, nothing more than collective hunches, then we need to ask, *Whose* reality? *Which* collective hunch?[12] And the answer is that it is the modern, Western construction of reality (the progress myth) that has most effectively dominated the globe and defined what is rational and normative for human life. But since this dominance is not due, on any post-modern account, to strict epistemological success (as if the progress myth is demon-strably "truer" than any other construction), what *is* it due to? Trudy may well ask of modernity, "Why is it *your* construction of reality, *your* collective hunch, that rules?" Why is any one construction of reality given privileged status, thereby mar-ginalizing all others?

### Violence and the Therapy of Deconstruction

As soon as we begin attending to the relation of reality and representation to marginalization and oppression we have entered that rarified postmodern world known as *deconstructionism*.[13] Jacques Derrida, the French philosopher most char-acteristically associated with deconstruction, names the realism of the dominant Western intellectual tradition a "metaphysics of presence."[14] In this tradition, what is assumed to be *present* in our conceptual systems of truth is seen as a real *given* which exists prior to language and thought and which we have adequately grasped by our language and thought. That is, the Western intellectual tradition, and espe-cially Western modernity, claims to reflect and represent reality so accurately that it simply *mirrors* the way things really are. It is this *mimetic* (i.e., imitative) theory of truth, with its assumption of a substantial convergence between reality and our description of reality, that Derrida and other deconstructionists attack. It is a central deconstructionist theme that we can never get to a prelinguistic or preconceptual "reality." Instead, deconstructionism insistently attempts to show us that what is claimed to be *present* is really *absent* and that the *given* is itself a construction of human discourse. Through this analysis the given is dismantled and we are dis-abused of our reifications.

To *reify* something is to treat it as if it were a thing (Latin *res*) external to ourselves.

Peter Berger and Thomas Luckmann describe reification as

> the apprehension of the products of human activity *as if* they were something else than human products—such as facts of nature, results of cosmic laws, or manifestations of divine will. Reification implies that man is capable of forgetting his own authorship of the human world, and further, that the dialectic between man, the producer, and his products is lost to consciousness.[15]

By uncovering our reifications deconstruction attempts not to destroy in any nihilistic sense but to play a positive, therapeutic role in the culture of late (and decomposing) modernity. We are to face up to our constructions and to own them as such.

But the therapist cuts deep. What is concealed in the realism of the metaphysics of presence and revealed by deconstructionism is the impulse to mastery and ultimately to violence. What is really at stake in our intellectual rhetoric about scientific objectivity, nonbiased observation and universal maxims, explains Jane Flax, is nothing less than the typically Western desire "to master the world once and for all by enclosing it within an illusory but absolute system" which, it is believed, "represents or corresponds to a unitary Being beyond history, particularity and change."[16] We desire, in other words, intellectual mastery and control. In the famous words of René Descartes, we seek to become "the masters and possessors of nature."[17]

But the claim to have grasped reality as it *really* is (beyond the contingencies of history, particularity and change) discloses our desire for another sort of mastery, that over human beings. By granting an aura of universal truth to our local conventions, the Western intellectual commitment to realism serves ideologically to legitimate Western conquest and political superiority. As Trudy's space chums put it, reality functions as a primitive form of crowd control. Thus Derrida can claim that "the entire philosophical tradition, in its meaning and at bottom, would make common cause with oppression."[18]

The realist metaphysics of presence is thus an "aggressive realism."[19] It is a metaphysics of violence. And that violence, explains deconstructionists, is the direct result of seeking to grasp the infinite, irreducible complexities of the world as a unified and homogeneous totality.[20] Since all such totalizing seeks to reduce the heterogeneous diversity of reality to a system which *I* (or *we*) can grasp, the deconstructionist is suspicious, says James Olthuis, that the "unity of truth is purchased only at the cost of violence, by repressing what doesn't fit and erasing the memory of those who have questioned it."[21] Recognizing that truth is a human, social construction, deconstructionists force us to inquire about what (and who) has been left out, silenced or suppressed in all constructions that aspire toward a *total* accounting of reality. The problem with such totalizing aspirations is that they necessarily result in a violent closure of human thought that denies all heterogeneous difference or dissolves it into a homogeneous unity, effectively co-opting, dominating or eliminating that which is perceived as "other."

A paradigm example of what deconstructionists are getting at is the cultural reality of racism. As a way to deal with the difference of those who are *other*, racism is a totalizing vision of the world in which the racist takes as normal (and normative!) that which is the same as himself. The racist thus finds it necessary to relegate anyone who is *other*, that is, heterogeneous to what is taken to be the norm, to an inferior status. That inferiority can be manifest in anything from slavery to neglect and quiet oppression.

The same cultural dynamics are evident in traditional U.S. approaches to immigration. Anyone who is not an American is termed an *alien*. For such persons to cease being aliens, they must first become *naturalized* citizens of the United States (since, presumably, to be American is to be natural). After this initial step, they must then find their way into the homogeneity of the American way of life by allowing their cultural difference to be dissolved in the great American melting pot.

What deconstructionists are saying is that the sort of homogenizing and naturalizing approach to otherness and difference that is illustrated by both racism and U.S. immigration policy has characterized Western thought and culture as a whole and modernity in particular. The difference of women, the otherness of non-Western cultures and the very complex heterogeneity of the world have been dissolved or repressed into a totalizing vision of the world. Such a vision is inherently violent because it necessarily excludes not just elements of reality that don't fit, but any *person* or *group* who sees things differently. "When convinced of the truth or right of a given worldview," notes Kenneth Gergen, "a culture has only two significant options: totalitarian control of the opposition or annihilation of it."[22] Whether or not these are the *only* options, this has in fact been the legacy of the last 500 years of Western history in relation to women, to non-Western, particularly nonwhite peoples, and to the nonhuman creation itself. It is no wonder, therefore, that postmodern author Jean-François Lyotard tells us that modernity has given us "as much terror as we can take."[23] Renouncing the nostalgia for a total scheme of things because it is both unattainable and inherently violent is a characteristic postmodern theme.[24]

If modernity attempted to make homogeneous, "naturalized" citizens of all of us,

then deconstructionists want to engage in a therapeutic process of "denaturalization." The initial postmodern concern, says Linda Hutcheon, "is to de-naturalize
some of the dominant features of our way of life; to point out that those entities
that we unthinkingly experience as 'natural' (they might even include capitalism,
patriarchy, liberal humanism) are in fact 'cultural'; made by us not given to us."[25]

And the purpose of this denaturalization is, laudably enough, to *stop* the violence,
or at least to lessen or mitigate it. Dismantling our reifications and undermining our
totalizing visions of reality are thus actions valorized in postmodern thought because they open up a positive space for "the free play of difference," as Derrida puts
it. Deconstructionism, in other words, potentially clears the ground for the possibility of doing justice to the marginal, for the liberation of those excluded or oppressed under the hegemony of modernity.

### Disorientation

The paradox, however, is that with liberation comes disorientation, for at least two
reasons. First of all, since it is precisely the function of a social construction of reality
to shield us from the abyss of meaninglessness by providing us with a "sacred
canopy" of meaning and order, the realization that this canopy is humanly constructed (not an inevitable given) leaves us with a sense of vertigo, unprotected
before the abyss.[26] For all its good intentions, deconstructive therapy can endanger
the patient: it can precipitate the loss of our safe "world" and our exposure to terror.
Although writing before the rise of deconstructionism, Peter Berger understood well
the sociological and psychological consequences of the loss of a "sacred canopy."

> This is the nightmare *par excellence,* in which the individual is submerged in a
> world of disorder, senselessness and madness. Reality and identity are malig-
> nantly transformed into meaningless figures of horror. To be in a society is to
> be "sane" precisely in the sense of being shielded from the ultimate "insanity"
> of anomic terror. Anomy is unbearable to the point where the individual may
> seek death in preference to it.[27]

*Anomie* is the loss of a *nomos*—the loss of any secure sense of a meaningful order
to the world. Deconstructionism confronts us with the claim that all order is arbitrary, imposed on the world by human beings, usually for self-serving and violent
reasons. But even if the reasons were honorable, the very realization that the order
of the world is a social construct, that we live and experience the world in terms
of belief-systems and worldviews that we have chosen, can be terrifying. It is indeed
paradoxical that worldviews best provide orientation to life when we are not aware

of them. They best provide a secure world and home for human activity when they are so internalized that we simply assume that we experience reality the way it truly is, that we picture the world "the way things in sheer actuality are."[28] Becoming aware of our worldview *as a worldview*, of its particularity, subjectivity and limitations, can have a profoundly anomic effect. An arbitrarily chosen worldview can scarcely function as a worldview anymore. We are left without a buffer against chaos, world-less and disoriented.

But deconstructive therapy is disorienting for another reason. If deconstructionism has done its job effectively, we become aware not just of the socially constructed character of reality but of *our part* in that construction. We come to realize nothing less than our complicity in violence, our implication in terror. If reality is socially constructed, then we have to admit that we have participated (whether actively or by acquiescence) in the construction of what is often a nightmare. Our Western collective hunch has turned out to be a largely destructive wager. Our "reality" is one of holes in the ozone layer, rampant environmental destruction, debilitating poverty, and worldwide inequity, oppression and terror. It is a reality of abuse, loneliness, fear and perpetual threat.[29] While it may seem a wonderful statement of our Promethean power to proclaim that we are the constructors of our own reality, it amounts, in the final analysis, to an admission of guilt. When confronted with the reality we have constructed, we are brought face to face with our arrogance—with our own brokenness, ambiguity and evil. According to literary critic Terry Eagleton,

> We are now in the process of wakening from the nightmare of modernity, with its manipulative reason and fetish of the totality, into the laid-back pluralism of the post-modern, that heterogeneous range of life-styles and language games which has renounced the nostalgic urge to totalize and legitimate itself.[30]

But our awakening is not as laid-back or complacent as Eagelton intimates. For those who (in varying degrees) naively shared in the modern dream of a progressive world of justice, wealth and peace, the postmodern therapy of deconstruction, if taken to heart, is profoundly painful. Whether, then, we have been exposed to the abyss of meaninglessness or have become aware of our complicity in evil, deconstructive therapy can be a disorienting experience.

### Hyperreality and a Culture of Images

Not all, however, have faced up to that difficult therapy. It is possible that many readers will never have even encountered deconstruction before, or, at least, not in a form that made any sense.[31] Nevertheless, disorientation is also our lot simply by living in the culture of late Western modernity. It is a characteristic feature of our times, even without the insights of deconstruction, to flaunt—indeed glory in— reality as construct. Take, for example, this headline from a Northern Telecom advertisement addressed to university students: "We call it the Intelligent Universe and we're building that vision into reality."[32]

Consider how this ad might answer the first worldview question, Where are we? Are we in an intelligent universe? Not quite. The Intelligent Universe does not yet exist. The Intelligent Universe is our vision which we are *building into reality*. This is modernity pushed to the extreme, self-consciously facing up to its own Promethean autonomy. And, since the Intelligent Universe is a human project and construct, which the ad exalts in its attempt to attract technologically trained university graduates, the construct is appropriately capitalized. The reality we are building looms larger than life, a brilliant improvement over the mundane natural order of things. The Intelligent Universe of Northern Telecom is an example of what various authors describe as "hyperreality."

A product of the information age of late modernity and heavily dependent on communications technology, the hyperreal is that which we have not just constructed, but glorified with media *hype* as "even better than the real thing."[33] Advanced information processing has allowed us to overcome and displace the naturally occurring world insofar as we are able to produce an artificial universe that is more brilliant, pliable and rich. Although we could cite the futuristic wonders of the holodeck in *Star Trek: The Next Generation* (and its spinoffs *Deep Space Nine* and *Star Trek: Voyager*), recent advances in computer-simulated "virtual reality" or even the multibillion-dollar movie *Jurassic Park*, we need not go so far afield. Hyperreality is as close to us as the shelves of the corner grocery store. As Albert Borgmann insightfully observes, "Cool Whip is hyperreal whipped cream, cheaper, more durable, and far less caloric than the real thing. Cool Whip does not need whipping and is free of cholesterol. Enormous efforts have been undertaken to provide us with fats and sugars devoid of calories."[34]

The culture of late, advanced modernity is a Cool Whip society. Or, in the words of French cultural critic Jean Baudrillard, it is an "age of simulacrum,"[35] by which he means, explains David Harvey, "a state of such near perfect replication that the difference between the original and the copy becomes almost impossible to spot."[36] This is a Disneyworld society of simulated reality.[37] Indeed, Disneyworld has been described as a "fully integrated hyperreal island."[38]

We in North America live in a Disneyworld culture, a Cool Whip society, in which we engage in autoerotic telephone sex in place of real intimacy, splash in simulated lakes and waterfalls at recreational waterparks rather than risk the pollution at the local lake or river, shop in climate-controlled malls that attempt to look like old-fashioned shopping neighborhoods and even watch the horrors of wars carefully sanitized on television to give us a sense that we are really there, yet not leave us uncomfortable with what we have seen.

Paradoxically, however, instead of heightening our experience of reality, the simulated world of image-enhanced hyperreality *distances* us from reality and is ultimately unsatisfying and desensitizing. There is something routinely numbing about all of this. Simulation never provides long-term stimulation. So we try to slap ourselves out of our numbness by watching a plethora of new "reality" shows on television, about "real cops," "real-life tragedies" and "real emergencies," only to find at the end of it all that there was something manipulative, cheap and even *unreal* about what we had just witnessed. Not only was it just *too* glamorous and brilliant, but the hype doesn't last; the glamour tarnishes and the brilliance fades.[39] When *Jurassic Park* is over, the ushers still have to clean up the popcorn and spilled drinks.

But hyperreality extends beyond the realms of traditional entertainment and advertizing. It permeates even contemporary politics. Consider the language commentators used to describe the U.S. presidential debates of 1992. "No one got a KO," "Bush needed a grand slam and struck out" and "Clinton stumbled out of the blocks." Such sporting metaphors could well justify Christopher Lasch's judgment that "the degeneration of politics into spectacle has . . . transformed policy making into publicity, debased political discourse, and turned elections into sporting events."[40]

But note that these are not events in which we *participate* in any significant way (except by voting). Politics, like a great deal else in our culture, has become a spectator sport, a theatrical performance, produced and packaged for our consumption. Our vote is simply our endorsement of the product. Through carefully crafted pseudoevents, photo opportunities, sound bites and image production, contemporary political theater is self-consciously staged for our benefit, to "sell" us on the merits of one candidate or another and the virtues of one political reality over another. Walter Truett Anderson's comments on the "job skills of the creator of social reality" could well apply to political campaign managers: these skills "include not only storytelling, but playwriting and playacting and many varieties of stage management."[41]

Anderson further suggests that Ronald Reagan was the first postmodern politician "because he understood the power of free-floating symbolism, rooted in nothing at all."[42] His politics was pure theater, the spectacle of the moment. Anderson is worth quoting at length:

> Reagan's unique qualification lay not merely in his speaking skills or camera savvy—those are not too hard to come by—but in a certain kind of intellectual training that had equipped him admirably to take a leading role in the politics of the nonevent: he had managed to go through a long and rather successful professional career that did not require him to develop any concept of truth; the truth was simply whatever entertained the audience.[43]

According to Anderson, the incredible success of Ronald Reagan during his years in office and the continuing esteem with which he is held in America are due to a sort of radical perspectivalism on his part: in Reagan we see the triumph of style over principle, rhetoric over argument and image over substance. It may, however, be more accurate to say that Reagan packaged an old-time modernist agenda in a new, postmodern wrapping. Indeed, he packaged a modern agenda in crisis, but this crisis was effectively disguised by that hyperreal, postmodern packaging. And it worked! Somehow the American people continued to believe, respect and even love a man who had dramatically increased the public debt (though he promised to do the opposite), heightened the gap between the rich and poor, multiplied military spending, waged, or funded, wars on democratically elected governments in Grenada and Nicaragua, lied to Congress and generally presided over the continual, ineluctable moral and economic decline of America. But the theater was so good that hardly anyone noticed. It was certainly better than the mundane realities of American life.

Our point, however, is not simply to pass judgment on the Reagan years in Washington. It is the theatricality of it all that merits comment.[44] It really does feel as if "all the world is a stage." Even geopolitical conflict has become a spectacle. Deadly and bloody battlefields in which human beings are being killed and maimed are called the "battle theater." World-shaking events like the demolition of the Berlin Wall, the protests in Tiananmen Square, the slaughter of hundreds in South Africa, the war against Iraq and the conflicts in Bosnia-Herzegovina all appear on the nightly television news as global spectacles. There is something perversely entertaining and strangely unreal about it all. Picture the U.S. troops landing in Somalia, tripping over the electrical wires of the TV networks, dogged by reporters, cameras and lights. What is reality anyway? Nothing but a collective hunch, a well-constructed theater piece.

By now the careful reader may have noticed that we have alternated between the terms *postmodern* and *late modern* throughout our discussion of hyperreality. What's the problem? Can't we make up our minds? Is hyperreality a postmodern phenomenon or not? Although there is at present a raging debate among social theorists between those, on the one hand, who think that modernity is bankrupt and we need (and are witnessing) the birth of a postmodern culture and those, on the other hand, who think that the Enlightenment dream has merely been sidetracked and thus remains essentially unfulfilled, our problem is somewhat different. While we do indeed believe that modernity is bankrupt, it is not at all clear that it has been superseded or replaced. We live in a time of cultural transition, where we are experiencing the continuance—even the heightening—of central features of modernity, side-by-side with genuinely novel, postmodern elements. One of these central features is a continuing commitment to human autonomy.

It is important to note that there are two equally important—yet perhaps ultimately incompatible—sides to the modern project. They may be represented symbolically by the names René Descartes and Francis Bacon, both important figures of the seventeenth century. While Descartes was a philosopher who sought an absolutely certain rational foundation for science, understood as an all-embracing "total" system of truth, Bacon was a popularizer of science, who valued knowledge as a powerful tool for controlling nature and improving the human condition. Where the Cartesian ideal was intellectual submission to reality as an external, inflexible given, the Baconian ideal was transformation of the world in accordance with utopian human values. Realism is thus central to the Cartesian ideal, but the Baconian ideal values human autonomy above all.[45]

Strictly speaking, however, the Cartesian ideal of a system of absolute Truth, with its attendant epistemological confidence, is not unique to modernity but is traceable back in the Western tradition (as Derrida saw) at least to Plato. It may be that what we call "modernity" was an inherently unstable hybrid of realism and autonomy, a transitional way station between classical and medieval culture, with its submission to the given, and postmodernity, with its frank admission of human construction. According to Richard Rorty, postmodernity is characterized by the rejection of the Cartesian ideal and the radicalization of the Baconian.[46] In a fundamental sense, then, the postmodern is a continuance and *intensification* of (one aspect of) the modern. This is certainly the case with the phenomenon of hyperreality, which takes human technological ability to transcend the limits of nature to new heights.

The hyperreal is thus quintessentially modern. We could say it is *hyper*modern or *ultra*modern. It is self-conscious social construction with a vengeance.[47]

Woody Allen explores something of the vengeance of hyperreality in his film *The Purple Rose of Cairo*, where the dashing, perfect hero Tom Baxter comes out of a movie portrayed within the film.[48] While at first this seems to fulfill the fantasies of the moviegoing heroine, Cecilia, the confusion becomes too thick, and Baxter finally returns to the "reel" world whence he came. Cecilia is both relieved and despondent. In the last scene she is seen wistfully watching a Fred Astaire and Ginger Rogers movie, still compelled by the escape of hyperreality. *The Purple Rose of Cairo* suggests that while the experience of the hyperreal can be profoundly disorienting, the return to reality is a letdown. Borgmann's interpretation is convincing: "It appears that we finally cannot escape from the real into the hyperreal, nor can we settle for reality and escape the allure of hyperreality."[49] Such no-win situations are the stuff of disorientation.

### From Babel to the Confusion of Tongues

But the disorientation is intensified by the fact that there is not just one movie going on. There is not just one reality being constructed and offered to us. Postmodernity is a cable culture. We can simply switch channels to sample other, easily available worlds.

To extend the metaphor, we could say that postmodern life is like a carnival. Unlike classic theater, in which one show is going on, postmodern culture "seems like a carnival with a never-ending array of sideshows."[50] There is no center to this production. Unlike even a three-ring circus, this carnival offers only the clamor of multifarious sideshow hawkers calling out for our momentary attention. They do not seek our commitment in any ultimate sense; they only want to entertain and titillate us with the weird and wonderful worlds they are peddling. And, of course, there is nothing heavy or serious about this. The heavy seriousness of classical theater and the heavy-handed domination of modernity are replaced by the lightness of the postmodern carnival. As Karl Marx insightfully put it more than a century ago in *The Communist Manifesto*, "all that is solid melts into air."[51]

The carnivalesque, pluralistic culture in which we live can be seen as a consequence of the breakdown of modernity (which touted itself as the "greatest show on earth") combined with a recognition of the socially constructed character of reality. Since the old construction has been discredited and is in a process of decomposition, the season is open on the construction of new realities which are produced with the same speed and ease with which temporary circus tents are raised. Far from the erosion or even eclipse of religious belief that the Enlightenment so confidently predicted, the Enlightenment itself has been eclipsed, resulting in a veritable smorgasbord of religions and worldviews for our consumption.[52] "Never before has any civilization openly made available to its populace such a smorgasborg of realities," Anderson notes. "Never before has a society allowed its people to become consumers of belief, and allowed belief—all beliefs—to become merchandise."[53]

Peter Berger insightfully anticipated the commodification of belief in a radically pluralist society. After our awareness of reality as a social construction has brought about the decline of the dominant construction, Berger explains,

> the religious tradition, which previously could be authoritatively imposed, now has to be *marketed*. It must be "sold" to a clientele that is no longer constrained to "buy." The pluralist situation is, above all, a *market situation*. In it, the religious institutions become marketing agencies and the religious traditions become consumer commodities.[54]

It is important to distinguish this radically pluralist postmodern situation from the sort of pluralism fostered by modern political liberalism. Liberalism allows, even promotes, tolerance for idiosyncratic private beliefs *that have no socially public significance*. It allows that such beliefs are constructions. But on the nature of *reality*, liberalism is clear. Reality is a privileged, nonnegotiable given. There is one public world accessible to all and no deviation is tolerated concerning public truths.[55] To put it another way, liberalism allows a proliferation of sideshows as long as they do not infringe on the centrality of the Big Top. In a postmodern culture, however, there are nothing but sideshows. We no longer have confidence in claims about a public world or public truths. Whereas modern liberalism allowed (in principle) for a plurality of private worlds in which people could hold a diversity of religious or personal beliefs, postmodernity insists that all worlds are equally private.[56]

Returning to the imagery of Babel that we employed in the last chapter, liberal pluralism is like the architects of the tower of Babel allowing the workers to erect mud huts in the shadow of the tower—as long as this didn't interfere with their jobs. Postmodern pluralism, however, corresponds to the situation after Babel, when construction on the tower had come to a grinding halt. Today, the tower is tottering, perhaps even on the verge of collapse. Construction has halted; indeed, deconstruction seems to have taken over. And those of us who have labored hard for this tower, whether we live in huts around the site or in the once-impressive dwellings in the tower itself, find ourselves immersed in a confusion of tongues, overwhelmed by a cacophony of private languages and tribal agendas, all clamoring for our attention. Not only has all meaningful construction stopped, there is open conflict and confusion on the work site. The cultural unity of the tower of Babel is replaced by the culture wars of the post-Babel situation.

But unlike the sense of tragedy that the biblical story conveys in the post-Babel situation, our postmodern context is populated by deconstructionists and others celebrating the confusion. "Here's to heterogeneity!"[57] could be the quintessential postmodern toast, as glasses are raised and clinked to the liberating chaos.[58]

There is, of course, some biblical warrant for the celebration. The fall of Babel in Genesis 11 is not unequivocally negative. There God's judgment is viewed as a preventive measure which limited the monolithic totalizing aspirations of an empire and created the possibility of the diversity of nations and cultures which follow. If the tower of Babel, in the context of Genesis 1—11, is understood as an imperial and Promethean attempt to thwart God's historical purposes for the world, then the failure of this building project can be seen as God's gracious intervention in human affairs. By dispersing the human race, confusing their tongues and undermining their pretentious tower, God in fact opens up new possibilities for human history that would have been impossible if the totalizing aspirations of Babel's architects had been realized. By analogy, then, the collapse of the tower of modernity is good news. Postmodernity opens up genuine new possibilities for human cultural formation and should be welcomed as a positive historical opportunity.

Nonetheless, the fall of the tower of Babel is still judgment. There is an undeniably tragic element to the fall of both Babel and modernity. That is why the book of Revelation calls for mourning at the passing of Babylon before there can be any rejoicing.[59]

> Woe! Woe, O great city,
>
>   O Babylon, city of power!
>
> In one hour your doom has come! (Rev 18:10)

And so we must mourn over the collapse of modernity.[60] For all of its ideological pretensions and moral ambiguity, modernity was an impressive project, resulting in genuinely valuable advances in technology, health care, democracy and the general betterment of human life. The progress ideal, after all, is not something invented out of thin air. It rests both on the God-given human ability to transform our world and improve our lot and on an impressive list of actual accomplishments. Nevertheless, God does not tolerate the hubris of idolatry, and the Bible is replete with examples of the exalted brought low and the proud made to sit in the dust.

At the end of modernity, totalizing aspirations are being dashed and reality isn't what it used to be. The deconstructive therapy, combined with the failure of modernity to deliver on its promises of progress, has irretrievably changed our world. Once we realize that the lofty perspective we enjoy from the heights of our Western tower neither guarantees us any final access to truth nor is built upon secure foundations, the roof caves in, the sacred canopy blows off and an uneasy vertigo overcomes us. And then we must ask again that foundational worldview question, Where are we? And the overwhelming answer that comes back is that we are in a world of our own construction. But no longer can that answer fill us with a giddy sense of accomplishment. Rather, it leaves us with a sense of dread and a paralyzing anxiety.

# 3/The Decentered Self

emember Trudy the bag lady? *She's the one who refused to be intimidated by reality.* That doesn't sound too sane, now does it? Well, Trudy is quite aware of that.

> It's my belief that we all, at one time or another,
> secretly ask ourselves the question,
> "Am I crazy?"
> in my case, the answer came back: A resounding
> YES![1]

Being out of touch with reality has its benefits. Sanity isn't one of them. After all, what is it to be insane but not to be at home in the world in which you live? An inability to answer the first worldview question, Where am I? necessarily results in psychological disorientation because you are out of touch with your environment and do not know where you are. But insanity also results from not knowing *who* you are, from being out of touch with yourself.

### Homo autonomous

Although it is true that modernity has spawned a wide diversity of theories about the nature of human selfhood, it is also fair to say that both these theories and the modernist project in human history have been grounded in a widely shared understanding of how to answer the second worldview question, Who am I?

Who are we? We are *Homo autonomous.*[2] Humans are independent, self-reliant, self-centering and self-integrating rational subjects. This is a fundamentally heroic understanding of human subjectivity. We are who we are by overcoming all that binds or inhibits us and by determining for ourselves who we will be.

Ernst Cassirer notes that this modernist anthropology was achieved during the Renaissance by means of a radical "inner transformation" or reinterpretation of the biblical story of Adam in the light of the Greek myth of Prometheus: "Man is a creature; but what distinguishes him above all other creatures is that his maker gave him the gift of creation. Man arrives at his determination, he fulfills his being, only by using this basic and primary power." Prometheus is, of course, "a human hero of culture, the bringer of wisdom and of political and moral order. Through these gifts, he 'reformed' man in the true sense, i.e., he impressed upon him a new form and a new essential character." But, Cassirer notes, "Renaissance philosophy moves farther and farther away even from this [original] version of the [Promethean] motif, for it transfers the power of giving form ever more definitely to the individual subject."[3]

Prometheus is no longer simply a symbol for humanity as a whole, but rather becomes the paradigm for the individual. The heroic individual is no longer a "slave of creative nature, . . . rather, he is its rival, completing, improving, and refining its works."[4]

Such a Promethean reinterpretation of the biblical view of Adam is given its quintessential articulation in Pico della Mirandola's 1487 *Oration on the Dignity of Man.*[5] In Pico's retelling of the creation story, God makes the human creature indeterminate, without any specific nature. Then God addresses this new creation: "We have given you, Oh Adam, no visage proper to yourself, nor any endowment properly your own, in order that whatever place, whatever form, whatever gifts you may, with premeditation, select, these same you may have and possess through your own judgment and decision."

Modern humanity has unlimited possibilities! We can have what we choose; we can be whatever we will to be. God further tells Adam: "The nature of all other creatures is defined and restricted within laws which We have laid down; you, by contrast, impeded by no such restrictions, may, by your own free will, to whose custody We have assigned you, trace for yourself the lineaments of your own nature."

Here we reach the core of the modernist answer to the Who are we? question: the postulate of human autonomy. In the modern worldview, man becomes a law *(nomos)* unto himself *(autos)*.[6] Pico's God tells this heroic individual that he has no specific, limited nature "in order that you may, as the free and proud shaper of your own being, fashion yourself in the form you prefer." This is, quite literally, a *self-centered* ego. The ego finds its center, its point of unity, cohesion and identity, precisely in itself. Or perhaps we could more accurately say that this is a self-centering ego—constantly in the process of constructing and reconstructing its own center, its own identity, its own place in the world. We see here the roots of the modernist, and now postmodernist, notion of the self-constructed self.

It is not an overstatement to say that the whole modernist project depends on this view of human selfhood. Without an independently rational self there would be no reason to trust the results and achievements of modern science. If the self were not an autonomous subject then the realist world of modernity would have no one to master it technologically. Moreover, this view of the self even underlies modern liberal democracy. "Systems of democratic governance," notes Kenneth Gergen, "depend on commitments of the citizens to certain definitions of the self. It makes sense for individuals to vote only if they are presumed to have 'powers of independent judgment,' 'political opinions,' and 'desire for the social good.' "[7]

Although the democratic impulse can be traced back to the Judeo-Christian tradition, the emergence of this impulse in modern history would not have occurred if it were not for the anthropologically self-assured view of the human subject that came to characterize the modern era.[8]

But if liberal democracy is a valuable byproduct of the modern view of the self, there are other byproducts that are more ambiguous, like the history of Western conquest. The modern self may accurately be described as an "imperial ego." This self, says Christopher Lasch, is "the endlessly acquisitive conqueror and pioneer"[9] who replaced the geocentric world of the ancients and medievals with an anthropocentric world of discovery and conquest and displaced the plurality of non-Western cultures with the hegemony of Western colonialism. *Homo autonomous,* we have discovered, is El Conquistador. The free and autonomous subject exercises his freedom and constructs his own identity by means of his mastery over the world of nonhuman (or subhuman!) objects. "Proudly conscious of his autonomy and freedom," suggests Herman Dooyeweerd, "modern man saw 'nature' as an expansive arena for the explorations of his free personality, as a field of infinite possibilities in which the sovereignty of human personality must be revealed by a complete *mastery* of the phenomena of nature."[10] This is another way in which the modernist self is appropriately described as a self-centered ego. Not only is the ego *self-centered* in the sense of self-constructed, it also constructs itself in such a way that it is the center of the world. The world, bound as it is by natural laws that are imposed upon it, is subjected to the impulses of mastery of the one creature that is autonomous, a law unto itself. Pico's Adam is placed in the center of the world, and from that vantage point exercises his sovereign rule.

No longer dependent on the superstitions of the past or the Bible as an external source of authoritative revelation, modern man champions his secular independence. Freed from the control of ecclesiastical authority and the imposition of identity by a rigid medieval social order, the modern person is found to be a self-made subject. And armed with the tools of modern science and technology the heroic modern individual can transform the world of objects into *subjects of* the human kingdom, serving the human sovereign and yielding its riches for human economic self-aggrandizement.

### I'm Just Not Feeling Myself Anymore: The Demise of the Modern Subject

Such anthropological self-assuredness, however, is just as difficult to sustain in a postmodern world as is the epistemological optimism we discussed in chapter two. And there are at least two reasons for this. In the first instance, it seems that when left to their own self-directed devices, the heroic individual and the culture of heroic individualism inevitably and invariably do violence. The heroic self can manifest its heroism only by engaging in acts of heroic mastery. The problem is that that mastery has returned to haunt us. Not only have we seen the wide-ranging consequences of the despoliation of the natural environment,[11] but we have also been confronted with the sad truth that the autonomous mastery of the heroic individual seems to always result in mastery over other human beings.[12] Today the voices of subjugated people (women, aboriginal peoples, African-Americans and others), echoed by the pained voice of an ecologically devastated creation, are heard raising loud complaint against the arrogant mastery of this autonomous ego that has placed itself at the center of the world.

In chapter two we saw that the aggressive realism of modernity is rooted in a *metaphysics of violence*. It is also apparent that such a metaphysics of violence finds its corollary in an autonomous *anthropology of violence.*

But this violence is not just against others. The violent mastery of the autonomous ego rebounds against itself. Whether we consider the massive bureaucracies and economic structures that modernity constructed to control nature more efficiently and guarantee economic progress or the manipulation of the public by means of advertising, the media and other forms of propaganda, the result has been that in Western culture the once proud self-centered ego "is no longer that autonomous subject who can sovereignly set processes in motion and who can also, at a moment of his own choice, stop these processes again." Rather, the modern self is "now caught in the predicament of being managed rather than of being the manager."[13] El Conquistador has the sinking feeling that he has become "the conquered" in the socioeconomic systems of modernity! The controlling and mastering subject who adjusts the world to accommodate its own self-realization begins to experience its life in modernity as the controlled, mastered and adjusted subject of a powerfully hegemonic worldview that requires constant accommodation.

And this gives rise to the second reason that our anthropological self-assuredness has been shaken. Simply stated, postmodern thought has come to recognize that the humanist understanding of the self-constructed and self-centered ego is itself a construct. This anthropology is a fiction. The very notion of the self as an autonomous, self-reliant individual is a modern invention. It is a construction that was conceived in a particular place and time (specifically, the Western world since the Renaissance), rather than a universally recognizable and timeless self-evident truth about human nature. Just as reality is a social construct (the answer to the first worldview question) so also is *Homo autonomous* a socially constructed answer to the second worldview question. Just as "we only know the world through a network of socially established meaning systems" or "the discourses of our culture," so also such meaning systems and discourses "structure how we see ourselves and how we construct our notions of self, in the past and in the present."[14]

There is an important point that needs to be underlined here. Not only are many postmodern theorists insisting that the self is a construct or a product of social systems, they are also making rather far-reaching claims about the role of discourse, or language, in this constitution of the self.[15] Rather than perpetuating the myth of the autonomous, self-constituting subject, Michel Foucault says that the modernist subject must be "stripped of its creative role and analyzed as a complex and variable function of discourse."[16] In this postmodern appraisal, language is more a producer of subjectivity than a meaningful product of autonomous subjects. Indeed, literary critic J. Hillis Miller claims that "language is not an instrument or tool in man's hands, a submissive means of thinking. Language rather thinks man and his 'world.' "[17]

Within such a worldview it is no longer humans who are autonomous, but language itself. *Homo autonomous* is reconstituted as *Homo linguisticus.* Commenting on Jacques Derrida's critique of the logocentric presumption that language is the product of an expressive autonomous mind, Kenneth Gergen explains that for Derrida,

> language is a system unto itself. Words derive their capacity to create a seeming world of essences from the properties of the system. This system of language *preexists* the individual; it is "always there," available for social usage. Thus, anything said about the world or the self should, in principle, be placed in quotations.[18]

Everything must be placed in quotations because it is just "words," mere "representations" of reality, not reality itself. Are human beings "really" self-constructing, autonomous and heroic individuals? That question cannot be answered. All that we can say is that this is the way that we have come to talk about human beings and that such discourse effectively has reimaged us in these terms. This has become the "natural" way to think about human beings, a "dogma" of Western culture. As we have seen in the last chapter, however, postmodernity is a process of "denaturalization."

Whether or not we agree with replacing the autonomous self of modernity with an even more abstract autonomous "language," it is clear that in a postmodern world, this autonomous self is effectively dismantled. We need to acknowledge that the autonomous self is a construct of a particular culture. Moreover, we need to admit that this way of answering the Who are we? question has proven to be a violent and oppressive disaster. And we might well join our voice with postmodernity and say good riddance to the humanist view of the self.

But while such dismantling is a good and necessary corrective to the pretensions of the imperial ego, we would not go as far as many postmoderns do in "valorizing the pulverization of the modern subject."[19] Indeed, the dismantling of the modern ego has an inevitable downside. When we come to realize that the autonomous self is a fiction which can no longer be believed, we are thrown into apocalyptic doubt about all previous beliefs about humanness and all courses of action that such beliefs sustained.[20] With the loss of our secure modern self-image, we are submerged in a postmodern identity crisis of immense proportions. These days more and more people are asking themselves Trudy's question, "Am I crazy?" And though the answer may not come back a resounding YES! many of us are honest enough to admit, "I'm just not feeling myself anymore."

So it is not surprising that a sensitive artist like Peter Gabriel chronicles this loss of modernist self-confidence in his song "Blood of Eden."[21] When this postmodern man catches a sight of his own reflection, he no longer sees the Promethean hero of modernity. Rather, Gabriel tells us, "I saw the signs of my undoing." In a similar way to Bruce Cockburn, who says that he needs a miracle "to keep this little thread from snapping,"[22] Gabriel describes the darkness of his heart as a process of unraveling and untying that has been going on from the beginning. To use postmodern language, this is a self in the process of deconstruction. And unlike those who are "so secure with everything they're buying," Gabriel later sings:

My grip is surely slipping
I think I've lost my hold . . .
I cannot get insurance any more
They don't take credit, only gold.

These lines depict a person who is losing his grip—on himself and on his world. It almost seems that he experiences the world as foreclosing on his soul. And in such a foreclosure the pretensions of the autonomous, self-sufficient ego are unmasked and the postmodern self finds itself asking again, "Who am I?" The question will not go away.

### Embracing the Decentered Self

Perhaps Kenneth Gergen can give us further insight into this postmodern anthropological dilemma. What we have called an identity crisis, Gergen describes as the process of "social saturation." The problem isn't just that in a postmodern situation we've lost the identifiable and unitary self of modernity, but that we are inundated by a multiplicity of clamoring voices proffering alternative identities. "As the voices expand in power and presence," Gergen observes, "all that seemed proper, right-minded, and well understood is subverted."[23] Instead of any clear alternative to the imperial ego, "social saturation provides us with a multiplicity of incoherent and unrelated languages of the self" with which we are perpetually bombarded, but between which it is impossible to choose. The result is that "the fully saturated self becomes no self at all."[24] Or to be more precise, we are left with an infinitely malleable self, capable of taking on an indefinite array of imprinted identities. Gergen explains:

Under postmodern conditions, persons exist in a state of continuous construction and reconstruction; it is a world where anything goes that can be negotiated. Each reality of self gives way to reflexive questioning, irony, and ultimately the playful probing of yet another reality. The center fails to hold.[25]

Not surprisingly, Woody Allen's films are often preoccupied with questions of individual identity in a postmodern world. This is nowhere more evident than in his cinematographic masterpiece, *Zelig*. This film portrays a chameleonlike individual who constantly changes his personality, his area of expertise and even his appearance to match whatever environment he finds himself in. Zelig represents the postmodern self that is unstable and decentered. Besides parodying the traditional subject of "normal" realist cinema, Allen here raises questions about the broader modernist view of the integral and whole self. When Zelig is finally healed of his psychosis, his case is given such worldwide media attention that he is transformed into yet another—perhaps even worse—aberration.[26] At the end of the film we are left wondering whether Zelig, or any of us, has any integral point of identity.

Far from bemoaning this lack of stable identity, however, many postmodern thinkers would have us celebrate the decentered self. Since there is no essential *me*, it follows that I can be whatever I construct myself to be. Gergen describes this "capacity to enter into identities or relationships of widely varying forms" as *ersatz being*.[27] He explains that "if identities are essentially forms of social construction, then one can be anything at any time so long as the roles, costumes, and settings have been commodiously arranged."[28]

This talk of costumes and roles recalls the theme of carnival we discussed in chapter two. Having recognized that we have no inherent or essential identities but only the various self-constructions that we project upon the world, we are encouraged to sit back and enjoy the show. Instead of taking ourselves too seriously we should honestly recognize and embrace a postmodern identity "lived out as a series of incoherent posturings."[29] Instead of seriousness, we are to "play with the truths of the day, shake them about, try them on like funny hats. Serious concerns are left at the carnival gate."[30]

It is this sense that ultimately nothing can be taken too seriously that informs the shift of perspective from modern to postmodern comedy. Comedy is often at the expense of another. But whereas modern comedy typically identifies the other as someone who is cruel, stupid, a despot or evil, the postmodern comedy of *Monty Python*, *Saturday Night Live* and David Letterman is essentially self-parody. We each become the other. It is in comedy, says Gergen,

that the implications of the carnival for the problem of self become most fully apparent. For as contemporary comedy warns, all actions are subject to satire from some perspective. All our attempts to do good works, to achieve, to improve, and to be responsible can be punctured with wit. The postmodern invitation is thus to carry the clown on one's shoulders—to always be ready to step out of "serious character" and locate its pretensions, to parody or ape oneself.[31]

Of course, it is not such a problem to "ape" or parody oneself when the self that is being poked fun at is just a stage persona anyway. There isn't really all that much at stake. No one need take this too personally, because that would assume that the brunt of the joke was somehow really "me." In reaction to the autonomous modern subject that took itself too seriously, postmodernity breeds a pluriform culture of jokesters, pranksters, jesters and carnival hustlers.

### Postmodern or Hypermodern?

But precisely this image of the carnival hustler betrays a fundamental paradox which we noted in chapter two. Whereas the carnival has become a classic postmodern symbol, with its evocative suggestion of multiplicity, playfulness and decentering, carnivals are in fact big business. And one consequence of the postmodern decentering of the self that is constructed and can be endlessly reconstructed is the proliferation of a vast array of service industries which cater to, facilitate—and profit from—postmodern self-construction. But this attempt to market the self is itself a quintessentially *modern*, not postmodern, phenomenon, going back at least to the rise of capitalism. Also essentially modern is the very notion that the self can be constructed. Charles Taylor has shown that "technologies of the self" developed out of the modern impulse to master and control nature.[32] This impulse was simply extended, by the nineteenth century, to *human* nature. If there is anything new about all of this, it is the incredible growth and tremendous success, at the end of the twentieth century, of a plethora of career counseling firms, business consultants, fitness centers, self-help groups, adult education programs and psychotherapeutic services. These are all predicated on the postmodern—or perhaps better, the hypermodern—understanding of the constructed (and reconstructible) self.

Further, since the electronic media are most prevalent in the saturation of the self, it is not surprising to see these media, in particular television, playing a formative role in the construction and reconstruction of our self-understandings. A constantly reconstructible self with no stable core requires a world of fleeting images to provide material for its reconstruction. Having no substance in itself, the saturated self must be constantly fed with images that it can take up, mimic, be entertained by and then discard. Television, of course, is custom-built for this task.[33] But it is Music Television (MTV) that is committed to image production with a vengeance. The postmodern subject does not need a coherent world; MTV makes sure that he or she does not get one. MTV is entertainment for a culture that is more interested in images, emotions and energy than in any plot that forms character either in the protagonists on the screen or the viewer at home. Bob Pittman, the founding chairman of the MTV network, said, "What we've introduced with MTV is nonnarrative form. . . . We rely on *mood* and *emotion*. We make you feel a certain way as opposed to you walking away with any particular knowledge."[34]

At issue in MTV is style, not substance, because the MTV viewer is the postmodern subject who has no substance.[35] But that means that such a person is infinitely open to the image manipulations of the media. When our kids today say, "But Dad, it's the style!" more is at stake than just peer pressure. The media will produce images and change them at a regular rate in order to provide us with styles to consume and identities to try out. Not only is this an extension—and heightening—of modern consciousness, but, like all consumer products, both styles and identities are essentially disposable.

This is the ultimate irony of the disposable society of advanced capitalism. Whatever is mastered, constructed and produced is, in the end, disposable—even identities! While the modern, centered self was consumptive of the world, the postmodern, decentered self is consumptive of images and experiences and will likely prove to be even more insatiable than its modern ancestor. On the level of socioeconomic analysis this would seem to indicate that postmodernity is little more than a logical extension of the culture of capitalism.[36] All of life has now been commodified, even personal identity. The heir of modernity's *Homo autonomous* is postmodernity's "solitary soul couched in front of the television set, seeking satisfaction for unspecified needs and ineffable desires."[37]

### Paralyzed in the Face of It All[38]

But this leads to another problem of the postmodern self. Gergen describes the condition resulting from the process of social saturation, especially as facilitated and accelerated by the media and recent communications technology, as a state of "multiphrenia," in which the individual is split "into a multiplicity of self-investments."[39] A multiphrenic person is populated by a plethora of selves. "In place of an enduring core of deep and indelible character, there is a chorus of invitations."[40] What Gergen describes as postmodern "multiphrenia" is strikingly similar to a pathological condition which is increasingly coming to light in the twentieth century. We are referring to "multiple personality disorder." People who suffer from this can usually trace the condition to physical, sexual or even ritual Satanic abuse as children. In order to cope with the terror of psychic violation, the self splits, as a defense mechanism, partitioning off the memory of abuse into a series of newly created, isolated personalities. Perhaps the culture of postmodernity suffers from something analogous to multiple personality disorder because the modernist understanding of the autonomous, independent, self-reliant, rational subject was, in fact, abusive of the human person. Multiphrenia would then be something to celebrate only insofar as it functions as a mechanism for coping with the violent imperial ego of the past. Beyond celebration, however, the decentered postmodern self testifies to the lingering trauma of modernity.

When we search for a biblical analogy to multiphrenia, the demon-possessed man of Mark 5 comes to mind. In answer to the second worldview question, Who are you? the postmodern self replies, "My name is Legion, for we are many" (v. 9). Controlled by many spirits, the man in the biblical story was tormented, homeless and in need of healing. So, it seems to us, is the contemporary postmodern psyche. Rather than valorizing the emerging postmodern worldview, we ought to recognize the tragic character of the answers to the first two worldview questions provided by contemporary culture:

*Where are we?* In a pluralistic world of our own construction.

*Who are we?* We are Legion.

It is important that we see the relationship between these two answers. Christopher Lasch notes that a sense of personal identity "has become uncertain and problematical not because people no longer occupy fixed social stations . . . but because they no longer inhabit a world that exists independently of themselves."[41] Rather than asking the second worldview question in the light of an assumed answer to the first, thus understanding human identity in the context of a broader world in which humans live, postmodernity—like modernity before it—makes the first worldview question a subspecies of the second. This is a crucial point. If we are in a world of our own constructions (the implicit postmodern answer to the first worldview question), and there is no accessible world beyond those constructions, then *where* we are depends on *who* we are. The tragedy of postmodernity, however, is that we are Legion. Therefore, the undecidability that has come to characterize our answer to the first worldview question is only heightened in the second worldview question. We know neither where we are nor who we are.

Well then, what are we to do? The second worldview question, Who are we? inquires about both the nature and task of being human.[42] How we are to live is deeply implicated in the vision we have of ourselves. This is the question of normativity, of ethics. But will we be able to offer any satisfying answer to this question if we have been caught in the quagmires of undecidability? How can we know what we should do if we can have no clear idea of ourselves or the world? This is precisely the problem at the root of the moral paralysis that characterizes the postmodern age.

This paralysis, confusion and undecidability can be discerned in the lyrics of some of the most sensitive artists in popular music. For example, the Indigo Girls' song "Closer to Fine" chronicles a quest for "insight between black and white."[43] This postmodern anthem about normativity is suffused with a sense of anomie and anxiety. The artist depicts a context in which "darkness has a hunger that's insatiable" and "lightness has a call that's hard to hear." And that is a context in which fear is the most appropriate emotional response—indeed, a fear that is so tangible that it can be wrapped around you like a blanket. It is a context in which the "ship of safety" has been sunk.[44] This is a situation of radical questioning, and the author tells the story of seeking clarity in various sources and finding none. She concludes that "there's more than one answer to these questions pointing me in a crooked line." But this answer is enough because, in the end, she decides that "the *less* I seek my source for some definitive / The closer I am to fine."

But can we live without definitive answers? Can we live without normative clarity? Or do we feel that once our "ship of safety" has sunk, we are submerged "in a world of disorder, senselessness and madness"?[45] And with such a massive sense of disappointment and normative confusion, what else can we do but be paralyzed in the face of it all? Such moral paralysis is constitutive of the postmodern condition.

How else could a postmodern, self-parodying jester end up? By definition, a saturated, multiphrenic self will find it problematic to enter into a relationship of commitment and intimacy. Such relationships necessarily assume that there is a real self (a real "me") that is being known and loved. How could a postmodern self ever make such a commitment? Who would be the *I* in the *I do*? Is this why we see an incredible difficulty with commitment in our culture?[46] Perhaps the problem is that we find ourselves unable to answer the Who am I? question, and thus we are without enough self-knowledge to be able to enter into a relationship of committed intimacy with another.

Christopher Lasch describes this as the condition of the "minimal self." In a postmodern context where the self is under siege, it "contracts to a defensive core, armed against adversity. Emotional equilibrium demands a minimal self, not the imperial self of yesteryear."[47] We find ourselves characterized by "selective apathy, emotional disengagement from others, renunciation of the past and the future, a determination to live one day at a time."[48] Such a beleaguered, minimal self is clearly in no position to make any commitments.

### Consumer Choice and Moral Undecidability

Indeed, instead of long-term commitment, the postmodern self just moves on—to the next game, to the next show, to the next relationship. This is a nomadic self, on the road with the carnival. The postmodern self thus finds itself ultimately homeless. The notion of a settled home or a stable world is, after all, an illusory modern (and premodern) construction that can no longer be believed. So, the emerging postmodern vision disallows any such settledness for human life. Don't get too comfortable, this vision tells us. After all, you're just playing a game of self-construction in the midst of a wide array of such games. This is the carnival. There is another show to put on, there are other worlds to play with, other selves to try on for size.

The moral crisis that ensues, however, is massive. Leonard Cohen is right:

Things are going to slide in all directions

Won't be nothing

Nothing you can measure anymore.[49]

Nothing can be measured because there are no measures that are not our own constructions. This is the radical meaning of postmodern incommensurability. No wonder Cohen goes on to say, "When they said REPENT / I wonder what they meant." The language of repentance is only understandable if there is a means to be measured and be found wanting.

Consequently, the genuine question facing postmodern culture is whether we can find norms to guide personal and societal development in a cultural context that has abandoned belief in moral standards as existing independently of particular human judgments and interests. How is it possible to live meaningfully if our ethical norms are simply our constructions, not given to us by either God or nature?

Perhaps the first thing to notice, by way of answer, is that in a socially constructed world, populated by either defensively minimal or playfully multiphrenic selves, ethical normativity becomes fundamentally a matter of choice. Since we can no longer hide behind the façade of universality, we must now openly and honestly decide which ethical framework we will adopt. Or better, we must decide on which ethical framework we will construct. This emphasis on choice and construction legitimately draws our attention to the responsibility we have in forming and articulating ethical frameworks and provides a helpful antidote to modernity's self-assured claims to universality.

However, more significant than the *content* of our choice (as if one option were better than another) is the act of choosing itself. As we have seen, postmodernity is a consumer culture, feasting (or picking, as the case may be) at the smorgasbord of worldviews pluralistically spread before it. As a society of consumers, we define choice "not as the freedom to choose one course of action over another but as the freedom to choose everything at once. This is the 'I-want-it-all' mentality. 'Freedom of choice' means 'keeping your options open.' "[50] However, in real life every choice of any consequence inevitably rules out a whole series of other options. It is literally impossible to "keep your options open" and live a life of any significance. A postmodern approach to choice in a pluralistic universe results in moral paralysis. In the end, no choices can be made—or at least no choices that really matter. Again, Lasch is helpful: "Unless the choice carries with it the possibility of making a difference, of changing the course of events, of setting in motion a chain of events that may prove irreversible, it negates the freedom it claims to uphold."[51]

Without taking seriously human limits and the need to choose between finite alternatives, *freedom* is trivialized into little more than market preference. So again we see that the postmodern self is the ethical product of late capitalism. Roger Lundin is undoubtedly right when he says that "the desiring and acquiring self of postmodern cultural theory bears more than a casual resemblance to the unit of consumption at the center of market economies and democratic societies."[52] But instead of the modern rational consumer, driven by the confidence of Western economic progress, the unencumbered postmodern self is driven and directed by nothing but its own arbitrary (and changing) preference. "There is no goal for the actions of the self save the fulfillment of its desires."[53] *Choice* thus becomes not an owning of responsibility but an escape from allowing oneself to be held accountable. Consequently, Albert Borgmann describes the current ethical mood as one of indolent sullenness:

> At times sullenness is voiced in telling phrases. Indolence comes to the fore in the expression, so often delivered with finality, "it's *my* choice." What sounds like the assumption of ultimate responsibility is usually the flourish of moral retreat,

the refusal to discuss, explain, and justify a decision, and the retirement to self-indulgence.[54]

Within the context of postmodernity, however, this retreat from moral accountability and retirement to self-indulgence is perfectly understandable. Postmodernity is, after all, a "mall culture." And, like carnivals, shopping malls can be exhausting. Being bombarded with a cacophony of voices, each calling us to enter into their world, and constantly being required to make world and identity-constructing choices before the postmodern smorgasbord results in a widespread feeling of consumer exhaustion. Shopping when you know exactly what you need and where to get it is often an enjoyable, even relaxing, experience. Aimlessly wandering through a mall with an incredible range of consumer options can be extremely tiring. It is not simply the multiplicity of options that exhausts us; at bottom it is the inability to make a normative choice.

But people *do* act. We *do* make ethical decisions every day. The problem is that we have no way to argue definitively with each other about the *grounds* of those actions because all such grounds are the limited and idiosyncratic perspectives of our particular moral community at best, and our own consumer desires at worst. If ethical norms are socially constructed, and if all criteria by which we would judge the legitimacy of social constructions are themselves embedded in other social constructions, then we find ourselves in a situation where it is impossible to come to any final ethical decisions. Modernity could confidently proclaim that rationality was the final adjudicator of all views of reality and the self, if it was applied scientifically and in service of progress. Postmodernity tells us that at best Enlightenment rationality is but one particular way of construing the world, which has no privileged epistemic status, and that at worst such rationality is an ideological tool of mastery and oppression. But this only deepens our sense of moral paralysis. If reason is no longer a final arbiter of what we can truly know about the world, or about right and wrong, then what is?[55]

Deconstructive patterns of thinking may have therapeutically served us well by uncovering our biases, interests, assumptions and reifications, but they leave us in a normless universe. Even the deconstructive critique of totalizing ways of thinking as inherently violent would lose its power. *So what* if this way of thinking is violent? On what basis are we to conclude that violence is a bad thing?[56]

This problem is illustrated by the narrator's despair in John Berger's novel *G.* Attempting to describe an actual historical event, the narrator finally says, "Write anything. Truth or untruth. It is unimportant. Speak but speak with tenderness, for that is all that you can do that may help a little. Build a barricade of words, no matter what they mean!"[57] Apart from problems of representation that the narrator is struggling with, there are also ethical quandaries to be addressed here. If truth doesn't matter, why does tenderness? Why write in a way that will help? What is *help*? Is a barricade of words conducive to tenderness? And if the writing can be true or untrue and it doesn't matter what the words mean, then how will we recognize tenderness when we meet it?

At the end of the deconstructive process we must ask, What *action* are we left with? What kind of *praxis* will a postmodern world engender? Won't any ethical action in a postmodern world, in the end, be subverted by its own deconstructive questioning?[58]

### From the Carnival to the Sea

Crushing normative confusion characterizes postmodern morality. Recognizing that there is no moral order apart from the moral order that we impose on our own socially constructed world leaves us submerged in anomic terror. The experience of the world as our *home*, in the sense of a place where we know the rules and responsibilities of the house, is lost and a nomadic homelessness dominates the ethical horizon.[59]

We find ourselves, ultimately, traveling with the carnival. Moral discourse is, like all discourse, a game to be played. And since it is a game, it should not be played with too much seriousness. As we have already noted, "serious concerns are left at the carnival gate."[60] Even the pained face of the other in his or her suffering could no longer be countenanced. In the end, normativity is another casualty of postmodernity.

The problem is that there is something in us that doesn't allow us to simply "play the dandy" and "piss against the wind" in the face of suffering and oppression.[61] Playing the language game begins to feel self-indulgent in the face of a broken world. Indeed, such game playing is an alienating self-indulgence that numbs us both to the pain of others and to our own pain. The ironic deconstruction of all meaningful discourse, including normative discourse, says Gergen, "is like a Pac-Man of social pattern, gobbling all that stands in its path."[62] Postmodern morality amounts to little more than "macho masturbation," "a celebration of self-serving autonomy."[63] Such self-serving autonomy is perhaps better seen as the heroic dying breath of late modernity than as an honest postmodern confrontation with our ethical confusion.[64]

Normativity is fundamentally a matter of direction in the midst of confusion. A normative framework functions as a navigational guide throughout life, with all of its dangers, quandaries and dead ends. So perhaps a better metaphor to express the postmodern ethical condition than the carnival would be being lost at sea. John Dominic Crossan puts it this way: "There is no lighthouse keeper. There is no lighthouse. There is no dry land. There are only people living on rafts made from their own imaginations. And there is the sea."[65] The modern era began with Columbus setting out to sea. He seemed to have had at least some idea as to where he was going. As that epoch ends and a postmodern era begins we find ourselves again at sea. But this time we have no navigational assistance and no direction. We are alone, adrift in a postmodern world.[66]

# 4/They Don't Tell Stories Like They Used To

H aving examined in the last two chapters the emerging postmodern answers to the worldview questions Where are we? and Who are we? in this chapter we will explore the answers postmodernity suggests in response to the third and fourth questions, What's wrong? and What's the remedy? Although these could be construed as asking about right and wrong human action, that is, about matters of ethical guidance or normativity, we are taking them in a broader and more fundamental sense. The issue here isn't simply How am I to live? though that is definitely implied. That question also arose in chapter three as an important aspect of the question of self-identity. More fundamentally, however, we are raising the question of how we are to understand evil and redemption. And these understandings are typically communicated in a narrative. The question of right and wrong action is here reframed in terms of the overarching worldview or story we tell about *what's wrong* with the world and human life and *what's the remedy* for this fundamental problem.

## The Nature of Narrative

It is perfectly natural to answer the third and fourth worldview questions in terms of a story. For every story has, minimally, a plot, and as far back as Aristotle's *Poetics* plots have been understood as involving movement from an initial complication or tension to the denouement or resolution of that tension, what Aristotle called literally "tying" (or "entanglement") and "loosing."[1] The tension may be the biblical story of the fall or the murder in a mystery novel. "It may not occur on page 1," says Michael Root, "but it sets the narrative tension that impels the plot's movement and whose resolution constitutes the story's end."[2] The formal structure of enplotment thus makes narratives perfect vehicles for exploring the worldview questions What's wrong? and What's the remedy? Whereas the introduction of plot conflict formally corresponds to the problem of evil, the movement toward resolution corresponds to redemption. This correspondence has led Michael Root to suggest that, at least in the biblical story, enplotment is equivalent to soteriology.[3]

But two other typical dimensions of narrative are important also for worldview analysis, namely *character* and *setting*. These might be seen to correspond to the questions Who are we? and Where are we? This shows just how inextricably the four worldview questions are interrelated. Our identity and task as human beings (who are we?) is fundamentally rooted in our sense of the world or reality which we inhabit (where are we?). But both our identity and sense of the world are themselves profoundly modified by the larger story we tell of evil (what's wrong?) and redemption (what's the remedy?). Although in *The Transforming Vision* we didn't explicitly use the category of story to describe the Christian worldview, it is precisely as *a narrative of God's intent to redeem a fallen creation* that the Bible answers the four worldview questions.[4] Although this was implicit throughout our exposition, it is worth stating clearly here.[5]

Both Judaism and Islam (the other "religions of the Book") also articulate their worldview in narrative form, appealing to the destiny of history as revelatory of God's intent. Even Eastern religions, such as Hinduism and Buddhism, which are often portrayed as suspicious of history (at least before their encounter with the West), have passed on a rich heritage of myths in storied form, including an epic narrative, the Mahabrata (of which the Bhagavad-Gita is a part). Myths and folktales of good, evil and redemption are also the stock-in-trade of the contemporary indigenous religions of Africa, North and South America, and Australia, as well as the classical religions of Greece, Rome, Egypt and Mesopotamia. In each case, ultimate truths about the world, humanity, evil and salvation are communicated in terms of stories which give guidance and set the parameters for ethical human action.

## The Universal Ideal of Modern Ethics

The only exception would seem to be in the case of modernity. If there is one point the history of modern ethics is agreed upon (granting, of course, the great diversity and conflict about what actually constitutes right living or the "good" life), it is that meaningful ethical action cannot be rooted in anything as naive, subjective or idiosyncratic as a story, since that would make ethics merely an expression of a particular cultural or religious attitude. On the contrary, ethical thinking in the modern period (since at least the seventeenth century), both among moral philosophers and in the broader society, is characterized by the quest for a purely rational, objective, abstract and universal foundation for human action, independent of and unimpeded by the subjective point of view of any existing religion, nation, social group or individual.

This quest is epitomized in Immanuel Kant's famous "categorical imperative." Although Kant was a Christian, he refused to ground ethical action in anything specific to the Christian faith. Every ethical judgment I make, claimed Kant, must be both derived from neutral human reason and universalizable—that is, capable of being treated as an invariant law, equally applicable to every rational human being in every possible circumstance.[6] "The hallmark of contemporary [that is, modern] ethical theory," explain David Burrell and Stanley Hauerwas, "has been to free moral behavior from the arbitrary and contingent nature of the agent's beliefs, dispositions and character."[7] Neither my context, identity nor worldview is regarded as significant in modern ethics, and such idiosyncratic factors must be bracketed out in moral decision-making. "Under the spell of Kantian accounts of rationality," explains Hauerwas, "there lingers the fear that if we recognize the historic nature of our moral convictions we will have to acknowledge them as arbitrary and possibly even false."[8] The underlying anxiety has been that anything less than absolute moral universality would open us up to an arbitrary subjectivism or relativism that would undermine modern progress.

It is important to note just how novel this ethical ideal really is. Even the Greek philosophical tradition, stretching back to Plato and Aristotle, did not think to extend its quest for objective knowledge of a universal and unchanging cosmic order to the realm of ethics. This is at the root of Aristotle's famous distinction between *theory* and *praxis*. Although some sort of absolutely certain knowledge of the way things "really" are could be claimed in the theoretical realm (only to be suitably deconstructed in postmodern times), the practical realm of ethical human action was regarded as inexorably intertwined with what we would today call subjective, historical and contextual matters. Thus Aristotle contrasted *theōria* (contemplative thought) with *phronēsis* (practical reasoning). By *phronēsis* he meant the essentially ad hoc attempt to discern and justify right and wrong in particular circumstances, a process which was always dependent on the identity, social roles, beliefs and tradition of the moral agent in question. Far from conceiving ethical decision-making to be a matter of applying some supposedly universal and objectively certain moral principles to human action, Aristotle understood ethical choices to be dependent on one's prior learning of a pattern of virtues by a sort of moral apprenticeship to a particular tradition.[9]

### From System to Story

And just as modern claims about the nature of reality and the self are being uncovered in a postmodern context as social constructions with no intrinsic necessity, so modern systems of ethics, with their claim to universality and objectivity, are also under suspicion. Perhaps no one has done more in recent times to dispel the illusion of neutrality under which modern ethics has labored than the Christian philosopher Alasdair MacIntyre. Although he is by no means alone in this exposé, MacIntyre's prominent position in mainstream North American philosophy has granted him a hearing beyond either the deconstructionists or Christian ethicists like Stanley Hauerwas (whose arguments, though similar to MacIntyre's, have addressed primarily the North American *theological* community).[10] It would not be an exaggeration to say that MacIntyre's 1981 book *After Virtue* precipitated a profound and widespread change in thinking about ethics on this continent.[11]

Although certainly not everyone has been convinced by all his arguments, MacIntyre's meticulous historical analysis has dealt a decisive blow to the dominant Western ethical ideal (both in the academy and in the wider society) of attaining universal, abstract moral norms for human action that are independent of, and uncontaminated by, social, cultural, historical and individual particularity. Not only has such contextless universality never been attained in the history of ethics, it never *can* be attained.

Furthermore, MacIntyre argues, this ethical ideal disguises the particular, conditioned, historical context in which it actually arose. The very ideal of a universal, contextless ethics—a perfectly objective rational system capable of grounding human behavior—is itself firmly rooted in and conditioned by the modern, Enlightenment project.[12] "At its core," notes Roger Lundin,

> the Enlightenment held to a bedrock faith in the ability of the self to discover
> universal, binding truths of science, politics and morality. Since it conceived of
> human nature as essentially rational, the Enlightenment could claim that every
> free individual would reach similar conclusions about the most crucial matters
> of civic, moral, and intellectual life.[13]

Lundin is right: this is a *faith*. Indeed, it is a faith which flies in the face of massive evidence to the contrary, namely the fact of wide-ranging moral disagreement.[14] Why would anyone believe that a self, centered in free and autonomous rationality, would achieve, together with all other enlightened selves, the same, universally valid, moral conclusions? For the simple reason that this is required by the progress myth, which until recently has guided Western culture. But, paradoxically, the very notion that in modern times we have outgrown the childish, prescientific stage of mythical thinking and progressed to the maturity of scientific reason and technological mastery is itself a *story*. It is, therefore, only by telling its own "tall tale" that modernity can claim to have surpassed the need for stories.[15]

But MacIntyre's attack on modern ethics goes further than pointing out how this modern ideal disguises its own subjective, particular, storied origins. According to MacIntyre, it is precisely this false ideal which is to blame for our present inability to grasp what is going on in the intractable moral disputes within both philosophical ethics and contemporary society. It is MacIntyre's claim that our public moral disputes (whether concerning abortion, war, the economy, homosexuality or even the nature of justice itself) are not accidental, temporary conflicts, which are in principle resolvable through rational public debate. We have long assumed, explains MacIntyre, "that there are standards of rationality, adequate for the evaluation of rival answers to such questions, equally available, at least in principle, to all persons, whatever tradition they may happen to find themselves in and whether or not they inhabit any tradition."[16] But this is a false assumption; there simply is no such tradition-neutral rationality available to us. And the residual quest for such a rationality impedes even meaningful conversation about moral disagreements.

Hence, MacIntyre does not argue simply that contemporary disagreements about justice and ethics arise from (and are traceable back to) different, conflicting traditions of inquiry or action. He makes the further point, explored at some length in his 1988 sequel to *After Virtue*, that contemporary ethical disagreements are themselves implicated in parallel disagreements about *phronēsis* or practical rationality.[17] The reason why public rational debate in Western society cannot resolve disputed questions of justice is that there are intractable disagreements about the rational process and criteria governing our decisions about what is just. Not only is justice tradition-bound, but reason is narrative-dependent. Hence the title of the 1988 sequel: *Whose Justice? Which Rationality?*

MacIntyre's basic point is that human subjectivity is intrinsic to ethics. But this subjectivity should not be conceived as disembodied, idiosyncratic or purely individual. The subjectivity he indicates is fundamentally communal.

> So theories of justice and practical rationality confront us as aspects of traditions, allegiance to which requires the living out of some more or less systematically embodied form of human life, each with its own specific modes of social relationship, each with its own canons of interpretation and explanation in respect of the behavior of others, each with its own evaluative practices.[18]

Right and wrong can thus only be discerned from *within* a particular tradition. Ethical action is dependent on indwelling a socially embodied narrative, on membership in a concrete community oriented to a distinctive perspective, heritage and vision of life. In MacIntyre's succinct formulation: "I can only answer the question 'What am I to do?' if I can answer the prior question 'Of what story or stories do I find myself a part?' "[19]

It is important to note that MacIntyre is not postmodern. Not only does he have little time for "Nietzscheans" (by which he typically means deconstructionists), but he further aspires to recover a premodern ideal of ethics rooted in an Aristotelian-Thomistic version of the Christian faith.[20] Without affirming this premodern aspiration in any way (indeed, at this point we would part ways with MacIntyre), it nevertheless seems to us that MacIntyre's narrative proposals concerning the nature of ethics constitute a healthy corrective to the modernist approach and one that we as Christians can wholeheartedly embrace. With MacIntyre, we are happy to say good riddance to the false modern ideal of formulating abstract, contextless systems of thought or action. And we applaud his turn to narrative (a turn which is echoed in many postmodern writers) as a central category for understanding human life, including our discernment of how we are to live ethically in the world.[21]

Furthermore, narrative is a helpful category (as we have suggested at the beginning of this chapter) for understanding the nature of worldviews, and, in particular, the nature of the Bible and the biblical worldview. Although we will engage in quite extensive narrative analysis of the Bible in chapter five, it is perhaps appropriate to emphasize this here because under the impact of modern ideals Christians have long ignored the narrative infrastructure of Scripture, as well as the specific literary narratives within the Bible, as so much extrinsic packaging for timeless theological or moral truths (or even for a Christian "worldview") which is what *really* matters. In N. T. Wright's picturesque phrase, many Christians use the Bible as "an unsorted edition of *Daily Light.*" They think it really ought to be arranged into neat little devotional chunks, but it "happens to have got all muddled up."[22] Employing the metaphor of the Bible as a large pot of narrative soup, Wright pictures our practice of biblical interpretation as our "attempts, as it were, to boil off certain timeless truths, models or challenges into a sort of ethereal [supra-narrative] realm" in order to transport these timeless truths from the biblical pot to our own soup bowls and then to "re-liquify them," thus making them tasty and relevant to our contemporary situation.[23] Or, to use Thomas Long's comparable image, we throw "the text into an exegetical winepress, squeezing out the ideational matter," and then try to find ways of applying these contextless "ideas" to our lives in the present. The essentially narrative shape of the text is simply "discarded as an ornament."[24] In light of this widespread exegetical *practice* (whatever our hermeneutical *theory* might be), it is imperative that the church unequivocally reclaim the Bible as narrative (whatever the consequences for our encounter with postmodernity).

This is not to say that the Bible consists exclusively of stories, that is, texts in the narrative genre. The Bible is more like a grand epic or, in David Kelsey's words, "a vast, loosely structured, non-fictional novel,"[25] in which is embedded a great diversity of nonnarrative material like proverbs, laws, psalms and epistles.[26] Yet all this material has its place and is to be interpreted in the context of the overarching narrative movement of creation, fall and redemption, the epic drama of God's purposes for the world and for humanity being worked out through Israel, Jesus and the church.

### Incredulity Toward Metanarratives

It is important to note here a dual sense of *story* (or *narrative* or *tradition*) in our analysis so far. This twofold usage is found not only in MacIntyre but also in other writers on the subject, and it can be quite confusing. On the one hand, *story* is taken to mean a *socially embodied* narrative. This is story in the sense of a first-order activity or practice, the way of life of an actual community of persons oriented toward (and guided by) a common heritage and common goals. On the other hand, however, *story* can refer to a *grounding or legitimating* narrative, the worldview which guides the practice of a given community. "Human life," says Wright, "can be seen as grounded in and constituted by the implicit or explicit stories which humans tell one another."[27] This is story in the sense of a second-order activity, the "mythic" account given *of* a way of life, which is taken as normative *for* that way of life.[28] Although MacIntyre usually means by story a socially embodied narrative (a *lived* story or tradition), he appeals to the second sense of the term when he writes: "There is no way to give us an understanding of any society, including our own, except through the stock of stories which constitute its own dramatic resources. Mythology, in its original sense, is at the heart of things."[29]

What is at stake in the distinction between these two senses of *story* is that while most postmoderns would applaud MacIntyre's view of ethics as always rooted in first-order *lived* stories or socially embodied narratives, they would part company on the role of second-order stories or *meta*narratives. Going beyond MacIntyre's laudable critique of abstract systems of truth that claim to transcend all particular contexts, postmodern thinkers tend to be suspicious of grounding or legitimating stories, whether the modern myth of autonomous progress or the Christian story of God's redemption, since such stories amount to little more than temporally extended versions of the same sort of absolute systems that MacIntyre inveighs against and that Derrida and company have attempted to deconstruct. This suspicion is epitomized in Jean-François Lyotard's famous statement: "Simplifying in the extreme, I define *postmodern* as incredulity toward metanarratives."[30]

From a postmodern perspective, there are two central problems with metanarratives, and the one flows from the other. The first problem is epistemological. Whereas conceiving truth in terms of lived narrative, as MacIntyre does, may be more honest about the socially embodied, contextual nature of human knowing, if a narrative purports to be not simply a local story (an ad hoc, first-order account of a community's experience) but the universal story of the world from *archē* to *telos*, a grand narrative encompassing world history from beginning to end, then such a narrative inevitably claims more than it can possibly know. If all knowledge is socially constructed, as we saw in our discussion of the Where are we? and Who are we? worldview questions (in chapters two and three), then the same is true of the stories we tell to answer the questions What's wrong? and What's the remedy? But if metanarratives are social constructions, then, like abstract ethical systems, they are simply particular moral visions dressed up in the guise of universality. And in falsely claiming universality while being blind to their own constructed character, metanarratives inevitably privilege unity, homogeneity and closure over difference, heterogeneity, otherness and openness.[31] The result is that all kinds of events and people end up being excluded from the way in which the story gets told. No meta-narrative, it appears, is large enough and open enough genuinely to include the experiences and realities of all people.

But this leads us to the second problem, namely the ethical objection that meta-narratives are inevitably oppressive and violent in their false claims to "totality." Whereas this objection begins with the postmodern critique of the hegemonic, imperial, absolutistic claims of modernity and the violence perpetuated in the name of its grand narrative of autonomous progress, the objection is expanded to encompass a widespread suspicion of any comprehensive metanarrative of world history that makes "total" claims.[32] Indeed, the typical postmodern answer to the third worldview question (what's wrong?) is that it is precisely metanarratives that are the main culprit.

To the postmodern mind, metanarratives are mere human constructs, fictive devices through which we impose an order on history and make it subject to us (hence they may be termed "master" narratives).[33] Claims to moral universality, whether rooted in systems or metanarratives, can be deconstructed in such a way that they are seen to be little more than the legitimation of the vested interests of those who have the power and authority to make such universal pronouncements. That is why Walter Truett Anderson can say that "social definitions of morality (which are of course another name for social constructions of reality) are power grabs and conspiracies."[34] On a postmodern reading, metanarratives, just like absolutist claims to "reality," invariably serve to legitimate the dominant power structures and to trivialize, marginalize or suppress those whose stories and experiences do not fit the metanarrative.[35] Postmodernism, says Terry Eagleton, thus "signals the death of such 'meta-narratives' whose secretly terroristic function was to ground and legitimate the illusion of a 'universal' human history."[36]

### What's Been Done in the Name of Jesus

A recent example serves to illustrate the totalizing character of metanarratives. In the summer of 1989 Francis Fukuyama published what has become a famous and widely read article in the neoconservative journal *The National Interest*. Entitled "The End of History?" the article discussed the meaning of the demise of Soviet communism.[37] The details of Fukuyama's argument do not concern us here.[38] Suffice it to say that he offers an interpretation of the events in the Soviet bloc at the end of the 1980s that has liberal capitalist democracy as the victor in the battle of ideologies. In fact, this victory is equivalent to the "end of history" because history is, according to Fukuyama, driven by the conflict of ideologies, and since 1989 there has been nothing left to fight about. Liberal capitalist democracy is the highest ideological achievement of the race. That this is a metanarrative, there is no doubt.[39]

But Fukuyama's reading of history also demonstrates precisely the kind of violent exclusion and marginalization of other perspectives and peoples that postmodernists criticize in metanarratives. Not only is Fukuyama's analysis blind to the ambiguities of democratic capitalism (manifest in such things as the inequitable distribution of wealth, a geopolitical track record that tends to support authoritarian regimes that are friendly toward capitalist economic interests, and the massive destruction of the environment at the hands of industrial capitalism), but his analysis systematically rules out the insights and contribution of any peoples who are not taken up by the spirit of capitalist democracy. This latter point is especially evident when Fukuyama declares that Western liberal democracy is nothing less than "the common ideological heritage of mankind."[40] This declaration effectively excludes the vast majority of the world's population from this "common" heritage and thus constitutes an ideological form of genocide. The grand narrative of Western progress, like all grand narratives, results in the devaluation and suppression of other stories.

But metanarratives also result in quite literal, physical and military violence against persons. Paradigm examples of this violence stretch from Neo-Babylonian imperial conquest throughout the ancient Near East in the sixth century B.C., buttressed by the mythology of the Enuma Elish, which pictured Babylon as the privileged dwelling of the gods and other nations as the forces of chaos, to the twentieth-century Nazi agenda for supremacy in Europe, legitimated by a narrative of blood, soil and racial destiny.[41] Alongside these examples we might cite the Christian crusades for possession of medieval Palestine, Islamic jihad against infidels, Marxist-Leninist aspirations to world domination and the consequences in Latin America of the Monroe Doctrine as part of the U.S. narrative of liberal democracy.

To put it in the words of the Christian (and, in this respect, quite postmodern) songwriter Bruce Cockburn: "Everybody / loves to see / justice done / on somebody else."[42] In "Justice," a song released the same year that the first edition of Alasdair MacIntyre's *After Virtue* was published, Cockburn highlights the politically and religiously self-interested nature of what passes for "justice" and the violence that is often perpetuated in the name of our cherished narratives. Self-critically, Cockburn starts with his own tradition:

What's been done in the name of Jesus

What's been done in the name of Buddha
What's been done in the name of Islam
What's been done in the name of man
And in the name of liberation
And in the name of civilization
And in the name of race
And in the name of peace!
    everybody
    loves to see
    justice done
    on somebody else.[43]

If MacIntyre claims that justice (what am I to do?) is intrinsically contextual, necessarily rooted in a socially embodied narrative (of what story do I find myself a part?), then his claim is to be applauded as a significant advance over the illusory neutrality and universality accorded ethics in the Enlightenment tradition. Narratively formed ethics holds great promise. But if we take either postmodern warnings or historical examples seriously, the promise of narratively formed ethics turns out to be a fundamentally ambiguous one. At the very least we will have to ask (playing with the title of MacIntyre's book), *Whose* story? *Which* tradition? Some narratives (like fascism and communism) seem to be intrinsically more oppressive than others.

### The Move Beyond Narrative

If the dominant postmodern answer to the question What's wrong? points to the violence inherent in totalizing systems and stories, then it becomes clear what the answer to What's the remedy? will be. We are to get rid of all such metanarratives and grand systems of truth. As a result, a recurring theme of localized narratives has arisen in postmodern discourse.[44] Just as all voices must be allowed to be heard in the carnival of postmodern culture, so also must we allow the proliferation of "little stories" in our culture. If no grand narrative is true, and if all narratives are constructed by individuals and communities, then no narrative must be privileged, and local, multiple and marginal narratives must be encouraged. Rather than requiring any grand narrative to ground or legitimate our actions, we must admit that all such grand narratives are simply particular and limited stories that have been imperialistically imposed on the world. If all we really have is the first-order narratives of our own particular, limited and finite communities, then we must acknowledge that our actions are locally legitimated in what is essentially an ad hoc manner, with no transcendent justification.[45] One story may legitimate a style of life and course of action very different from another story. And since there is no transcendent court of appeal—no finally true story for everyone and everything—the postmodern condition requires us to find a way in which to live with radical plurality.

But some postmoderns would go even further in their embrace of heterogeneity and difference. Some, like Friedrich Nietzsche (arguably the first postmodern philosopher), have emphatically refused to construct or participate even in *narratives* since even local stories have a structure or plot and thus impose an order on the world.[46] Nietzsche's radical position led him to favor *aphorisms* as a means of communicating. Aphorisms are typically a set of loosely connected, often randomly sequenced, assorted comments. At most, they may be arranged topically. They may be short pithy statements (such as proverbial sayings) or more poetic, lyrical discourses, but the consistent point is that no series of aphorisms constitutes a unified, totalizing structure. Gilles Deleuze has described the Nietzschean aphorism as a "play of forces."[47] It is a vector through which energy is transmitted but no conclusion reached. And while various isolated aphorisms might hit or strike us powerfully, there is in the choice of the aphoristic genre a calculated absence of systematic or narrative argument.

A progressive increase in this absence of argument is observable in the writings of Norman O. Brown, the classical scholar who translated Hesiod's *Theogony* in the early 1950s.[48] Brown later embraced a radical (postmodern) form of Freudian psychology and wrote *Life Against Death: The Psychoanalytic Meaning of History*, a sustained argument for what we might today call a postmodern reading of Freud that goes beyond Freud.[49] Having thus *argued* for a postmodern position, his next book, *Love's Body*, abandoned argument altogether.[50] Described in reviews as Nietzschean, it was aphoristic in form and contained a lengthy section (chapters 10 to 16) on the problem of language.[51] Next came a book entitled *Closing Time*, also aphoristic, though more radically so, which contained a fifth and final chapter on language (containing Brown's aphoristic reflections on aphorisms, poetry and silence, and calling for a return to the language of the gods).[52] Finally Brown stopped publishing his writing altogether (presumably the written format was too fixed and contextual), and audiotapes of his aphorisms, entitled "To Greet the Return of the Gods," were made available to the public.[53]

It is fascinating that the noncanonical Gnostic Gospels (like the Gospel of Thomas discovered at Nag Hammadi) are basically aphoristic in character, unlike the canonical Gospels, which tell a definite story.[54] The literary form in this case matches Gnosticism's refusal to take seriously the local, embodied, narrative shape of the life of Jesus.[55] Aphorisms are also the genre of choice in Zen Buddhism, in the form of koans, and in Taoist thought, exemplified in the Tao te Ching and the I Ching.[56] This helps explain why numerous postmodern thinkers who are suspicious of narrative are attracted to gnosticism, Zen and Taoism.[57]

## A Critical Response

It must be admitted that some of this postmodern suspicion is justified, since many metanarratives have indeed functioned ideologically, imposing their view of reality and suppressing minority stories in the process. We are, therefore, sympathetic to the postmodern diagnosis that implicates metanarratives in violence. And we are sympathetic also to the postmodern remedy, namely the proliferation of little, local stories. We affirm that it is a good thing that minority voices which have long been silenced should now be heard. Indeed, it is of the utmost importance for Christians to listen to others and learn from other traditions in a relationship of mutuality and respect.

Nevertheless, there are a number of significant problems with the postmodern diagnosis and prescription. In the first place, it is not obvious that metanarratives have any exclusive claims to totalization and violence. On the contrary, the embrace of local stories can legitimate violence on a scale to match any metanarrative. Take for example the present tribal violence and "ethnic cleansing" in the Balkan states that was actually held in check by the political dominance of the Soviet Union with its modernist metanarrative of Marxist social engineering and universal class struggle. With the dissolution of the Soviet Union, we now have the intensification of conflict between small states—and between ethnic communities *within* states—each with its own local identity, agenda and narrative.[58]

If we look at South Africa, we see that as the hegemony of white Afrikaner rule (legitimated by the metanarrative of apartheid) has been weakening in recent years, leading to a democratic constitution and free elections, there has been an escalation of tribal violence between Zulus and the ANC, and even intra-Zulu fighting, local faction pitted against local faction. This tribal violence is reproduced in the recent genocide in Rwanda, in the history of conflict between Israel and the PLO, and now between the PLO and the Palestinian terrorist faction known as Hamas.[59] In each of these cases, horrendous bloodshed has been motivated by a local narrative, which makes no explicit claims to universality, but which legitimates total war against some community or group identified as the enemy.[60]

Humans, it seems, constitutionally need metanarratives. We require some over-arching framework that makes sense of the totality of life and that gives meaning to our place in the grand scheme of things. Hence even local narratives pertaining initially to even a small tribe or community end up being *treated as if* they were universal. An example of this is the fact that many aboriginal peoples of the Amer-icas have traditionally named their own tribe "the people," thus disenfranchising, by implication, all other tribes from that honorific. Perhaps a local narrative leg-itimating a particular people's way of life would be relatively harmless *if* the group in question were isolated from all others who were different. But when a group with a local narrative encounters those who are "other," such others must be accounted for in terms of the narrative. Tragically, on most occasions, the other becomes the enemy, embodying the forces of evil, impurity and chaos, resulting in an imperative of opposition, even extermination, in the name of the originally local story.[61]

But our problems with the postmodern diagnosis and remedy go further than noting that even local narratives can legitimate violence. We would claim, further, that the postmodern answers to the third and fourth worldview questions make sense only in terms of a postmodern metanarrative, though this metanarrative is surreptitiously introduced and remains implicit. The very term *postmodern*, which is self-consciously used by many contemporary thinkers as a term of self-identification, implies a discernment of a particular stage in world history, that we live after or at the end of modernity. Thus Stephen Best and Douglas Kellner inquire: "Does not the very concept of postmodernity or of a postmodern condition presuppose a master narrative, a totalizing perspective, which envisions the transition from a previous stage of society to a new one?"[62]

But more than simply positing a transition from an old to a new stage in history, postmodernists typically think this is a good thing and so frame this transition in terms of what we might call soteriological enplotment. That is, they typically tell us a large-scale story in which modernity, with its totalizing metanarrative, functions as the complication or problem that is to be historically/narratively resolved by transcending the need for metanarratives. But isn't this itself a tall tale, a meta-narrative of universal scope which is simply unacknowledged?

The metanarrative character of postmodernity is clear if we attend to the meta-phor we previously used (in chapter two) of the postmodern smorgasbord, with its multiplicity of worldviews offered for our consumption. If among the variety of offerings we find Western modernist soup, Marxist rice, Christian stew and Muslim bread (so to speak), is there also a postmodern dish of some sort? Do postmodernists consider their own worldview as simply one option among many? Not at all. Post-modernity, as the master discourse which guides our understanding that all stories are mere human constructs, does not appear on the table. It *is* the table on which all the other dishes are served.[63] Postmodernity thus functions as the larger interpretive frame that relativizes all other worldviews as simply local stories with no legitimate claims to reality or universality. The postmodern worldview asserts that reality isn't what it used to be, that the self is multiple and decentered, and it answers the questions What's wrong? and What's the remedy? by recourse to a tall tale meant to guide ethical action after the demise of modernity. How else to make sense of Walter Truett Anderson's optimistic exhortation, "Lacking absolutes, we will have to encounter one another as people with different information, different stories, different visions—and trust the outcome"?[64] Given the clash of ideologies and aggressive violence which so characterizes postmodern plurality, why should we trust the outcome, unless we are rooted in a metanarrative that demands this? The postmodernist is thus caught in a performative contradiction, arguing against the necessity of metanarratives precisely by (surreptitious) appeal to a metanarrative.

But this appeal is not something to fault postmoderns for, since it is rooted in the valid human need for a worldview, a universal perspective that allows us to understand our place in the world and gives us guidance for living in the world. This need is so great that without a coherent metanarrative we are left morally adrift, at the mercy of random violence and brutality. In this light, we would suggest that the rising tide of violent crime over the past thirty years in the inner cities of North America, Europe and many Third World countries is testimony to the past power of both the modern metanarrative and alternative traditions of identity that had served to give life meaning and coherence. It is precisely the demise of modernity, accompanied by the absence of alternative narratives, that has left a worldview gap for many dispirited and hopeless urban youth who then act out their hopelessness, often in violent ways. The escalation of fascist ideology among teens in Europe and the multiplication of inner-city gangs in North America, often with a narrowly conceived ethnic identity, is further evidence of the desperate need to belong to a group and inhabit a meaningful story, even a narrow and violent one, so long as it gives an identity and purpose.[65]

Walter Truett Anderson recognizes that "the human mind continues to think in terms of stories" and "naturally seeks to order experience, looks for explanations of sequences of events, is attracted to dramas."[66] The postmodern world, however, is characterized by a loss of trust in stories. Not only can no story or tradition be regarded as absolute, but postmodern people have come to experience themselves more and more as storyless. In this respect the postmodern situation is analogous to the plight of the replicants in Ridley Scott's science-fiction film *Blade Runner*.

*Blade Runner* has been described as one of the finest examples of its genre and as a quintessentially postmodern film.[67] Situated in a decaying, deindustrialized Los Angeles in 2019, the film tells the story of a small group of genetically produced humans called replicants and the task of Deckard (the "blade runner") to hunt them down and retire them (a euphemism for destroying them). The problem is that these replicants are such perfectly simulated human beings that it is difficult to discern who is human and what is a replicant.[68] Indeed, their maker, Tyrell, insists that they are "more human than human." What they lack, however, is both a future and a past. They have no future because they are all programmed to serve particular functions for a limited period of time. But it is the lack of a past that is most determinative for the human/replicant distinction. Replicants are constructed, they have no story, no history. At the end of the film, the voice-over of Deckard reflects that replicants are just like most of us. They want to know "where they have come from, where they are going to and how much time they've got."[69] These are all worldview questions. The problem is that replicants have no way in which to answer them. And in their quest for answers and for survival, they act out their anomie with a violent intensity and brutality, insensitive to the suffering of others.

It is the tragedy of our postmodern times that humans are becoming more and more like replicants. This is because the postmodern metanarrative, while calling into question the universal claims of all other stories and traditions, does not itself have the resources to enable us to live with integrity and hope in a postmodern world. In its relativizing of all stories as merely local constructs, coupled with its inability to recognize its own character as a metanarrative, the postmodern world-view cannot sustain hope or empower us to live in the face of the ethical chaos and brutality that characterizes the ending of modernity. Indeed, if we seriously shaped our life by the typical postmodern answers to the four worldview questions, we would be at the mercy of whatever socially embodied narrative we found ourselves in. We would be unable to resist oppression since we would have no coherent way of appealing to any larger, transcendent story which might call into question whatever story was presently dominant.[70]

So we conclude our exploration of the postmodern worldview by questioning the typical postmodern suspicion of metanarratives as the root of the problem and the concomitant celebration of radical plurality and the free play of difference. Things are not that simple. Here, indeed, we have none other than Jacques Derrida himself on our side. For in a famous essay, "Plato's Pharmacy," in which he engages in a deconstructive reading of Plato's *Phaedrus*, Derrida comments on the complexity of the recurring term *pharmakon* ("drug") which Socrates applies to writing (as opposed to oral speech) and which can have a positive or a negative meaning. The issue in the *Phaedrus* is the value of writing, whether it is a good thing or not. Derrida comments:

> This *pharmakon*, this "medicine," this philter, which acts as both remedy and poison, already introduces itself into the body of the discourse with all its ambivalence. This charm, this spellbinding virtue, this power of fascination, can be—alternately or simultaneously—beneficent or maleficent.[71]

Just as Derrida applies this notion of *pharmakon* as both remedy and poison well beyond the topic of writing, as in effect a symbol of the ambiguity of all of life, we, for our part, would apply it to metanarratives and local stories, arguing that they are "pharmacological," both medicine and poison, able to be used for good or ill.[72] The problem, we suggest, lies at a much deeper level than metanarratives. It is rooted ultimately in the violence of the human heart and thus requires a remedy considerably more radical than that suggested by postmodernity.

# Interlude

**W**e have now reached a turning point in this book. Thus far we have attempted to sketch the historical rise of our contemporary postmodern crisis (chapter one) and to outline typical postmodern answers to the four worldview questions (chapters two through four). Although we have not, of course, been "objective" (since that is quite literally impossible), we have tried to be fair and sympathetic in our presentation. That is because we are convinced that it is impossible to live faithful to the gospel in any timeless, abstract fashion. Christian discipleship, as lived faithfulness, always requires discernment of, and serious struggle with, our particular cultural context.

But although we have tried to be fair about postmodernity, we have not been uncritical. On the contrary, we have highlighted a number of problems that we have with postmodernity. The question before us now, in the second half of this book, is whether we can move beyond criticism to positive proposals. Does the Christian faith have the resources to face the postmodern challenge, withstand it, even learn from it? What is more, can a Christianity that is open to such learning remain faithful to the Scriptures and empower the church to live out its faith as we move into the twenty-first century?

We believe that the Christian faith indeed has the resources both to learn from postmodernity and to address our contemporary cultural situation with compassion and power. But for these resources we need to return to the Scriptures, which Christians confess are a canon (a rule or norm) for faith and life. This requires a shift in discourse from part one of this book to part two. Whereas we have been engaging in cultural analysis, largely in a philosophical idiom, from here on we embark on a serious study of Scripture informed by the best of biblical scholarship.

In the chapters which follow we will attempt to plumb the depths of this incredibly rich canonical text, a text which we believe is God's gift to the church for guidance and direction—in *any* cultural situation. This means that we cannot be guided simply by our postmodern context, since that context is not in itself normative. Not only does postmodernity not raise all the important questions, but on certain points, as we have attempted to show, postmodernity is itself in need of serious critique. Thus, in part two, although we are sensitive to the postmodern situation, we will be guided also by the internal norms disclosed by the Scriptures themselves. Our purpose will be to discern and formulate biblical answers to the four worldview questions that speak to the issues and concerns of our postmodern times.

We will, however, address the four worldview questions in the *reverse* order in which we have just discussed them. This book thus has what literary critics call a chiastic structure: each chapter in part two responds to a chapter in part one. In chapter five, as in chapter four, we address questions of evil and redemption (what's wrong? and what's the remedy?). In chapter six, corresponding to chapter three, we move on the question of self-identity (who am I?). And in chapter seven, as in chapter two, we tackle the question of the nature of reality (where am I?). In each case, we will attempt to show how a Christian worldview rooted in the Scriptures can speak to a postmodern age. In our concluding chapter we will look imaginatively to the future. As chapter one looked to the past, examining the roots of the postmodern crisis, in chapter eight we will explore the hope of our times. This interlude thus functions as the *hinge* of the chiasmus.

Our choice of a chiastic structure is not arbitrary. Indeed, it is more difficult (we have found) to write a book according to a formal preordained structure. Our choice, however, is based on a problem we are confronted with at the outset of part two. We believe that postmodernity, if taken seriously, constitutes an enormous challenge to the very foundations of a faith which claims to be *biblical*. It is not just that Christians accept, in one way or another, the authority of the Bible as a sacred text. That would be a problem for the modern worldview, with its idealization of the autonomous self, free from all external constraints. Genuine postmodern consciousness, however, is pervaded by awareness of allegiance and commitment.

The problem, from a postmodern point of view, is that the Scriptures, in which Christians claim to ground their faith and in which we will seek answers to the worldview questions we have raised, constitute a metanarrative that makes universal claims. This is another way of saying that the Scriptures disclose a *world*view in storied form. It is difficult to see how anyone could take the biblical presentation of creation, fall and redemption as merely a local tale. Indeed, it is difficult to find a *grander* narrative, a more comprehensive story, anywhere. Christianity is undeniably rooted in a metanarrative that claims to tell the true story of the world from creation to eschaton, from origin to consummation.

The trouble is that from a postmodern perspective the deepest answer to the question What's wrong? points to the tendency to oppress and exclude minority voices and peoples precisely by recourse to a totalizing metanarrative which claims to tell the story of the world. And we saw that the remedy most typically prescribed by postmodern thinkers was the free play of difference. We are to renounce the desire for metanarratives and, instead, to embrace heterogeneity, allowing for a radical plurality of local stories, each giving voice to the history and aspirations of a different group.

So the question we are confronted with at the outset of part two is whether the Christian faith, rooted as it is in a metanarrative of cosmic proportions, is subject to the postmodern charge of totalizing violence. Does the postmodern suspicion of metanarratives apply, legitimately, to the biblical story? Are we required, in the name of justice and compassion, to give up the biblical metanarrative and opt for a merely local tale? If we do not at least *attempt* to answer this question, then our exposition of the biblical worldview which follows will certainly lack integrity. We have therefore decided to start part two by articulating the biblical answers to the questions about evil and redemption in a manner which explicitly addresses the postmodern suspicion of metanarratives. This requires us to start part two with a response to chapter four; thus we have adopted a chiastic structure.

At the outset it must be admitted that the postmodern suspicion of metanarratives is rooted both in a systematic insight and in a historical observation. The insight is that those who articulate metanarratives and worldviews are inevitably finite, fallible (indeed, fallen) human beings. Not only is it quite literally impossible for any human articulation of a metanarrative to be genuinely universal in scope (and thus not exclude, devalue, co-opt or oppress, either explicitly or implicitly), but our fallen human tendency is to use our overarching value systems as ideologies to legitimate our own interests. The historical observation follows from this, namely that the biblical story has, in fact, often been used ideologically to oppress and exclude those regarded as infidels or heretics. In the hands of some Christians and communities, the biblical metanarrative has indeed been wielded as a weapon, legitimating prejudice and perpetuating violence against those perceived as the enemy, those on the outside of God's purposes. There simply is no innocent, no intrinsically just narrative, not even the biblical one.

Having said that, however, let us recall that we noted in the last chapter that local stories are no less inherently totalizing than metanarratives. As recent events in Bosnia and Rwanda indicate, local ethnic stories have profound potential for legitimating tribal violence on a scale to rival any metanarrative. Furthermore, in the last chapter we attempted to uncover the hidden (though ultimately vacuous) postmodern metanarrative that functions as the surreptitious table on which the smorgasbord of competing worldviews is offered for our consumption. It is this metanarrative that frames the postmodern answers to the questions What's wrong? and What's the remedy?

But if even tribal narratives may do violence and postmodernity tries to sneak in a metanarrative by the back door, perhaps the problem isn't metanarratives per se. Perhaps metanarratives, as we suggested, are *pharmacological* (both poison and remedy), harboring the potential for both oppression and justice, violence and healing. The important question, then, would not be *whether* the Christian faith is rooted in a metanarrative, but *what sort of* metanarrative the Scriptures contain.

# Part II/The Resources of Scripture

# 5/The Biblical Metanarrative

**W**hat we want to do in this chapter is to tell the biblical story in some detail, showing how the story paradigmatically answers the worldview questions about evil and redemption and, in the process, highlighting its inbuilt ethical thrust and antitotalizing potential.[1]

It is our contention that the Bible, as the normative, canonical, founding Christian story, works ultimately *against* totalization. It is able to do this because it contains two identifiable counterideological dimensions or antitotalizing factors. These dimensions do not, of course, *guarantee* innocence (or justice, or compassion for the other) on the part of those who adhere to this narrative. But these dimensions *incline* the Christian story toward delegitimating and subverting violent, totalizing uses of the story by those who claim to live out of it. The first of these dimensions consists in *a radical sensitivity to suffering* that pervades the biblical narrative from the exodus to the cross. The second consists in the rooting of the story in *God's overarching creational intent* that delegitimates any narrow, partisan use of the story. And these two dimensions, we submit, are intrinsic not only to the content, but also to the very structure of the canon.[2]

## The Exodus as Israel's Worldview

We are not going to start at the beginning of the story, with creation. Nor are we starting with Jesus, who Christians confess is the center of the entire story. Although we will eventually attempt to sketch the biblical story as a comprehensive meta-narrative, displaying its overall plot structure and dramatic movement, with Jesus as the denouement and turning point of the narrative, we are going to begin with that central event of the Old Testament, the exodus from Egyptian bondage.[3]

We are doing this not only because many Christians tend to ignore the Old Testament in general, and the exodus in particular, and thus risk missing the significance of this important event, but also because the exodus provides the essential background for understanding the historical mission of Jesus—his life, death and resurrection. Thus, without an extended engagement with the exodus story, we risk missing something crucial both to the Old Testament and to the Jesus story, indeed, something crucial to the entire metanarrative.

But there is another reason for starting here. Although the biblical canon, in its final form, tells the story of the world from creation to eschaton, Israel's first and decisive encounter with God was at the exodus. Yahweh's deliverance of the Hebrews from Egyptian bondage when they cried out to him against their oppressors and their subsequent constitution as a people at Sinai are widely regarded by Jews as the founding and pivotal event in their own narrative and by Christians as the central event in the Old Testament. Here is where we find the origin, historically speaking, both of God's people and of the Scriptures themselves. It is this incredible event which is first sung about, recited, reflected upon, written about. It is this event, in other words, which ultimately generated the Bible. So, starting with the exodus can help us understand the canon "from below," so to speak, in the process of formation. Not only is this an approach eminently consonant with our postmodern times (which tends to be suspicious of ahistorical absolute claims), but starting with the exodus can then provide insight into the finished product of the entire biblical metanarrative.[4]

What is crucial about the exodus as it is remembered in the Old Testament is that God graciously intervened "with a mighty hand and an outstretched arm" (Deut 26:8) in what seemed to be a hopeless, "no-exit" historical situation to provide for his people precisely a way out (hence *exodus*). Yahweh was so moved by human suffering that he acted to relieve that suffering, breaking the bonds of slavery underwritten by the mightiest empire of the day and setting the Israelites free. Here we find *in nuce* the first biblical answers to the worldview questions What's wrong?

and What's the remedy? And these answers are given in the form of a story. Whereas the introduction of plot conflict corresponds formally to What's wrong? the climax of plot resolution constitutes the remedy to that problem.

The story begins, as the book of Exodus tells it, with the Hebrew people having migrated from Canaan to Egypt to escape the ravages of famine. Descended from the line of Abraham, Isaac and Jacob (to whom God had appeared and entered into covenant), they have grown into a large and numerous people. But as aliens, living in a foreign land, the Israelites have been reduced to slavery, subject to the corvée (or forced labor) which the Egyptian empire has imposed on them. When the book of Exodus opens, the Israelites are being ruthlessly put to work in the fields and on building projects.

One motive given for this harsh treatment is fear—the Egyptian king's fear of a possible uprising in which the Hebrews would be a formidable enemy. But, as if forced labor were not enough, Pharaoh makes a rash attempt at population control, first by instructing the Hebrew midwives to kill all Hebrew males at birth (an instruction they surreptitiously disobey) and then by ordering all Hebrew boys to be drowned in the Nile. It is no wonder, then, that the people cry out to God for deliverance.

> The Israelites groaned in their slavery and cried out, and their cry for help because of their slavery went up to God. God heard their groaning and he remembered his covenant with Abraham, with Isaac and with Jacob. So God looked on the Israelites and was concerned about them. (Ex 2:23-25)

As the story unfolds, it becomes clear that God has already acted, *before* this cry, in protecting a newborn Hebrew boy from drowning by the authorities. Indeed, this boy, Moses, in a strange twist of events, is adopted by Pharaoh's daughter and raised in the royal palace of Egypt. But when in outrage Moses kills an Egyptian slave master who is whipping a Hebrew, he is exposed and flees for his life across the desert to the land of Midian. But all this is preparation. For there God reveals himself to Moses, in a decisive encounter, as Yahweh, the living God, who was known to Abraham, Isaac and Jacob, and commissions him for a momentous task. Yahweh says to Moses:

> I have indeed seen the misery of my people in Egypt; I have heard them crying out because of their slave drivers, and I am concerned about their sufferings. So I have come down to rescue them from the Egyptians and to bring them up out of that land into a good and spacious land, a land flowing with milk and honey. (Ex 3:7-8)

Yahweh thus calls Moses out of Midian to return to Egypt and confront Pharaoh (by this time a new pharaoh, for the earlier one had died). It is Moses' mission to get Pharaoh to release the Israelites from their bondage so they can leave Egypt for a new land God is going to give them, a land in which they can be free.

The story of this confrontation between the desert wanderer who speaks on behalf of Yahweh and the imperial monarch backed by the power of the empire is told at great length, with dramatic effect. At first Pharaoh refuses to release the Israelites (Ex 5). It takes a series of terrible plagues which God brings on Egypt (from which, miraculously, the Israelites are protected) before Pharaoh will listen (Ex 7—11). It is not until the death of the king's own son (along with every firstborn Egyptian male—human and animal) that the mighty empire finally buckles and the Israelites leave in haste (Ex 12—13).

But Pharaoh, out of anger and revenge, changes his mind and pursues them across the desert. The final showdown comes with the Israelites trapped between the Red Sea and the crush of the Egyptian war chariots (Ex 14). But once again God acts on his people's behalf, parting the waters so that they could cross over to dry ground. When the Egyptians try to follow, the waters return, drowning Pharaoh and the entire army.

Already we can begin to discern how the exodus story articulates a set of answers to the worldview questions What's wrong? and What's the remedy? The fundamental problem portrayed in the story is that of human suffering caused by injustice. In particular, it is the suffering of those who are relatively powerless at the hands of an oppressive imperial regime. That this is not a problem to be solved by human bargaining or ingenuity is made clear by the systemic and long-term character of the Israelite bondage, not to mention the recurring theme of the hardness of Pharaoh's heart. The only hope is the action of Yahweh, a God of compassion and justice. This God is concerned about human suffering and is moved by his people's agonized cry for help. The remedy for the massive problem of Egyptian bondage is thus God's decisive intervention in history to break the bonds of slavery and lead his people out on a journey to a land where they can live in freedom, justice and peace. As the foundational event in which Israel first encountered God, a God who acted on their behalf for deliverance, the exodus was etched indelibly on Israelite consciousness. It provided the paradigmatic answers to the worldview questions concerning evil and redemption, the vision in terms of which God's people would then view the world and live in it.

The people's immediate response to this amazing event was the so-called Song of the Sea (Ex 15), in which the newly liberated slaves celebrated their release and exalted Yahweh for his victory over Pharaoh's army. But that was only the beginning. This incredible event so captured Israelite imagination that the story is told over and over again. In Deuteronomy 26, for example, one of those texts that Old Testament scholar Gerhard von Rad called "little historical credos," the Israelites are given instructions they are to carry out when they enter the land of Canaan, the land God is giving them.[5] Once they have had their first harvest, they are to present the firstfruits of that harvest as an offering to God. As they present the offering, they are to tell the story:

> My father was a wandering Aramean, and he went down into Egypt with a few people and lived there and became a great nation, powerful and numerous. But the Egyptians mistreated us and made us suffer, putting us to hard labor. Then we cried out to Yahweh, the God of our fathers, and Yahweh heard our voice and saw our misery, toil and oppression. So Yahweh brought us out of Egypt with a mighty hand and an outstretched arm, with great terror and with miraculous signs and wonders. He brought us to this place and gave us this land, a land flowing with milk and honey; and now I bring the firstfruits of the soil that you, O Yahweh, have given me. (Deut 26:5-10)[6]

Here the story is told extending back before the exodus to the patriarchs or ancestors of Israel (Jacob was from Aram), and it continues right up to the entrance into the promised land. Effectively summarizing from the latter part of Genesis to the end of Numbers, the story is here recounted out of gratitude as the basis of and motivation for returning to God a portion of his prior gifts.

We find a similar retelling of the story in Psalm 136, one of the storytelling psalms (or psalms of "historical recital") that were sung by worshipers in the Jerusalem temple.[7] This time the story starts not with the ancestors but even further back with creation (vv. 4-9), moving then to the plagues in Egypt and the parting of the Red Sea (vv. 10-15), continuing through the wilderness journey and the entry into the Promised Land (vv. 16-22). The purpose of this telling, like that of Deuteronomy 26, is gratitude and praise. "Give thanks to Yahweh, for he is good," the psalm begins, and the antiphonal refrain, which the worshipers sing after each line, is "his love endures forever." The conclusion of the psalm, declaring the heart of the story, encourages the worshipers to give thanks

> to the One who remembered us in our low estate
>
> *His love endures forever.*
>
> and freed us from our enemies,

> *His love endures forever.*
> and who gives food to every creature,
> *His love endures forever.*
> Give thanks to the God of heaven.
> *His love endures forever.* (vv. 23-26)

Whether it was in corporate worship at the Red Sea (Ex 15) or in the Jerusalem temple (Ps 136), or in an individual act of worship at harvest time (Deut 26), God's people told and retold the story of the exodus in thanksgiving and praise.

### The Ethical Thrust of the Exodus Story

But they told the story for other reasons as well. Note, for example, how the Ten Commandments begin: "I am Yahweh your God who brought you out of Egypt, out of the land of slavery" (Ex 20:2). The commandments don't come out of the blue as some sort of absolute, timeless principles. They are guidelines for living that are given by the God who has a history with these people. This is the God who has acted in a wondrous way for their deliverance and is now entering into covenant with them at Mount Sinai. The commandments are thus meant to shape the contours of a newly formed community of freedom, and the story is told (in briefest possible form) as part of God's self-identification, to provide the basis and motivation for the community's obedience. Indeed, Deuteronomy 6 (another "historical credo") says that when your children ask you, "What's the meaning of these laws and commandments?" you shall answer:

> We were slaves of Pharaoh in Egypt, but Yahweh brought us out of Egypt with a mighty hand. Before our eyes Yahweh sent miraculous signs and wonders— great and terrible—upon Egypt and Pharaoh and his whole household. But he brought us out from there to bring us in and give us the land that he promised on oath to our forefathers. Yahweh commanded us to obey all these decrees and to fear Yahweh our God, so that we might always prosper and be kept alive, as is the case today. And if we are careful to obey all this law before Yahweh our God, as he has commanded us, that will be our righteousness. (vv. 21-25)

What we find recounted in abbreviated form in Exodus 20 and Deuteronomy 6 we find in greatly expanded form in Psalm 105, another psalm of historical recital. Here we have a detailed telling of the story of the exodus, beginning with God's promise to Abraham, recounting how God delivered his people from Egypt and led them through the wilderness into the Promised Land (vv. 1-44). And what is the purpose of telling this amazing story of God's marvelous deeds on behalf of his people? The punch line comes in the last verse: "that they might keep his precepts and observe his laws" (v. 45).

In these (and numerous other) Old Testament texts we find fascinating evidence of what biblical scholars call variously midrash, the traditioning process or inner-biblical exegesis.[8] That is, at some later stage in a community's development, as they face a changed existential situation, that community remembers, retells and rearticulates crucial aspects of their dramatic narrative as the basis for self-understanding and renewed ethical action in that changed situation. Alasdair MacIntyre is entirely correct here. For later Israel to answer the question What am I to do? it had first to answer the question Of what story am I a part?[9] So the founding Torah story (the call of Abraham, bondage in Egypt, deliverance by God, the wilderness journey and the gift of the Promised Land) is retold by particular individuals and groups at later stages *within* the overarching biblical narrative as the explicit basis for ethical action. In Israel's case, ethical action is clearly narratively formed.

But what sort of ethical action is formed by Israel's narrative? What are the implications for living that flow from the founding Torah story? The significance of this founding story, in which the exodus from Egyptian bondage is central, is that Israel's narrative memory was shaped decisively by the crucible of oppressive suffering and liberation unto justice. The memory of suffering (what's wrong?) and God's desire to relieve this suffering (what's the remedy?) was kept alive in the constant retelling of the story.

But this memory was kept alive also in the numerous psalms of lament which became part of the liturgical repertoire of ancient Israel. Constituting almost one-third of the Psalter, lament psalms (such as Psalm 22, which Jesus prayed on the cross) are abrasive prayers that give voice to pain. Refusing to repress such pain in favor of business-as-usual, these psalms honestly articulate suffering as intolerable and complain to God for redress and deliverance. In other words, the paradigm of the Hebrews' agonized groaning and complaint to Yahweh about Egyptian bondage in Exodus 2:23-25 and 3:7-10 found a settled home in the genre of psalms of individual and communal lament. These psalms, sung in Israel's worship, would have reinforced Israel's exodus memory and further shaped Israelite sensitivity to suffering.[10]

Eloquent testimony to that sensitivity is found in the contemporary tradition of Jewish Passover celebration, in which the exodus narrative is remembered and rearticulated. During the course of the Passover meal, wine is ritually spilled in compassion for, and solidarity with, the suffering caused to the Egyptians by God's deliverance of Israel at the exodus. While this suffering is realistically recognized as part of the process of historical and political liberation from a brutal regime, it is nevertheless mourned since God does not desire that any of his creatures perish.[11]

This sensitivity to the suffering of others is made explicit in the motivational clauses found in the so-called Book of the Covenant, that collection of laws which follows the Ten Commandments in Exodus. Two sorts of motivational clauses stand out as the basis for doing justice to aliens, widows and orphans, that is, to those who are relatively powerless or marginal in the community. These clauses both appeal to the exodus story. The one says, "Do not oppress an alien; you yourselves know how it feels to be aliens, because you were aliens in Egypt" (Ex 23:9). The other says, "Do not take advantage of a widow or an orphan. If you do and they cry out to me, I will certainly hear their cry" (Ex 22:22-23).[12]

What has become clear in recent biblical scholarship, especially since the groundbreaking sociological study of Norman Gottwald, is that the whole purpose of the exodus-Sinai event was for Yahweh to found a community with an ethical pattern of life alternative to that of imperial Egypt.[13] Because of the distinctive ongoing story it told, remembered and participated in, this was to be a community which refused to cause oppression and instead was committed to fostering justice and compassion toward the marginal.[14] This sensitivity to suffering is a major thrust or trajectory within the Bible, and it constitutes the first (and most foundational) counterideological dimension of the biblical story.

Old Testament scholar Walter Brueggemann has referred to this biblical trajectory as the "embrace of pain," since it involves ruthless honesty about (rather than denial of) suffering. To use a postmodern metaphor, this biblical trajectory does not make false claims to *presence* but instead highlights *absence*—the absence of God, the absence of justice, the absence of shalom. Biblical texts in this trajectory thus critique the unjust status quo in the name of Yahweh, the God of justice and liberation, and call for social transformation in the name of the founding narrative.[15]

Brueggemann also calls this biblical trajectory the "prophetic imagination," since it is the prophets par excellence who (at a later stage in the story) give voice to the suffering of the people, and even (in sections of Jeremiah and Isaiah) to the suffering of God. Furthermore, the Old Testament prophets rearticulate the founding exodus story as the basis of both their critique of later (corrupt) stages in Israel's narrative and their proposal of an alternative, eschatological future.[16]

### Israel's New Bondage

But alongside the prophetic trajectory of the embrace of pain (a trajectory which goes back to Moses, regarded in Deut 18:15 as the first prophet), there is a royal or imperial trajectory, which Brueggemann names "structure legitimation," since it is typically the role of kings, at least in the ancient Near East, to enforce order, often without concern for the suffering of their subjects.[17] This is what is behind both Samuel's and God's opposition to Israel's request for a king "such as all the other nations have" (1 Sam 8:4-8). True, God ultimately allows the people to have their way (1 Sam 8:22), testimony to the radical role of human freedom in the biblical story whereby we are invited to participate in, even to shape, the direction of the story. Yet not only does Deuteronomy 17 attempt to limit significantly the power of Israel's kings, but Samuel (at God's instruction) warns the people in no uncertain terms of the likely social oppression which will follow the introduction of the monarchy (1 Sam 8:9-18).

The prophetic tradition in the Old Testament (as far back as Elijah and Elisha in the ninth century and Nathan in the tenth) arose largely in response to the abuses of the Israelite kings. In one way or another the prophets all critique the policies and practices of the monarchy as essentially a recapitulation of Egyptian bondage. From a prophetic point of view, the hegemonic and totalizing tendencies of monarchy bring a regressive twist to the overall plot of Yahweh's story with Israel. Indeed, the narrative of 1 Kings 3—11 (part of the "Former Prophets") itself portrays Solomon's grandiose reign as directly contradicting the legislation of Deuteronomy 17 and as similar to the empire of Egypt. The description of his reign as including a large harem, a standing army of horses and chariots, and the proliferation of wisdom literature rivaling that of Egypt, along with the introduction of the corvée for building Solomon's magnificent palace and the Jerusalem temple, shows that it was regarded, in George Mendenhall's vivid phrase, as the beginning of the "paganization" of Israel. Solomon was a new Pharaoh, and Israel was returning to Egyptian bondage.[18]

It is not, however, just that the two trajectories, the Mosaic/prophetic and the imperial or royal, are found in tension within the Bible, but that the second trajectory is numb to, and indeed causes, suffering and injustice.[19] It therefore constitutes a fundamental contradiction of Israel's founding exodus story and thus a contradiction of Israel's identity and intended ethical pattern of life, both of which derive from that founding story.

What we have with the rise of the monarchy in Israel (somewhat ambiguously with David, more clearly with Solomon, and with great vividness after the kingdom is divided by civil war into north and south) is nothing less than a massive, new plot conflict introduced into the biblical story, a conflict that cries out for resolution. Just as the oppression of Egyptian bondage required God's deliverance at the exodus, so the pervasive abuses of the corrupt kings of Israel (the northern kingdom) and Judah (the southern kingdom) required a new narrative resolution. But that resolution would not be a new mighty act of deliverance on God's part—at least not initially. On the contrary, the prophets announced judgment. It was the unanimous message of Isaiah of Jerusalem, Jeremiah, Hosea, Amos and Ezekiel (among others) that God would judge his people for their injustice, which was rooted in idolatry— that is, in following not the Yahweh story of exodus from bondage but typically the Canaanite Baal story of cyclical fertility and guaranteed security. Even when there is no explicit accusation of Canaanite idolatry, the indictment of injustice stands, injustice stemming from the royal establishment's usurpation of power at the expense of the marginal within Israel, which amounts to an abandonment of Israel's founding exodus story.

The canonical prophets of the sixth century B.C. argued that just as God had delivered Israel from Egyptian bondage, so God would deliver Israel *over to a new bondage*, the Babylonian captivity. Yahweh was against all injustice, whether Egyptian or Israelite. Scripture testifies amply to other prophets, judged in the text to be false, who, like the canonical prophets, appealed to the founding exodus story, but with the opposite conclusion. These status quo prophets argued, against the canonical prophets, that just as God had delivered Israel from Egyptian bondage, so God would deliver them also *from the hands of the Babylonians*. Yahweh was fundamentally on Israel's side. The two sorts of prophets appealed to the same narrative but drew contradictory implications and conclusions. The status quo prophets, in the service of the royal court, employed the narrative for ideological self-justification. The canonical prophets, however, allowed the counterideological force of the narrative to break through royal numbness and subvert royal ideology.

As we know, the canonical prophets, who were largely dismissed as seditious madmen (Jeremiah, for example, was imprisoned for treason), were proved to be right.[20] Israel did go into Babylonian exile, and so the story which started with the exodus seemed to come to a dead end. The Israelites, whom God had freed fr⁓ bondage in Egypt, constituted as a people at Sinai and granted their own land, we once more in bondage, living as aliens in Babylon. In this situation, the newly uprooted and now dispirited exiles suffered a fundamental crisis of worldview, identity and life-pattern. The future seemed closed to them.[21] So they cried out to Ezekiel by the river Chebar in Babylon: "How then can we live?" (Ezek 33:10).

## The Place of the Exodus in the Creator's Purposes

And the answer is, as always, we live out of our narratives. We need only think of the power of Psalm 106, a psalm of historical recital. Written in the midst of Babylonian exile, Psalm 106 tells the founding story in great detail, moving from the exodus and the Red Sea (vv. 7-12) through the wilderness experience (vv. 13-33) to life in the land of promise (vv. 34-46). But unlike Psalm 105, which tells the story as motivation for obedience, Psalm 106 highlights the people's persistent rebellion and unfaithfulness *despite* Yahweh's mighty deeds on their behalf. Far from being a song of despair, however, the psalm appeals directly to the exodus in a radical act of hope. Although, due to their sin, Israel's enemies oppressed them many times, God never forgot his people.

But he took note of their distress
> when he heard their cry;
for their sake he remembered his covenant
> and out of his great love he relented.
He caused them to be pitied
> by all who held them captive. (vv. 44-46)

Taking as its central motivation this paradigmatic move from bondage to liberation, rooted in God's love, the psalm ends with a passionate plea:

Save us, O Yahweh our God,
> and gather us from the nations,
that we may give thanks to your holy name
> and glory in your praise. (v. 47)

Even in exile Israel returned to its founding narrative, which after more than half a millennium had not lost its power. Only in the memory of this radical story could a vision of hope for the future be found.

But not only did exilic Israel return to the exodus story as the basis for their hope, they returned to the prophets of judgment whom they had previously dismissed. James Sanders, a pioneer in the field known as canonical criticism, argues that it was precisely the experience of land loss and exile that engendered a rehearing of these prophets, whose message had previously been highly unpopular.[22] And they were reheard not just because they were factually correct or had predictive accuracy, but also because they somehow did not think that exile annulled the story that began with the exodus and the deliverance from bondage. It is not just that Yahweh would, in the fullness of time, again deliver the people from Babylonian exile. They certainly said that. But they went considerably further than predicting a new exodus.

Because what would the point of a new exodus be? Indeed, what was the point of the original exodus?

More fundamental than the prediction of a new exodus was the conviction of the canonical prophets that Yahweh's purposes were not simply to establish Israel as an alternative, countercommunity to the imperial tradition of the ancient Near East. Israel's existence as a nation, even an egalitarian nation, practicing justice toward the marginal, was not ultimately what God had in mind. On the contrary, going back to God's promise to bless all nations through Abraham's seed (Gen 12:1-3), the canonical prophets discerned what was always there but often misunderstood, that Israel's distinctive practice of justice was meant to shine as a beacon in the ancient Near East, attracting other nations to the distinctive God who wills such justice. If it was Moses' task to be God's agent in the exodus for Israel's deliverance, God's overarching purpose in the exodus was for Israel to be the bearer of a universal, cosmic metanarrative, a drama of God's intent to mend the world, to bring justice and healing to all nations and even to the nonhuman realm.[23] This was the meaning of Israel's election as a "royal priesthood and holy nation" (Ex 19:6). Their role was mediational; their calling was to restore the nations to God.[24]

Therefore it was not crucial that Israel was landless, that their national identity was gone, that the monarchy was ended, that the temple was destroyed, that the sacrificial system and the cultic, ritual tradition had ceased. None of these constituted the ultimate purpose of Israel's election. Yahweh could sustain Israel even on the margins, and he could further his cosmic purposes even through the suffering of his servant people.

The canonical prophets discerned, in other words, that Yahweh was not simply Israel's God (as the status quo prophets had assumed) but the Creator of heaven and earth who had a redemptive purpose for all peoples. It was the insight that *this* was the sort of God with whom they had to do that distinguished the true from the false prophets and that allowed them to bring a message of judgment.

This universal perspective (or "monotheizing" insight, as Sanders calls it) into God as Creator constitutes the second counterideological or antitotalizing dimension of the biblical metanarrative. If the experience of the exodus generates a profound sensitivity to suffering (especially the suffering of the powerless), the affirmation of God as Creator prevents any merely nationalistic, partisan interpretation of the story (as if only the suffering of *Israel* mattered).

## The Shape of the Canonical Metanarrative

Two important consequences for the very shape of the biblical canon followed from the insight into God as Creator, argues Sanders. The first is that the Torah or Pentateuch, the first and foundational grouping of books in the Bible, ends with Deuteronomy, not Joshua. Whereas every retelling of the story within the Old Testament (whether von Rad's "credos" or the storytelling psalms) contains minimally (1) the exodus from bondage and (2) the entrance into the promised land, the Torah ends surprisingly *before* the entry into the land. This should give us pause. The book of Joshua, which tells the story of the entry, is relegated to the second grouping of books, the Former Prophets or Historical Books.[25] But Torah, the founding story, ends with the Israelites still in the wilderness, as poignant testimony to the nonessential (or at least secondary and derivative) character of Israel's settled, national identity.[26]

Just as the traditioning process of repeating the story in new situations inevitably changed the story in subtle or explicit ways (note how *different* the retellings are in Ps 105 and 106), so the exilic retelling effected a decisive change, reflected in the final shape of the canonical text.[27] Sanders cogently argues that only a Torah story that excluded land settlement could have provided a meaningful narrative for landless exiles (especially since it was a distorted narrative of national identity and land possession that had led to exile).[28] Israel learned that even in a chaotic, marginal state of diaspora, they could still be God's people and act ethically in accordance with their story. So the first consequence for canonical shape of this inner-biblical monotheizing process (this insight into God as universal Creator) is the exclusion of land possession from Torah.

The other consequence for the shape of the canon that follows from this monotheizing insight is the placing of the Genesis creation story as the prologue or introduction to Torah, and ultimately to the entire biblical metanarrative. It is noteworthy that while none of the early retellings of the story within the canon start with creation, by the time of the exile creation is explicitly articulated at the beginning of Israel's narrative. Thus Jeremiah, on the brink of exile, with the Babylonian army besieging Jerusalem, prays to Yahweh and recounts God's mighty deeds as the basis for hope beyond exile (Jer 32:16-25). But he tellingly starts not with the exodus or even the call of Abraham: "Ah, sovereign Yahweh, you have made the heavens and the earth by your great power and outstretched arm. Nothing is too hard for you" (32:17).

And in the answer to Jeremiah's prayer, it is likewise God's status as universal

Creator that is highlighted as the ground of both Israel's judgment (32:28-35) and hope (32:36-44): "I am Yahweh, the God of all flesh. Is anything too hard for me?" (32:27).

Note also the contrast between the two covenant renewal ceremonies recorded in Joshua 24 and Nehemiah 9. In the former case, Joshua, as Moses' successor, retells the Torah story to the second generation of Israelites, who have newly entered the promised land. In order to gain their commitment to the covenant that God made with their ancestors at Sinai, Joshua recounts Yahweh's mighty acts on their behalf, from the call of Abraham, through the exodus, to the entry into the land (vv. 2-13), ending with the famous challenge: "Choose for yourselves this day whom you will serve. . . . But as for me and my household, we will serve Yahweh" (v. 15). In Nehemiah 9, however, some eight centuries after Joshua, the situation is that of Israel's *return* to the land after exile. In an extended communal prayer led by the Levites (chap. 9), which precedes a renewal of the covenant (chap. 10), the story of God's mighty deeds is recounted. Significantly, the story starts (as in Jer 32) with *creation* rather than exodus (Neh 9:5-6).[29]

This placing of creation at the start of Israel's story, evident both in the retellings of Jeremiah 32 and Nehemiah 9 and in the opening of the entire Bible, has ramifications for how we are to answer the worldview questions about evil and redemption. The answer to What's wrong? is no longer simply Israel's bondage, nor can the remedy be simply their deliverance. Instead, from the point of view of the overall metanarrative, it is humanity that is in bondage and the remedy must be likewise universal. Something of this broad perspective is seen in Amos's warning to Israel not to be presumptuous about the meaning of their election.

"Are not you Israelites
    the same to me as the Cushites?"
        declares Yahweh.
"Did I not bring Israel up from Egypt,
    the Philistines from Caphtor
    and the Arameans from Kir?" (Amos 9:7)

The same "monotheizing" insight, whereby it is recognized that God has acted for the deliverance of nations beyond Israel, was also the basis of the so-called prophecies against the nations, collections of judgment oracles found in every major canonical prophetic book (Is 13—21, Jer 46—51, Ezek 25—32) and in some minor ones.[30] Whereas judgments against Israel could cite infringements of the Sinai covenant laws, judgments against other nations could only be rooted in God's purposes and claims as universal Creator of all. This universal reading of human sin is given explicit canonical shape in the story of the fall recorded in Genesis 2—3, followed by the account in Genesis 4—11 of humanity's increasing depravity and violence. Just as the canonical story now starts with creation, so both problem and remedy affect all people. Hence God's call of Abraham in Genesis 12, leading to the election of Israel, is meant ultimately to impact the entire human race.

But if both the problem and the remedy become broadened in terms of the canonical metanarrative, they also become deepened. It is, after all, Jeremiah and Ezekiel, two prophets on the edge of exile, who come to the most profound awareness of the evil that resides deep in each human heart. Living as they did after centuries of Israel's recalcitrance to Yahweh, pervasively evident despite the exodus and God's other mighty deeds, these prophets speak of individual responsibility for sin and its seemingly indelible and deep-seated character.[31] It is likewise these same prophets who announce God's most radical plan to deal with the problem: a "new" and "everlasting" covenant, which God will write not on tablets of stone but on the human heart.[32]

It thus becomes clear, even within the pages of the Old Testament, that the exodus-Sinai story is not an end in itself. Israel's "election" as the chosen people, which was often treated as election for privilege and elite status (in opposition to the *gôyîm*, the nations), is decisively reinterpreted in the context of the canonical metanarrative as election *for service*.[33] Although a nationalistic reading of election is possible (though not required) in terms of a local narrative of exodus to land possession, in the context of the larger metanarrative this reading is subverted. Instead, Israel is called to be the particular, historically conditioned means of mediating a universal story of the healing of the world. As the servant of Yahweh, Israel exists for the sake of other nations.[34] It is this monotheizing metanarrative rooted in the Creator's purposes that constitutes the second counterideological dimension of the biblical story.

It is important to note, however, that these two counterideological dimensions do not simply exist side by side. On the contrary, they are integrally connected, as Psalm 146 indicates.[35]

> Blessed are those whose help is the God of Jacob,
> 　whose hope is in Yahweh their God,
> the Maker of heaven and earth,
> 　the sea and everything in them—
> 　Yahweh, who remains faithful forever.

Who upholds the cause of the oppressed
  and gives food to the hungry;
Yahweh sets prisoners free.
Yahweh watches over the alien
  and sustains the fatherless and the widow,
    but frustrates the ways of the wicked. (vv. 5-7, 9)

It is precisely *because* (1) Yahweh is the universal Creator and Judge of all nations, indeed of heaven and earth, that (2) the marginal and the suffering other have a normative court of appeal against all injustice. The upshot of this twofold counter-ideological dynamic is that the biblical God has an overarching narrative purpose alternative to the many oppressive systems and stories in which we find ourselves. Not only is this God not to be identified with such systems and stories, but as sovereign Creator, Yahweh is able to fulfill his purpose of shalom for his creation, a purpose which includes the liberation of the oppressed and the empowerment of the marginal. It is thus crucial to hold together *both* dimensions of this counter-ideological dynamic in creative interaction.

A merely one-sided emphasis on God as sovereign Creator without attentiveness to human suffering might well result in an arid, totalitarian view of deity and an ethos of legalism and blindness to the marginal.[36] Attention to pain, on the other hand, without the possibility of appeal to a sovereign Creator, may result in either a disempowered theology of suffering and survival or a vengeful sectarian attempt at heroic self-assertion in the face of overwhelming odds.[37]

### The Antitotalizing Mission of Jesus

It is arguably this latter possibility which was realized in first-century Israel, with its plethora of messianic revolutionary movements seeking liberation from Roman oppression. In the tradition of the Maccabean revolts some centuries earlier against their Seleucid overlords, many Jews in the time of Jesus positioned themselves in a generalized stance of opposition not just to the Romans but toward all Gentiles, as outsiders. Even within Israel, as Marcus Borg has shown, a complicated ritual system of clean and unclean (or same and other) was imposed on sociopolitical and economic classes of Israelites, such that vast multitudes of the poor were considered as ritual outcasts, officially non-Jewish, excluded from the benefits of the covenant.[38]

Into this situation Jesus came, mounting a scathing prophetic critique of the religious and political center on behalf of the excluded other—the tax collectors, Gentiles, prostitutes and, in general, "sinners."[39] This prophetic stance is pervasive in the Gospels and is especially indicated by the almost complete absence of the popular first-century religious category *holiness* from the teaching of Jesus. Whereas the idea of holiness was central to the worldview of the Pharisees and scribes, Jesus himself seems to have avoided the term on principle because it had come to function as a category of self-righteous exclusion which betrayed the heart of Israel's exodus faith. Israel's election from among the nations, described in Exodus 19:4-6 as a priestly calling to be a "holy nation," was widely interpreted in the time of Jesus as election unto separation, purity and boundary setting.

Jesus, however, understood Israel's vocation to be one of priestly *reconciliation*. That is why he replaces the commandment "Be holy because I, Yahweh your God, am holy" (Lev 19:2; also see 11:44) with "Be merciful, just as your Father is merciful" (Lk 6:36).[40] Jesus reinterprets holiness as loving inclusion of the marginal and he enacted this reinterpretation by befriending the outcasts of Jewish society. In so doing, Jesus clearly stands in the prophetic tradition of the "embrace of pain." He embodied the counterideological dynamic of sensitivity to suffering.[41]

But Jesus also stands in the creation tradition. Indeed, we suggest that his essential critique of first-century Judaism was that tne vision of the canonical metanarrative, which N. T. Wright calls "creational covenantal monotheism," had become compromised, being reductively replaced by a nationalistic, sectarian narrative of "covenantal monotheism."[42] That is, first-century Judaism had ignored both the creational prologue to Torah and the exclusion of land possession from Torah, which resulted in a totalizing form of "justice" both toward Gentiles and toward the marginal even within Israel. Hence, in place of the teaching of Leviticus 19:18 to "love your neighbor" (to which some religious teachers had added "and hate your enemy"), Jesus enjoined his disciples, in a radical, antitotalizing move, to "love your enemies" (Mt 5:43-44). What is more, he specifically grounded this injunction in the example of God's universal love as Creator, who causes sun and rain to nourish both the just and the unjust, without discrimination (Mt 5:45).

That Jesus could side vigorously with the marginal within Israel (pervasively evident in his frequent clashes with the Jewish religious and political center) and at the same time resist the allure of militant messianic movements which sought, on behalf of the marginal, the violent overthrow of Rome (evident in his persistent refusal to be acclaimed king by the crowds) is testimony to his profound discernment of the fundamental contours and intent of the canonical metanarrative.

This discernment is illustrated in what was perhaps his most controversial and subversive action, the so-called cleansing of the temple, when he overturned the moneychangers' tables (Mt 21:12-16; Mk 11:15-18; Lk 19:45-46), an action following directly on the heels of what has come to be known as the triumphal entry.

As the Gospel text has it, Jesus had entered Jerusalem during the Passover week to shouts of messianic acclaim ("Hosanna! Blessed is he who comes in the name of the Lord!"). In response to the growing expectation that he would throw off the yoke of the Romans and liberate Israel (an expectation which always ran high during Passover, when Israel celebrated the original exodus), Jesus entered the temple and decisively called into question the heart of Jewish self-understanding. Whereas Israel as elect nation and the temple as symbol of that election (representing God's presence among the chosen people) were meant, in the context of the canonical metanarrative, to be a vehicle for the reconciliation of the world, both nation and temple had become impediments to this overarching narrative purpose. Quoting two Old Testament prophetic texts (Is 56:7 and Jer 7:11), Jesus declared that the temple, which should have been "a house of prayer for all nations" had become instead "a den of robbers" (Mk 11:17).[43]

Since the term "robbers" *(lēstai)* acquired, possibly as early as 40 B.C., the technical connotation of militant brigands or insurrectionists resistant to Roman rule,[44] it is significant that when Jesus was crucified between two *lēstai* by a Jewish-Roman coalition, it is Barabbas, a true *lēstēs*, who goes free in his stead (Mt 26:55; Mk 14:48; Lk 22:52; Jn 18:40). It is further significant that what precipitated Jesus' arrest, leading eventually to crucifixion, supposedly on charges of insurrection against the Roman state, was precisely his challenge to Jewish self-identity in the temple.[45]

The irony is thus complete. The one who discerned the anti-ideological thrust of the canonical story, that Israel is God's servant to bring blessing to the nations (including the Romans), and who came to restore the faithful remnant to that vocation, is sacrificed on the altar of Roman and Jewish self-protective ideology. Jesus quite literally suffers for the sins of the (Jewish and Gentile) world.

In this he fulfills a vocation adumbrated in the Old Testament of both Israel and the prophets as the "servant of Yahweh," rejected by those to whom they are sent.[46] Here we have the historical basis of the New Testament claim about the atoning sacrifice of Jesus' death. It is not simply that Jesus rightly discerned the thrust of the canonical metanarrative, evident in his antitotalizing critique of the center, but that through his passion and death he *recapitulated* in his person the suffering of the rejected prophets and of exilic Israel before him. Jesus, in other words, was more than just a prophet. It is the Christian claim that Jesus paradigmatically embodied the central biblical trajectory of embracing marginality and pain—ultimately death—on behalf of *both* the margins and the center, thus bearing the sins of the world. This radical embrace was vivid testimony to his trust in the Creator of both center and margins, a Creator who is able to bring life even out of death. The person of Jesus, and especially his death on a cross, thus becomes in the New Testament a symbol of the counterideological intent of the biblical metanarrative and the paradigm or model of ethical human action, even in the face of massive injustice.[47]

**Decisive Plot Resolution Is at Hand**
But according to the New Testament the cross of Jesus is not merely symbolic. Christians confess that in the death and resurrection of this marginal one we find (paradoxically) the center of the biblical metanarrative. The centrality of these events is evident from the fact that Jesus' death and resurrection take up fully one-third of the Gospels. But it is also evident from Paul's succinct summary of the Gospel in 1 Corinthians 15.

> For what I received I passed on to you as of first importance: that Christ died for our sins according to the Scriptures, that he was buried, that he was raised on the third day according to the Scriptures, and that he appeared to Peter, and then to the Twelve. (vv. 3-5)

"According to the Scriptures" does not mean simply that Paul had a set of proof texts he could appeal to. On the contrary, it refers to the embeddedness of the Jesus story in the Torah story, indeed in the entire biblical metanarrative.[48]

Thus when Paul is invited, in the early years of the Christian movement, to speak "a message of encouragement" to his fellow Jews and God-fearing Gentiles in the synagogue in Pisidian Antioch (in Acts 13), he tells the Jesus story. But, like a good Israelite, he puts Jesus in context. Starting with the ancestors and the sojourn in Egypt, Paul recounts God's mighty deeds of the exodus and the gift of land, up to the beginning of the monarchy (13:16-22). But when he reaches David he decisively updates the story—beyond David, beyond the prophets, beyond the exile, and beyond the return from exile, which was not a genuine return anyway. For ever since they had returned to their land in the fifth century the Jews had been continuously dominated by foreign nations, first by the Greeks and then by the Romans. Thus, in Jewish self-awareness during the time of Jesus and Paul, Israel was regarded as still in exile, awaiting God's redemption. God's people were still in bondage, awaiting a new exodus.[49]

So Paul, who has experienced this new exodus on the road to Damascus (Acts

9), updates the Old Testament story once more in Acts 13, recounting God's next, decisive, mighty act in history: "From this man's [i.e., David's] descendants God has brought to Israel the Savior Jesus, as he promised" (13:23). And he proceeds to tell the story of Jesus, focusing on its most decisive moments: his death for sin and resurrection to new life (vv. 27-37).

It is not just that Paul updates the Israel story to include Jesus. Rather, Paul understands that Jesus is the center of the story, the denouement and climactic turning point of the entire narrative, the central page in the book God is writing. For the death of Jesus constitutes nothing less than the voluntary subjection of the Messiah to the bondage of death on behalf of Israel, and ultimately on behalf of the world, while his resurrection constitutes his exodus—his way out—in which Israel and all humanity may now participate, by trusting in the God who has acted decisively on their behalf. In Jesus' atoning death and resurrection victory over the grave, the fundamental plot conflict introduced by the fall has been in principle reversed. Although we still await the eschatological kingdom of God, the finale of the story, when the Creator shall make all things new (the Scriptures anticipate "a new heaven and a new earth"), in Jesus "the kingdom of God is near" (Mk 1:15; Mt 4:17). Decisive plot resolution is at hand.[50]

Furthermore, as Paul makes clear, the story to which Jesus brings resolution is not simply Israel's story, but the story of the world, read precisely through the lens of Israel's story. Gathering up his own people's accumulated centuries of suffering and their deep-seated yearning for deliverance, Paul vividly portrays the groaning of all creation, now in bondage to futility, and its eager expectation to be liberated when the Messiah returns (Rom 8:19-22). And all who have tasted of this liberation through faith, says the apostle, groan within themselves, as they too await this coming redemption, this final cosmic exodus from the bondage of sin and death (Rom 8:23-25).

By the time we reach the New Testament it thus becomes crystal clear (if it was not clear before) that the story the Scriptures tell is fundamentally the story of all creation. It is thus *our* story, no matter who we are, capable of speaking to us even in the midst of a postmodern crisis. In answer to the question What's wrong? the Scriptures tell of our rebellion against our Creator, of our willful bondage to futility and our entrapment in no-exit situations (even the situation of postmodernity). And they tell, further, of our deep-seated, often inarticulate yearning for release, healing and transformation.

In answer to the question What's the remedy? the Scriptures speak of God's passionate desire to answer our cries of desperation and meet us in our need, intervening in our no-exit situations, to turn our bondage into freedom. This is the story of the Creator's unsurpassing love for a world gone astray, a love that would lead him ultimately to the cross, to enter into our pain, bearing our suffering and sin, to hand it back to us as redemption. This is the story of the unswerving narrative intent of the Author of creation to liberate his creatures from their bondage, untangling the dead-end plots of their stories by incorporating them into his grand design, through what Jesus has done.

### An Antitotalizing Metanarrative?

The biblical metanarrative thus addresses our postmodern situation with both compassion and power. But does this metanarrative escape the postmodern charge of totalization and violence? On our analysis, it does far more than that. Far from promoting violence, the story the Scriptures tell contains the resources to shatter totalizing readings, to convert the reader, to align us with God's purposes of shalom, compassion and justice.

Such transformation is, of course, never guaranteed. It is not a mechanical function of the text but depends on our response, we who claim this text as canonical. This means that we must be willing for the biblical text to judge our constructions, to call us into question, to convert us. In one sense, then, the charge of totalization addressed to Christianity can only be answered by the concrete, nontotalizing life of actual Christians, the body of Christ who as living epistles (as Paul calls the church in 2 Cor 3:1-3) take up and continue the ministry of Jesus to a suffering and broken world. *That* is ultimately the only answer that counts. Thus, the point of our articulation of Scripture as nontotalizing and counterideological is not simply an apologetic ploy, a pat answer to the postmodern objection so we can get back to business as usual. Instead, we tell this liberating story so that the Scriptures might be a living resource, contributing to the genuine empowerment of the church in the exercise of its mission in a postmodern world.

# 6/The Empowered Self

ver a century ago *Lewis Carroll inadvertently summed up* the postmodern crisis of self-identity in the last verse of the Mad Gardener's song:[1]

> He thought he saw an Argument
> 　That proved he was the Pope:
> He looked again and found it was
> 　A Bar of Mottled Soap.
> "A fact so dread," he faintly said,
> 　"Extinguishes all hope!"

If modernity was the "argument" (the plausibility structure or metanarrative) that legitimated the old sense of human autonomy (proving we were each the secular equivalent of the pope), we have now discovered just how mistaken we have been. Having got our hopes up, having raised our self-image, thinking we had caught sight of our glorious reflection in the mirror, we looked again and saw a paltry thing. And this postmodern discovery fills us with overpowering dread. We no longer know who we are or what we may legitimately hope for.

Our aim in this chapter is to show how the Scriptures provide a basis for realistic hope concerning human identity and purpose. We will attempt to articulate a biblically rooted answer to the worldview question Who are we? that takes seriously the postmodern experience of social saturation and personal fragmentation. We want to address, through Scripture, the loss of significant agency and the resultant sense of impotence and victimization that many in Western culture are experiencing, even if they cannot articulate it.

Our starting point will be the biblical portrayal of the self articulated in Genesis 1 as *imago Dei*, that is, created to be the "image of God."² This notion, which grounds all later biblical portrayals of what it means to be human, presents us with an important alternative both to the modern "imperial self of yesteryear" with its grandiose pretensions to autonomy³ and to the postmodern self—decentered, disoriented, fragmented and tossed by the wind of every impinging image and context.⁴ We hope to show that this unique vision of being human is empowering and liberating for living as human beings (and as Christians) before the face of God in a pluralistic, decentered, fragmented culture.

### The Dialectic of Tyrant and Victim

Yet it is not accurate to describe our culture as simply pluralistic and fragmented; it is also, in some sense, monolithic and imperial. For all its fragmentation and decentering, we do not live in a culture that is genuinely postmodern. Mingled with postmodernity is the enhanced, hypermodern tendency to idealize infinite consumer choice, decontextualized from any given tradition, community or norms. While is is not simply identical with the modern quest for autonomy through old-fashioned control of nature in the service of the progress ideal, it is a yearning for autonomy nonetheless, and a yearning which is enhanced by hyperreal advertising and the plethora of consumer images with which we are daily bombarded.

If the modern autonomous self sought to dominate the world (and other human beings) in the name of what we now recognize to be a fictitious and ideological ideal (universal, rational human progress), the postmodern (or hypermodern) self fluctuates between the quest for a new form of autonomy and the experience of victimization. Compulsively seeking personal advancement (ungrounded in any grandiose ideal) via aggressive control of one's situation and refashioning of one's image, fueled all the while by an insatiable desire for unlimited experience of the carnivalesque smorgasbord of life, the postmodern/hypermodern self is nevertheless overcome by a sense of meaninglessness, powerlessness, rootlessness, homelessness and fragmentation, where the self is incapacitated before its infinite possibilities, reduced to an effect of its plural contexts and consequently haunted by a deep-rooted sense of anomie. The "I want it all" attitude is easily transmuted into "I'm paralyzed in the face of it all."[5] The postmodern self thus exists in a perpetual state of dialectical self-contradiction.

For that matter, it is not at all clear that the modern self was uniformly or monolithically imperial. Modernity itself has been characterized from the beginning by the paradox that the progress ideal, though touted as universal, has functioned as an ideological cover for certain less-than-universal interests. Modern ideals have served to legitimate patriarchal, European (and later American) violence against native peoples, blacks, other people of color, women and nature itself. That is, under modernity, as under present postmodern conditions, humanity is pulled in two contrary directions, offered two contradictory alternatives for being human, which we may characterize as tyrant and victim, or centered and decentered, or imperial and impotent. The difference is that in postmodern times, the imperial self is stripped of its ideological pretensions (though its violence has not abated) and the decentered or victimized self has come to be valorized.

How then does Scripture, and the biblical worldview, address this anthropological dilemma? To answer this question, let us go back to the beginning of the biblical story in Genesis 1, which sets the stage for all that is to follow. Genesis 1 proclaims the foundational biblical answer to the Who are we? question, an answer which is elaborated throughout the remainder of the biblical story in its portrayal of human beings as either advancing or thwarting God's narrative purposes. But since the nature of the human calling and the contribution (positive or negative) that humanity is able to make to God's purposes is grounded in our creation as the image of God, it is important for us to start there.

It is also important, however, to realize that although Genesis 1 portrays the opening scene in the unfolding biblical metanarrative, it probably wasn't the earliest written text of Scripture. This is similar to the New Testament, where Paul's letters (especially 1 Corinthians and Galatians) are the earliest written Christian documents, and the Gospels, with which the New Testament begins, were actually written later (between ten and fifty years later, depending on the Gospel in question and the dating scheme) but tell the story of what came earlier.[6] Likewise, in the Old Testament, it is the story of the exodus that is earliest, and the book of Genesis is probably somewhat later, as Israel filled out its understanding of God's larger metanarrative purposes that went back *before* the exodus.[7] But whenever the substance of Genesis was actually written, the final form of the book, including its prologue (1:1—2:3) setting the stage for all that is to come, likely dates from the sixth century B.C., when Israel was in exile in Babylon.[8]

This makes perfect sense for a number of reasons. Apart from the fact that most authors tend to write their introductions or prefaces after they have completed the body of their work, the notion of humans as the image of God is found in the Old Testament only in Genesis 1:26-27, 5:1 and 9:6. Although the essential meaning of this term, we hope to show, is consistent with the portrayal of humans throughout the biblical story as agents able to advance or retard God's purposes in history, the fact that the term itself is strangely absent from the rest of the Old Testament suggests that its use in Genesis is relatively late.[9] But, more importantly, Genesis 1, though depicting the initial conditions of the entire biblical metanarrative, addresses a particular historical crisis of faith (a crisis of world and of self) in Israel. It was a crisis precipitated by Babylonian exile.

### Israel's Exilic Crisis

If we, living in a hypermodern/postmodern culture, experience fragmentation and loss of agency as we are pulled in multiple directions and sucked dry of significant selfhood by our pluralistic contexts, the Israelites in Babylon found themselves in an analogous situation. Granted, their problem wasn't pluralism. Babylon was a monolithic empire, more akin to modernity than to postmodernity. But like modernity, the Babylonian empire gave rise to tyrants and victims. And like us, at the end of modernity, Israel in the sixth century was plunged into a disorienting identity crisis of immense proportions.

Israel had been literally wiped out as a nation by the monstrous Babylonian empire, which had been sweeping over the ancient Near East and gobbling up those who stood in its way. And the Israelites, who had been in the way, found themselves vanquished by Babylon, their nation eradicated, their temple destroyed, their hopes decimated and their populace taken as prisoners of war. They were stripped of their familiar world, deported to Babylon, the center of the empire, and resettled right in the jaws of the beast.[10] And there in an alien land, among a pagan people, they had to try and salvage something of their life and regain some sense of meaning and hope.

That this was a difficult undertaking is indicated by Psalm 137, a psalm of lament written during the Babylonian captivity. The mere fact of captivity would be difficult enough, but the difficulty is compounded when you are taunted by your captors.

In the poignant words of the psalmist:

> By the rivers of Babylon we sat and wept
>> when we remembered Zion.
>
> There on the poplars
>> we hung our harps,
>
> for there our captors asked us for songs,
>> our tormentors demanded songs of joy;
>> they said, "Sing us one of the songs of Zion!"
>
> How can we sing the songs of Yahweh
>> while in a foreign land? (vv. 1-4)

How is it possible to praise God when you are still reeling from the shock of disorientation? Even if it were possible to praise God in the heart of ancient Babylon, it would be a futile enterprise, like "dancing in the dragon's jaws."[11] At any moment the jaws would snap shut, and that would be the end.[12]

And even if you were ultimately spared death, what sort of life would you have? If those terrifying jaws did not suddenly snap shut, if you survived in Babylon, what would be the cost of survival? Instead of snapping shut, those monstrous jaws would likely grind down on you slowly, crushing the life and faith out of you like some oppressive weight—the weight of empire, of a culture (ancient, modern or postmodern) that dominates the horizon, that shapes you into its image, that reduces you to an effect, that robs you of your identity, because it robs you of your world.

Although some Israelites came to survive and even thrive in Babylon, for many others exile precipitated a profound crisis of immense proportions. Ultimately exile was perceived as the failure of God. If this imperial pagan culture centered around the worship of the god Marduk—a culture which lives by sticking its clenched fist in the face of Yahweh-God, the God of Israel, the only true God—has overpowered the people of God, then what sort of God is this? Can this God still be trusted? After all, it was Yahweh who let the dragon devour his people, who allowed them to be swallowed by the beast. Or maybe God just can't help it. Maybe the dragon is just more powerful. What can God do about a massive empire anyway?

It's all well and good to talk and even sing about Yahweh, the God of our fathers, delivering his people of old from the hand of Pharaoh, or holding in *his* hand the royal palace in Babylon. But come on! Those are just words. Words the prophets tell us. Words from an ancient story. Paper-thin words. Meaningless words that have no more power. Because whatever was true in the past, the empires of today gobble up God's people and play their power-politics at the expense of the elect, imposing their alien values and worldview on us, subjugating us till we are no more than leftover morsels trapped in the jaws of a dragon. God's people are no better than insignificant motes, crushed and molded by the jaws of the monstrous culture in which they live.

And it's not as if awareness of your surroundings helps. If anything, it makes things worse. When you're in a dragon's jaws and look around, what do you see? You see teeth, the sharp white teeth of your captivity. Standing tall and sleek, gleaming with danger, ready to impale you. Not everyone is a victim, a mote being ground down. Some do the grinding.

### The Elite of the Gods

And the presence of those riding the crest of the empire, flaunting their tyrannical power, would certainly exacerbate the exilic crisis for sensitive Israelites. Take the writer of Psalm 73, for example. Whether he was writing about Israelites or Babylonians is not clear, but as a perceptive person of faith he noticed the "sharp teeth" all around him. And he admits that his faith was severely tested. Starting with a declaration of what is supposed to be true for God's people ("Surely God is good to Israel, to those who are pure in heart"), the psalmist goes on to confess honestly that this "truth" was contradicted by what he saw in the dragon's jaws.

But as for me, my feet had almost slipped;
    I had nearly lost my foothold.
For I envied the arrogant
    when I saw the prosperity of the wicked.
They have no struggles;
    their bodies are healthy and strong.
They are free from the burdens common to man;
    they are not plagued by human ills. . . .
Surely in vain have I kept my heart pure;
    in vain have I washed my hands in innocence. (Ps 73:2-5, 13)

When this psalmist looked around at those with power and success, he nearly slipped and lost his foothold; it's hard to keep your balance in a dragon's jaws. Although God is supposed to bless those who are faithful and pure in heart, it was the arrogant who prospered. What is more, these sharp people seemed almost superhuman, untroubled by the normal crises of life.

In ancient Babylon there were indeed people who seemed superhuman. Preeminent above all would be the king, understood in the ancient Near Eastern worldview to be the unique son and representative of the gods, who mediated social harmony and cosmic fertility from heaven to earth. Whereas the ancient Sumerian king Gilgamesh is described as two-thirds god and one-third man, and Egyptian pharaohs were thought to be eternally begotten in the womb of the gods, the kings of Babylon and Assyria were believed to be elected, chosen or adopted by the gods for their royal task.[13] They were described as the "image" of Marduk or Shamash, or likened to the gods in their wisdom and power.[14]

Although it was the rule of this preeminent quasi-divine figure on behalf of the gods that was thought to guarantee the success of the Babylonian empire, he was not alone in his task. Associated with the king would be the other members of the royal court, as well as the priests and priestesses of the many gods of the land. Together they were the bright and shining elite of Babylon, neither like the dull Babylonian masses nor like the captive Israelites. They were living icons who exuded divinity, manifesting in their opulence the glory of the divine realm. The gods were magnificently present in them and ruled through them.[15]

It is important to understand the theology of images in the ancient Near East. Throughout Egyptian, Canaanite, Sumerian and Akkadian (that is, Babylonian and Assyrian) cultures, images were thought to mediate the presence and blessing of deity, making the gods visibly and tangibly present to the worshipers. Idols or cult statues were not regarded as mere inert blocks of wood or stone. Through elaborate rituals of consecration, cult statues were thought to be transubstantiated (much as the bread and wine are in the Roman Catholic Eucharist) such that they ceased being mere statues and became living manifestations of the gods whom they represented, suffused with their unique power and glory.[16]

But just as important as the theology of images was their social function. The fact that cult statues, kings and sometimes priests were described as images of particular gods served both to distance the masses from direct contact with the gods and to enhance the status and power of those who stood between the divine and human realms. Access to deity was thus strictly controlled by the priesthood and the royal court. Indeed, in the ancient Near East, contact with the gods was simply impossible without the mediation either of shrines and temples, with their cult statues and priests, or of the royal court, supervised by the personage of the king, who was typically regarded as the high priest of the national cult.[17]

### Slaves of the Gods

But what about the masses of Babylon? What about those who were not divinely privileged? What were ordinary human beings understood to be like in ancient Babylon? Typically they were regarded as slaves or indentured servants of the gods, created for the express purpose of ministering to their needs. This is a widespread understanding of humanity throughout Mesopotamian history, beginning in the days of ancient Sumerian civilization and persisting through the rise and fall of the old Babylonian and Assyrian empires, down to the resurgence of Babylon under Nebuchadnezzar in the sixth century. It is stated in numerous myths and stories of human origin over an immensely long time span. For our purposes, however, we would do well to look at its statement in the Babylonian creation myth, the Enuma Elish, which though dating from well before the exile was enjoying unparalleled popularity in the sixth century as the defining charter myth of the Neo-Babylonian empire.[18] Indeed, there is evidence that this myth was dramatized or ritually enacted at the annual Babylonian new year festival, with the king representing Marduk, the head of the Babylonian pantheon, whose son and image he was.[19]

The Enuma Elish is a very lengthy myth, only a small part of which is concerned with the creation of humanity, or indeed with creation at all.[20] Most of the myth is dominated by a theogony, an account of the birth of numerous gods and goddesses, who line up into two major camps: the older gods, led by Tiamat, the ocean mother (who is portrayed more and more as a monster or dragon), and the younger gods, with newly born Marduk as their champion. From the beginning, however, the theogony turns into a theomachy, a battle of the gods, a story filled with deicide, followed by revenge and counterrevenge slayings. After a great deal of blood and gore, in which the older forces of chaos come close to triumphing, Marduk (who later in the story becomes the patron god of Babylon) is commissioned to engage Tiamat in single combat. He is victorious, and having slaughtered the monster of the chaos-waters, he dismembers her and uses her body parts to create the cosmos.

For this he receives great praise from the assembly of the gods and is granted perpetual kingship over them all. He then decrees the construction of Babylon and its many temples and shrines as, in effect, overnight hostels for the gods on their journeys, places where they might rest and be fed. And it becomes the lot of all those who were associated with the defeated Tiamat, a vast number of captured and demoted divinities, to tend the shrines and temples, feeding the superior gods by offering the appointed sacrifices before their cult statues and seeing to the efficient running of the entire temple economy.

Either because the captive gods willingly devote themselves to the task or because the work proves to be too menial or burdensome for them (the text is fragmentary at this point), Marduk proposes the ingenious solution of relieving their toil by the creation of human beings.

Blood I will mass and cause bones to be.

I will establish a savage, "man" shall be his name.

Verily, savage-man I will create.

He shall be charged with the service of the gods

That they might be at ease![21]

Here, what was well known throughout ancient Mesopotamian cultures, that humanity was created specifically to serve the gods, working the temple estates of their divine masters and providing for their upkeep, is repeated. But there is a new twist. At the suggestion of Marduk's father, Ea, the god of wisdom, it is decided that one of the captured rebel gods should be sacrificed as representative punishment for all the rebels and humanity fashioned out of his blood. The one chosen for slaughter is Kingu, the leader of Tiamat's forces in the most recent battle as well as her consort and second husband (her first husband, Apsu, having been killed earlier in the story).

They bound him, holding him before Ea.

They imposed on him his guilt and severed his blood [vessels].

Out of his blood they fashioned mankind.

He [Ea] imposed the service and let free the gods.[22]

Although the theme of humanity's creation out of the blood of a slain god is not as common in Mesopotamian writings as is the reason given for their creation (to serve the gods), it does occur in a number of ancient texts, including the famous Atrahasis epic (which also contains the closest ancient Near Eastern parallel to the biblical flood story).[23] There the reason given for the selection of the deity to be sacrificed is that he had either "intelligence" or "personality" (depending on how the word in question is translated), thus implying that humanity inherits this laudable divine attribute.[24]

In the Enuma Elish, however, there is nothing laudable about what humanity inherits. Just as the cosmos is fashioned out of the dead carcass of the primordial chaos monster, thus representing evil as intrinsic to the fabric of the world, always having to be repressed and controlled, so humanity is created from the blood of one of the chief enemies of Marduk, patron god of Babylon, thus representing our demonic origin and essentially degraded and subservient status vis-à-vis the divine. Although it might be possible in the Atrahasis epic to see the divine blood pulsing through human veins as evidence of our elevated status in the cosmic scheme of things, by the time of the sixth-century exile Babylonian culture was decisively influenced by the mythology of the Enuma Elish, which proclaimed in no uncertain terms the servitude (even bondage) of humanity, created as cheap slave labor to do the dirty work of the lower gods.[25]

When we realize that this service of the gods was mediated in practice by the entire cultic system of temple and priesthood, over which the Babylonian king presided, the ideological function of the Enuma Elish becomes clear.[26] Since the cultic and royal personnel of Babylon not only channeled blessing from the gods but organized and controlled the service which was rendered to the gods by the mass of humanity, the Enuma Elish, in concert with the Babylonian royal ideology and theology of images, would have contributed to an overarching plausibility structure or metanarrative legitimating the Babylonian social order in which the displaced Israelites found themselves.

**Exilic Alternatives for Being Human**
The appeal of this plausibility structure would have been immensely powerful and difficult to resist. Having recently lost their literal and symbolic world of land, city and temple, with their narrative of election in tatters and even the power and faithfulness of their God in doubt, the exilic Israelites would have been plunged into a massive identity crisis. The new ideological world in which they found themselves would have provided an ever-present, alternative vision of what it meant to be human that would have exerted a powerful pull.

How might Israelites in Babylonian exile have answered the worldview question Who are we? What alternatives for being human were available to them? When the Israelites in ancient Babylon looked in the mirror, what image would they have seen staring back at them?

They had essentially two options, two mirrors placed on opposite walls, so to speak. In one mirror they could, with the vast majority of Babylonian citizens, see an insignificant nobody, a mere slave of the gods, one who had no other purpose than to serve the king and the gods of Babylon. And this ideological alternative would be reinforced by the brutal fact of Israelite defeat and captivity. In this mirror, the Israelites would catch sight of themselves as mere motes in the dragon's jaws, impotent victims of an imperial power beyond their control, effectively enslaved to the gods and social hierarchy of Babylon. In this mirror they were stripped of power, without dignity, without hope. They were, in other words, remarkably like many today in our postmodern world, robbed of agency, reduced to a product or an effect of the action of others.

In the other mirror, on the opposite wall, however, the exilic Israelites could, if they strained hard enough, catch sight of the image of a veritable god in human form, one of the quasi-divine elite. True, this elite, being human, were also created for the express purpose of serving the gods, but they served in a position of privilege. Their service elevated them above the ordinary masses and granted them an extraordinary dignity, accompanied by the benefits of social power.

Although many in ancient Babylon would never have dared look in this mirror, the Babylonian hierarchy admitted of some degree of social mobility, and there were undoubtedly those who aspired to the ideals of power and privilege. Without aspiring exactly to *become* king, could not a young Babylonian nevertheless take the king as his model, aspiring to be like this shining image of Marduk? Especially appealing would be the king's symbolic enactment of Marduk's role in the Enuma Elish at the annual new year's festival, when he engaged in ritual battle with Tiamat (representing the enemies of Babylon and all the forces of evil) and slew the evil dragon of chaos as the heroic defender of the empire.

And would not the Israelites in exile, especially if they sought to resist the dehumanization and victimization of the role assigned them by the Enuma Elish, be drawn to this alternative model of being human, one which was more in keeping with their own narrative of election and privilege? It did not matter whether exilic Israelites were more tempted to acculturate to Babylonian values and seek success in terms of the existing social hierarchy or to adopt a confrontational stance vis-à-vis Babylon as the enemy of God, embodying the forces of evil and chaos, against which they must fight in Yahweh's holy name. In either case, the second mirror would have had its allure and certainly offered the more appealing self-image.

God's people in Babylonian exile would therefore have found themselves in a situation remarkably like our own, offered contradictory self-images, pulled in the directions of imperial tyrant and impotent victim. Possibly, like us, they found themselves assuming first one, then the other self-image, fluctuating between the extremes. Indeed, in a postmodern culture we find it difficult to assume any one posture consistently, since each engenders its opposite. As the experience of victimization often generates violent resistance, only to dissipate finally into despair, so our stance of autonomy can be maintained only as a hollowed-out façade, masking a deep-seated sense of insecurity and powerlessness. It is as if the alternatives of victim and tyrant, like mirrors on opposite walls into which we are invited to look, each reflect the other, until the image splinters and we see an infinite number of reflections diminishing into nothingness in the distance. We are left wondering who we are, feeling fragmented, confused and small, like a little kid lost in a hall of mirrors or a tunnel of horrors, desperately wanting to get out but not knowing where to turn. Our world and our lives seem embroiled in chaos, and we often have no sense of control over our circumstances. So we wonder where God is in the midst of postmodernity. And why doesn't God speak and address our exilic crisis?

Yes, we have God's Word, the Scriptures of old. But those are just words on a page which pale into insignificance beside the crushing reality of the dragon's jaws. Sometimes we feel like that perceptive psalmist aware of the encircling teeth, comparing himself unfavorably against those sharp people who seem to have it all together. Yet it is clear that these very people who seem to be blessed by God do not act in a very godly way.

Their mouths lay claim to heaven,
 and their tongues take possession of the earth.
Therefore their people turn to them
 and drink up waters in abundance.
They say, "How can God know?
 Does the Most High have knowledge?"
This is what the wicked are like—
 always carefree, they increase in wealth.
Surely in vain have I kept my heart pure;
 in vain have I washed my hands in innocence. (Ps 73:9-13)

That psalmist almost slipped in the dragon's jaws.

### A Fresh Vision of God

And it was for him, and for people like him, that Genesis 1 was written. Words, the psalmist might respond; just words on a piece of paper. Yes, but the word of *God.* And God's word is so powerful, says Genesis 1, that when God spoke in the beginning ("Let there be") the whole world came into being.[27] God didn't have to fight any sea-monster or dragon to create the cosmos. There was no opposition to the authority of the true Creator. It wasn't a struggle as it was for Marduk, that poor posturing god of Babylon. The Sovereign Lord of the universe simply decreed into existence day and night, sky and earth, waters and land, plants, animals and human beings. God commanded; and it was so.

Yahweh-God rules the entire creation. Sure you are in a dragon's jaws; but do you think the Creator of the cosmos can't handle dragons? Take, for example, the dragon Leviathan described in various poetic texts throughout the Old Testament.[28] Well known in Canaanite mythology as the seven-headed water serpent who does battle with the god Baal (thus the equivalent to Tiamat in the Babylonian myth), Leviathan is described in Job 41 as a huge wild beast that no one can conquer.[29]

> If you lay a hand on him,
>> you will remember the struggle
>> and never do it again!
> Any hope of subduing him is false;
>> the mere sight of him is overpowering. (vv. 8-9)

Portrayed as an armor-plated, fire-breathing monster who regards iron as straw and bronze as rotten wood, this terrible beast makes the depths churn like a boiling cauldron (vv. 15-32). But Leviathan is not God's enemy; far from it. "Everything under heaven belongs to me," says the Lord (v. 11). Even Leviathan is a creature of God. More than that, Psalm 104:26 proclaims that God formed Leviathan to frolic in the ocean depths. You might say God sports with Leviathan as his "rubber duckie"!

Are we scared of dragons? We're talking about a God who makes a dragon look like a pussycat! Sure, *we* can't treat empires that way. And we can't simply wish postmodernity away. But we can at least begin to put on our dancing shoes as we get ready to celebrate the good news of Genesis 1. Because Genesis 1 challenges our perception of the dragon's jaws. It redescribes Babylonian exile—and postmodernity—in terms of the larger, prior reality of the cosmos as God's good creation, a multifaceted, harmonious world brought into being and granted life and blessing by the word of God.[30]

Yes, Genesis will soon go on (in chapters 3—11) to speak of a creation corrupted and filled with violence, the exilic experience being a prime example of this. But between God's good creation and this violence comes the amazing story of God's creation of humanity. For Genesis 1 does not stop with telling us about the incredible Creator we have, behind and beyond all empires—the God who rules creation itself as his empire, as his kingdom. Genesis 1 doesn't only tell us about God and the world; it also tells us about ourselves. Genesis 1 holds up a mirror to us, in which we see a radical alternative to the Babylonian—and modern and postmodern—visions of humanity. Genesis 1 shatters the false dilemma of having to choose between being an impotent slave of the gods and an autonomous demigod ourselves.

### An Alternative to Victimization

Take that slave-of-the-gods mirror, that mirror in which you see an insignificant nobody staring back at you. Genesis 1 shatters that mirror with its amazing declaration. Having exhibited his creative rule over the cosmos in Genesis 1:1-25, God goes on to say,

"Let us make humanity in our image, in our likeness, and let *them* rule over the fish of the sea and the birds of the air, over the livestock, over all the earth, and over all the creatures that move along the ground."

So God created humanity in his own image,
in the image of God he created him;
male and female he created them.

God blessed them and said to them, "Be fruitful and increase in number; fill the earth and subdue it. Rule over the fish of the sea and the birds of the air and over every living creature that moves on the ground." (vv. 26-28)[51]

The sovereign Ruler over all creation here grants to the human race, at the outset of the biblical story, a royal status and dignity in the earth. Analogous to God's own rule of the cosmos, humanity (both male and female) has been appointed to the office of viceregent over the earth and its creatures. This causes the writer of Psalm 8 to burst out in wonder and amazement:

O Yahweh, our Lord,
how majestic is your name in all the earth! . . .

When I consider your heavens,
the work of your fingers,
the moon and the stars,
which you have set in place,
what are human beings that you are mindful of them,
mere mortals that you care for them?

Yet you made them little lower than God,
and crowned them with glory and honor.

You made them rulers over the works of your hands;
you put everything under their feet:
all flocks and herds,
and the beasts of the field,
the birds of the air,
and the fish of the sea,
all that swim the paths of the seas. (vv. 1, 3-8)

Without using the technical term *image of God* the writer of Psalm 8 nevertheless speaks of the royal glory and honor with which humans have been crowned as the rulers over God's works. And he boldly describes this elevated, royal status as being godlike or almost divine, which is the import of our having been made "little lower than God."[32] But while the terminology varies between Psalm 8 and Genesis 1, the point is the same. In an extraordinary democratizing move, the Scriptures declare that it is *not* some imperial or priestly Babylonian elite who stand between God and the world, exercising divinely authorized power as God's image. On the contrary, that task is granted to the entire human race.

To a people submerged in exile—uprooted, homeless, powerless victims of a monstrous empire—the Creator of the universe proclaims that he has granted all human beings (no matter how frail or fragile they might feel) a share in his rule of the earth. Even in exile, this text proclaims, we have been made royal dignitaries in God's world, placed in a position of power, agency and responsibility as the Creator's representatives on earth. In the face of both the Babylonian worldview and postmodern fragmentation, Genesis 1 calls into question an ideology of victimization which would reduce us to an effect. We are neither the products of a vanquished Babylonian deity, destined to serve the gods of the empire, nor the multiphrenic constructs of media-saturated postmodern society. Instead, the text empowers God's people to resist the dehumanization of their culture and to stand tall with dignity—even to dance joyfully—as they exercise their limited, though real, God-given power, even in the dragon's jaws. The good news of Genesis 1 to fragmented exiles is that God has granted to us very ordinary human beings the privilege and task of ruling the world.

But that doesn't make sense. That's *God's* job—to rule the world—isn't it? Precisely! Genesis 1 tells us that we weren't created to do the dirty work of the lower gods, but to do the proper work of the one true God. In the Enuma Elish human beings work so the defeated gods can take a break—they are so tired out! But in Genesis 1, when the Creator of the universe rests on the seventh day, it is not a petty deity's abdication of a burdensome task. On the contrary, God entrusts to human beings significant responsibility for the world he has created. We have been made stewards of the earth, and history is now in our hands!

The creation account in Genesis 1:1—2:3 reinforces this point by its very literary structure. Most people familiar with the Bible realize that the account is organized around seven days, and they realize further that a recurring refrain brings closure to each day of creation: "And there was evening, and there was morning—the first [second, third, etc.] day." That refrain marks the conclusion and completion of each day of God's creative work. But what is not usually noticed is that this refrain continues only to day six, on which humans are created in God's image to rule the earth. After God's work is complete and he rests on the seventh day, just where we would expect a final, concluding refrain ("And there was evening, and there was morning—the seventh day"), there is none.

The reason is simple: we are still in the seventh day. God has indeed rested from creating, but that is not the end of the story. On the contrary, God has appointed human beings as agents of his kingdom, royal ambassadors of his rule, precisely that the story might continue. Just as God over six days developed the original creation which was "formless and empty" (Gen 1:2) into a beautiful, harmonious world inhabited by a complex variety of creatures, so we are called on the seventh day to continue God's work of unfolding and developing the inbuilt potential of creation throughout human history. We have been granted real historical power by our Creator to represent him as his *image* and manifest his purposes by the way in which we live out our lives as stewards of the earth, and that power has never been taken back! Not even in exile. Babylonian exile, like the entire story the Bible tells from Genesis 2:4 on, takes place on the seventh day, the day of human historical responsibility.

To a people experiencing the despair and fragmentation of exile, crushed in the dragon's jaws, Genesis 1 proclaims the good news that we are not impotent, servile, insignificant nobodies, enslaved to the gods of the age. Genesis 1 shatters that false slave-of-the-gods mirror. We don't have to believe that lie any more.

### An Alternative to Autonomy

But neither are we quasi-divine dragon slayers. Genesis 1 also shatters that other false mirror—Babylonian, modern or postmodern—in which we can catch sight of our own autonomous power. It shatters that elitist mirror by making crystal clear that though we are indeed entrusted with a royal task, we are nevertheless *creatures*, dependent on the sovereign word of the Creator for our being, fundamentally one with all that is not-God, whether trees, galaxies, animals or the earth. Indeed, our solidarity with the nonhuman realm is indicated by our creation along with other land animals on the sixth day (1:24-28) and our sharing the same food with them (1:29-30).

Thus, although we have been made stewards over the earth with genuine power to effect significant change over our environment, this does not mean that humans may legitimately assume the oppressive role vis-à-vis the nonhuman realm that the Babylonian elite exercised over the masses. Unlike the actual practice of those who were called images in ancient Babylon, the true purpose of human imaging is not to control and disempower others but to mediate God's blessing and enhance the life and well-being of all creatures, *just as God did in creating the world.* As the sovereign Lord of creation did not use his power selfishly or oppressively but engendered a multifarious cosmos, blessing its creatures with life and fertility—and, in particular, *sharing his power* with humans—in the same way humans, as the *image and likeness* of this God, are to use their power and rule for the benefit of others.[33] Thus Genesis 2:15 portrays the original and normative human task of ruling the earth as equivalent to that of lovingly tending and caring for the ground from which we came.

This relationship of nurture, grounded in a primordial harmony between humans and the earth, is reinforced by a pun or wordplay that Genesis 2:7 makes on the Hebrew words for humanity *('ādām)* and ground *('ªdāmâ).* This resonance of humans with the humus (for that would be the equivalent English pun[34]) is broken only by the discord of the fall in Genesis 3, when humans attempt to transcend their creaturely limits, resulting in their expulsion from the Garden and their estrangement from the very ground from which they were taken.

And if it is clear that human rule of the earth consists in loving nurture rather than oppressive control, it should be even clearer that human power as *imago Dei* is not to be used for the oppression of other persons. It is significant that while humans (both male and female) are explicitly commissioned to rule the earth as God's image, there is no reference in either Genesis 1 or 2 to humans ruling *each other.* Indeed, Genesis 2 portrays the original and normative relationship between man and woman as one of mutuality and harmony. The original couple deeply desire, and resonate with, each other (2:23-24), and this resonance is reinforced by the wordplay on the Hebrew words for man *('îš)* and woman *('îššâ),* much like that between human and ground. It is only after the primal rebellion of Genesis 3 that we find for the first time man ruling over woman in an asymmetrical relationship of power (3:16), an act of violence which disrupts God's intent for creation and which is soon followed in Genesis 4 by Cain's impulsive murder of his brother Abel and the boastful revenge killing of a youth by Lamech (who, not so coincidentally, is the first polygamist in the Bible). These brutal acts multiply in a downward spiral of violence which fills the earth, precipitating the flood as God's judgment (6:11-13).[35]

The structural similarity between Cain's and Lamech's murders, the oppressive treatment of the masses by the Babylonian elite and Marduk's primordial act of violence against Tiamat is intriguing. Such acts require us to position ourselves in a stance of superior or righteous opposition over against some enemy which we have demonized that we might control or destroy with impunity. This totalizing stance was also at the root of the Neo-Babylonian imperial expansionist program in the sixth century, which resulted in the captivity of Israel. This expansionist political program was a natural outworking of the mythology of the Enuma Elish. Paul Ricoeur describes Marduk's battle with Tiamat as a theology of holy war in which the king represents Marduk and mediates the cosmic victory against chaos. The creation myth is then transposed to human history, in which the political enemies of the empire are vanquished as the agents of chaos.[36] Ricoeur explains:

> It will be seen what human violence is thus justified by the primordial violence. Creation is a victory over an Enemy older than the creator; that Enemy, immanent in the divine, will be represented in history by all the enemies whom the king in his turn, as servant of the god, will have as his mission to destroy. Thus Violence is inscribed in the origin of things, in the principle that establishes while it destroys.[37]

And if Israelites in exile were severely tempted to assume the stance of heroic dragon slayer, not necessarily against any individual, but against the Babylonian empire itself (which clearly was God's enemy), Genesis 1 nevertheless proclaims an alternative vision of reality in which God subdues no primordial monster to bring creation into being and in which each creature is good and all together are "very good" (1:31).[38] And that includes even Leviathan, as Job 41 and Psalm 104 suggest, and perhaps even Genesis 1:21 too, by its mention of the "great creatures of the sea" which God created on the fifth day.[39] If a theology of holy war grows naturally out of the worldview exemplified by the Enuma Elish (that is, evil is primordial chaos, while goodness, represented by cosmic order, is later, founded by the vanquishing of chaos—a mythological theme which biblical scholars have called *Chaoskampf* or the combat myth), it becomes evident that a creation which is originally very good would sustain an entirely different sort of historical action.[40]

**The Place of Violence in the Biblical Story**

It is crucial to understand the relationship between the creation account of Genesis 1:1—2:3 and what follows. Immediately after this account comes a literary inscription in 2:4 which reads, "These are the *tôlᵉdôt* of the heavens and the earth when they were created." The Hebrew noun *tôlᵉdôt* (literally "generations") is derived from the verb "to beget" or "to give birth," and the entire book of Genesis is structured by these headings (the next one is 5:1, "the *tôlᵉdôt* of Adam"). In each case, these inscriptions come before either genealogies or narrative episodes and serve to introduce that which was *born of* or *developed out of* the person named (whether Adam, Shem, Terah, Isaac, etc.).[41] But the first such heading, in Genesis 2:4, is unique in naming not a person but the heavens and the earth. It thus serves to introduce not only the next episode of the biblical story (Genesis 2—4) but also in a sense the entirety of human history that follows, both in the book of Genesis and in the rest of Scripture. It is as if Genesis 1:1—2:3 sets up the initial conditions of the entire biblical metanarrative, consisting in a harmonious world of creatures judged very good by its Creator (where are we?) and a special creature granted agency and historical power, mandated to exercise that power for the benefit of all the rest (who are we?). The remainder of the Bible thus consists of the extended story of how we fared historically in this world with this gift and mandate.

It is clear that the story the early chapters of Genesis tells is one of violence and the abuse of power in which God's rule is *not* represented or imaged. That is, the initial conditions of the story are soon disrupted by the introduction of plot tension. God's narrative intent, set forth in Genesis 1:1—2:3, is from the beginning effectively blocked. Although it is clearly the human vocation to rule the earth (Genesis 1:26, 28) or to tend the Garden (Genesis 2:5, 15), it is significant that the first humans *do not* fulfill this vocation. Although it is explicitly stated that this tending is the reason for God's creation of humanity, there is simply no reference in Genesis 2—3 to humans fulfilling their raison d'être.[42] Instead, the story focuses on the first human couple's illicit attempt to transcend their God-given limits and become *as God*, prototypically embodying the very Babylonian aspirations the *imago Dei* notion was meant to counter. The illicit aspirations of chapter 3 then lead to the violence of chapter 4, which is *not* resolved by the birth of Seth to replace murdered Abel (4:25) even though the creation of humanity in God's image is once more affirmed and the transmission of this image to Seth is implied (5:1-3). Neither is the violence of chapter 6 resolved by the flood which temporarily cleanses the earth. Although Noah, who survives the devastation along with his family, functions somewhat as a new Adam—it is even reaffirmed that humanity is in God's image (9:6)—plot conflict increases once again. Indeed, as the story of the tower of Babel illustrates, this conflict is so massive that God is worried (11:6) and intervenes to put a stop to it. Genesis 11, however, does not explicitly mention violence, but portrays the human race after the flood multiplying in numbers and, instead of filling the earth, deciding to settle in one place (the plains of Shinar) in order to make a name for themselves by building an immense civilization symbolized by a city with a tower, called Babel (which is simply the Hebrew word the Bible regularly uses for Babylon).

Perhaps we, with our developed sense of historical perspective, would make fine distinctions between the civilization of ancient Sumer, which seems to be the historical setting for the tower of Babel episode (we are told that Abraham was from Ur, an ancient Sumerian city), and the later Babylonian and Assyrian empires which were the cultural inheritors of the ancient Sumerians (though they spoke another language, known as Akkadian). The writer of Genesis, however, simply utilized conventions of his own time in describing the entire stretch of Sumero-Akkadian civilization under the rubric "Babel," a rubric that would have vivid meaning for his audience if they were indeed exiles in the Neo-Babylonian empire.

The problem with "Babylonian" civilization, from the perspective of Genesis 11, is precisely the systemic centralization of power that comes with empire building, which results not simply in the impulsive violent outbreaks of Cain or Lamech, but in the organized violence of an oppressive social order legitimated and sustained by a powerful myth of origins. Contrary to the ancient idealization of Babylonian culture as the epitome of human aspiration and achievement, the writer of Genesis 11 declares that this aspiration is exactly what impedes God's purposes in history, in effect bringing the story to a screeching halt.[43] It therefore does not matter that violence is not explicitly mentioned in the story of Babel. The centralization of social power for imperial, oppressive uses is the direct opposite of the loving empowerment of others which is the genuine human calling. Instead of Babel being a normative ordering of the human world, which embodies divine blessing, it reaps the curse of God's judgment, and its ultimate outcome is chaos, the confusion of tongues. Contrary to the intentions of the builders, this chaos is the only name they make for themselves, says the writer of Genesis 11, engaging in an ironic wordplay between Babel and *bālal* (the Hebrew word for "to confuse").[44]

Genesis 2—11 thus tells of the first phase of universal human history, a phase characterized by a spiraling increase in the misuse of human power, until the story seems to have reached an impasse. God's original purpose to bring blessing to all creatures through humanity seems to have been rendered null and void. The rest of the biblical metanarrative may then be seen as God's attempts to get the story line back on track, to bring resolution to the plot gone awry.

### A Narrative Reading of Election

God's response to the massive violence which has filled creation is to choose one person (Abraham) and his descendants (Israel) to be the central agents of plot resolution, in order to ultimately reverse this violence and bring blessing instead. Since Israel's calling or "election" (Ex 19:3-6) is essentially an extension of Abraham's (Gen 12:1-3), it is perhaps to be expected that there are important similarities between them. More unexpected, perhaps, is the striking similarity between the election of Abraham and Israel, on the one hand, and the human vocation to image God, on the other.

In Genesis 12 God calls Abraham (then known as Abram) out of his own land and culture for a specific purpose which will ultimately benefit this very culture. Although Abraham is blessed by God and promised both his own land and numerous descendants who will one day constitute a nation (12:2), none of this is an end in itself. It is meant to serve a larger purpose: "All peoples on earth will be blessed through you" (12:3). Likewise, Exodus 19 sets Israel's election in an international, even cosmic, context ("the whole earth is mine," v. 5). If the Israelites, newly delivered by the grace of God from Egyptian bondage, live faithfully to the Sinai covenant, says the Lord, then "out of all the nations you will be my treasured possession" (Ex 19:5). Certainly, both Abraham and Israel are special to God and gifted with a unique status, in much the same way that humanity is singled out from among all creatures in Genesis 1:26-28 as God's unique image in the world. But in both Abraham's and Israel's election and the primal calling of humanity, it is not election for privilege, but for service. God's purpose in both cases is that the chosen agent function as a mediator of divine blessing in the world, in much the same way that ancient Near Eastern kings and priests *claimed* to do. Hence the particular aptness of describing elect Israel as "a kingdom of priests and a holy nation" (Ex 19:6). The entire nation is *imago Dei!*

But for Israel to function as God's agent to bring blessing to the nations (and thus, ultimately, plot resolution to the biblical story), God's intermediate promises to Abraham concerning descendants and a land must be fulfilled. The book of Genesis ends, however, with the children of Israel numbering only seventy persons and living as famine refugees in Egypt (46:27). Although the book of Exodus goes on to tell of their rapid increase in number while in Egypt, they soon lose their status as honored guests of the empire and are reduced to slavery.[45] Israel is thus forcibly prevented from fulfilling its vocation as mediator of God's blessing to the nations. The story has got stuck once again.

Enter Moses, who is called to be God's unique agent to bring Israel out of Egyptian bondage, to mediate the covenant at Sinai which will constitute them as a people, and to lead them to the Promised Land, all of which is a necessary prelude to Israel's fulfilling its historical mission to the world.[46] Moses' mission thus functions as a *subplot* within the larger biblical story, since it is not *his* task to bring blessing to the nations, but to make it possible for Israel to fulfill that task (in effect, restoring them to that vocation). Yet Moses' election is similar to both Abraham's and Israel's and to the human calling to image God because in each case God calls his human servants to significant agency in history that they might impact the larger story for the benefit of others.[47]

Nevertheless the *imago Dei* and election are not simply identical. Whereas the original vocation to image God to the nonhuman creation does not explicitly take into account the plot tension of human violence, election is a postfall rearticulation of *imago Dei,* the purpose of which is to further plot resolution so that God's purposes from the beginning might be realized.

It is significant that the Bible understands Moses as the first and prototypical prophet (Deut 18:15, 18), since it is also the calling of the prophets to recall the people of Israel to their vocation and thus bring plot resolution to the biblical story. In this connection, the story of Moses' election (Ex 3:1—4:17) is remarkably similar to the call narratives of Isaiah and Jeremiah (Is 6; Jer 1), which describe these prophets' sense of inadequacy for their task. Whereas Isaiah was overwhelmed by his uncleanness in the presence of God and had to be purified that he might deliver a difficult message (Is 6:5-8), Jeremiah responded to his call by admitting, "I do not know how to speak; I am only a child" and was reassured that God would be with him to deliver him (Jer 1:6-8). This sense of inadequacy, reflected both in Moses' claim (like Jeremiah) that he is not eloquent with words (Ex 4:10) and in his question, "Who am I, that I should go to Pharaoh and bring the Israelites out of Egypt?" (Ex 3:11), might well be similar to the psalmist's amazed query when confronted with the royal calling of humanity: "What are human beings that you are mindful of them, mere mortals that you care for them?" (Ps 8:4). The point is that God uses fragile, fallible human beings (aware of their own inadequacies) to accomplish his momentous purposes in history.[48]

But between Moses and the prophets comes a great deal of Israelite history in which the narrative gets stuck over and over again. One such place is the book of Judges, which portrays Israel in recurring cycles of apostasy and military threat. The people continually abandon the covenant God made with them at Sinai and follow other gods, thus losing their distinctiveness as God's unique vehicle for blessing. But this religious assimilation is accompanied by a precarious political situation as they are constantly under attack by a variety of Canaanite peoples in whose vicinity they live. Therefore God raises up "judges" (Judg 2:16) to deliver them from military threat and to restore them to covenant faithfulness.

One such judge is Gideon, whose call narrative is remarkably like those of Moses and the prophets. Gideon protests his call with a confession of inadequacy ("But Lord, . . . how can I save Israel? My clan is the weakest in Manasseh, and I am the least in my family," Judg 6:15), but God promises to be with him that he might accomplish his mission (6:16). As in the case of Moses and the prophets, Gideon's story is a subplot within Israel's story; he is called to restore God's elect people to their (as yet unfulfilled) vocation in world history. By the end of the book of Judges it is clear that this has not happened. Something new is needed to bring plot resolution.

And that something new seems to be the monarchy, the next major institution to develop in Israel, replacing that of the judges. But this raises an interesting problem in biblical interpretation. We have election texts or call narratives (or their equivalent) for Abraham, Moses, Israel, Gideon, various prophets and the entire human race, but do we have any such texts for the kings of Israel? In short, are the kings also God's elect, called to restore Israel to its original vocation of mediating God's blessing to all humanity? The evidence is decidedly ambiguous.

On the one hand, the narrative of 1 Samuel 16:1-13 certainly indicates that Israel's second king, David, is chosen by God to rule Israel. And when his election is confirmed in 2 Samuel 7 through the prophet Nathan, David responds in a manner reminiscent of Moses and the prophets: "Who am I, Sovereign Yahweh, and what is my family, that you have brought me this far?" (2 Sam 7:19) Furthermore, God promises to grant David a dynasty, implying that all subsequent Davidic kings will be God's elect.[49]

On the other hand, God did not initiate the monarchy, but accepted it as a concession to Israel's request for a king "such as all the other nations have" (1 Sam 8:5). We discussed in the last chapter the controversy between God and the people regarding this request, in which God warned them of the oppressive consequences of the historical choice they were making (1 Sam 8:9-18).

Nevertheless God allows this new development (1 Sam 8:22) and tells Samuel to anoint Saul king over Israel that he might deliver the nation from the Philistine threat (1 Sam 9:15-16). This military purpose, hinted at also in the people's desire that the king might "go out before us and fight our battles" (1 Sam 8:20), confirms the sense of perpetual threat portrayed in the book of Judges as Israel is besieged and continually attacked by the surrounding nations. And Judges is peppered with the recurring statement that "in those days Israel had no king" (18:1; 19:1; 21:25), suggesting that monarchy might be the solution to this threat. Indeed, for Israel to carry out its vocation to the nations, it had first minimally to survive as a nation in its own right.

But the book of Judges makes it clear that the threat to Israel was not only external and military; it was also internal and ethical, stemming from its people's forgetting the covenant. Hence the massive bloodbath with which the latter part of the book is filled; Israelites kill each other in preemptive raids and mass acts of revenge, justifying the other important statement in the book, with which it also ends: in those days "everyone did as he saw fit" (Judg 21:25). Both internal and external threats constituted major impediments to the biblical story in that they prevented Israel from fulfilling the mission for which God chose them. The question with which the book of Judges thus leaves us is whether a monarchy would solve these threats.

It is clear that it did not. As the sordid history of the house of David shows, his successors (with few exceptions) did not even abide by the Sinai covenant,[50] much less restore Israel to their vocation (and this is to say nothing of the multiple dynasties of the northern kingdom which followed one upon the heel of the other as successive kings were assassinated in a series of political coups). Suffice it to say that the Bible seems to indicate it was precisely the corruption of kings which initially required the rise of prophets to restore Israel to their vocation. Whereas Moses locks horns with Pharaoh, Samuel rebukes Saul, Nathan challenges David, and Elijah confronts Ahab, as we approach the seventh century we find the kings of both Israel and Judah so persistently ignoring the prophets that they more and more address the people directly instead. Even then, however, the people by and large do not listen to the prophets, and first the northern then the southern kingdom is vanquished and taken into exile. The story again seems to have hit a dead end.[51]

### The Dialectic of Idolatry

The book of Ecclesiastes may be regarded as an inner-biblical commentary on the failure of the Israelite monarchy. Attributed to the "teacher," who seems to be identified with Solomon, the book takes the form of a personal meditation on the value (or lack thereof) of a king's power and prestige.[52] Ecclesiastes describes, from a first-person standpoint, the quest for wisdom, the immense building projects, the extravagant accumulation of wealth and the uninhibited search for pleasure of Israel's greatest, wisest and most glorious king. The conclusion of the book, stated persistently throughout, is that all this striving was "meaningless, a chasing after the wind" (Eccles 1:14). Both at the outset and near the end of the book we find the emphatic words:

"Meaningless! Meaningless!"
says the Teacher.
"Utterly meaningless!
Everything is meaningless." (1:2; 12:8)

*Meaningless (hebel)* is the key word in Ecclesiastes, repeated some thirty-six times throughout the book, which accounts for at least half of its occurrences in the Bible. But its other occurrences are also instructive and shed light on the failure of the monarchy. Apart from those places in Scripture where *hebel* refers, as it does in Ecclesiastes, to the sense of meaninglessness or futility experienced by particular persons, the term is found in two other important contexts.

The first is in reference to idols. Especially in the book of Jeremiah, *hebel* becomes a virtual synonym for idols.[53] In the covenant lawsuit Yahweh brings against Israel in Jeremiah 2, the central accusation is that Israel has forsaken the true God to follow "worthlessness" (either *hebel* in v. 5 or *lô yô'îl* in vv. 8, 11). Hammering home the utter futility of serving idols, Yahweh declares:

Has a nation ever changed its gods?
(Yet they are not gods at all.)
But my people have exchanged their Glory
for worthless idols.
Be appalled at this, O heavens,
and shudder with great horror. (vv. 11-12)[54]

The contrast between glory (*kābôd*) and worthlessness (here *lô yô'îl* as a synonym for *hebel*) is instructive. That is because *kābôd* and *hebel* are in Hebrew strict opposites, denoting that which is weighty, important or of true value versus that which is empty, ephemeral and vaporous, hence ultimately futile.[55] The terms thus aptly contrast the true God, who alone can bring judgment and salvation, with idols, which are powerless to act. But *kābôd* and *hebel* would also be apt terms to describe the central options for being human available throughout the ancient Near East. Whereas the powerful royal and priestly elites were thought to bear the *kābôd* of the divine presence, the impotent masses would be reduced to the futility of *hebel*.

Against this background, Psalm 115 takes on significant depth. Without using the term *heḇel* (or any of its synonyms), the psalm nevertheless contrasts the true God, to whom alone belongs glory (115:1) and who alone has power to act, with the utter impotence of idols, which can do nothing.

> Our God is in heaven;
>> he does whatever pleases him.
> But their idols are silver and gold,
>> made by human hands.
> They have mouths, but cannot speak,
>> eyes, but they cannot see;
> They have ears, but cannot hear,
>> noses, but they cannot smell;
> they have hands, but cannot feel,
>> feet, but they cannot walk;
> nor can they utter a sound with their throats. (vv. 3-7)

As mere human constructs, idols are without real power. Contrary to what was claimed in the ancient Near East, cult images have no agency; they cannot perform even basic *human*—much less divine—actions. What is more, says the psalmist, "Those who make them will be like them, and so will all who trust in them" (v. 8).

This amazing declaration subverts, by implication, the entire ancient Near Eastern ideology concerning being human. Although it might be thought that those who manufacture images and preside over the cultic system are the ones with real power, in contrast to the subservient masses who are dependent on this system, Psalm 115 claims that the same fate awaits both groups: they will become impotent, just like their gods. Created to be *imago Dei*, human beings inevitably reflect the image of whatever it is they give their allegiance to. The covenant lawsuit of Jeremiah 2 makes the same point even more vividly. Referring to Israel's entire history of idolatry, Yahweh declares: "They followed *heḇel* and became *heḇel* themselves" (Jer 2:5).

This statement brings us back to Solomon and the book of Ecclesiastes. Whether the historical Solomon ever came to the perspective of Ecclesiastes or the book reflects the judgment of a later wisdom teacher makes no difference. The point is that from the perspective of Scripture this most powerful and glorious Israelite king, who increasingly modeled himself on the ancient Near Eastern pattern, is in the end reduced to *heḇel.* This signifies more than the fact that Solomon introduced the cult statues of pagan nations into the Jerusalem temple and at the end of his life worshiped many himself. More fundamentally, this claim is a judgment that the sort of self-exaltation and autonomous grasping at power which Solomon exemplified results ultimately in futility. Just as the only name Babel made for itself was confusion, and just as Israel's grasping at the privilege of special-nation status, which precluded the fulfilling of their calling to bring blessing to the nations, resulted in the futility of exile, so the monumental accomplishments of Israel's greatest king are in the end meaningless.

It does not matter whether one seeks divine blessing through the mediation of cult images or appropriates to oneself the status of such an image (as kings and priests did in the ancient Near East); the dialectic of idolatry is such that the genuine glory of human nature is destroyed in the process, and we are rendered *hebel.* The same is true in our contemporary postmodern situation. Both our unlimited yearning for the consumption of new experiences and images at the postmodern carnival and our paralyzed acquiescence before the multiplicity of sideshows rob us of our genuine human dignity. We find ourselves becoming hollow, ephemeral reflections of the chaos around us, populated by multiple selves, robbed of historical power and agency. This hollowness has been described as the "unbearable lightness of being postmodern," which may be seen as the contemporary experience of *hebel.*[56]

The profound irony of this dialectic or reversal (from glory to futility) is at the root of the second important biblical context in which the term *hebel* occurs. In Genesis 4, *hebel* is a personal name. It is rendered in English as Abel. Describing one whose life seemed futile and meaningless, snuffed out in the fit of a brother's rage, *hebel* is a fitting name for the first murder victim in the Bible. Yet as the story unfolds, it becomes clear that it is the life of the murderer, not of the victim, that is reduced to futility. Not only is the murderer, Cain, placed under a curse and banished from the fertile ground to a restless nomadic existence characterized by perpetual fear and threat (Gen 4:11-13), but ultimately the line of Cain comes to naught in God's plan. It is effectively written out of the story of redemption.[57]

### The Paradox of Redemption

Paradoxically, however, Abel has staying power. In the words of the New Testament book of Hebrews, Abel "still speaks, even though he is dead" (Heb 11:4). What can this possibly mean? What does a dead person symbolically named *hebel* have to say to us who are struggling to live meaningful lives in a postmodern culture? Since Abel is characterized as a person of faith (indeed, he is the first in a long list of heroes of faith in Hebrews 11), perhaps it is Abel's *faith* that speaks to us.[58] Since faith is defined in Hebrews 11:1 as "the assurance of things hoped for, the conviction of things not seen," perhaps Abel points to nothing less than the biblical hope of an eschatological reversal when the last shall be first, those who mourn shall be comforted, those who weep shall laugh, the meek shall inherit the earth and those rendered *hebel* by human violence shall be raised in glory.

Ultimately this eschatological reversal, the Bible makes clear, pertains not just to humanity but to the entire creation, which was "subjected to futility, not of its own will" (Rom 8:20). Since the entire creation was rendered futile by the human race, to whom God had granted responsibility and stewardship as the *imago Dei*, the creation is waiting eagerly for the redeemed humanity (the meek who will inherit the earth), for that will signal its redemption. Then "the creation itself will be set free from its bondage to decay and will obtain the freedom of the glory of the children of God" (Rom 8:21).[59] If the violent grasping at power and glory results in a tragic reversal which renders the entire creation *hebel*, then Scripture points to a coming reversal of that reversal. If the misuse of the human power of *imago Dei* results in such massive plot conflict that it brings to a tragic halt God's story of blessing and redemption for the world, then dead Abel's faith tells us that God will one day unravel this plot conflict and bring resolution to the biblical story.

But it is clear from the Scriptures that this resolution does not come easily. When God's original purpose to bring blessing to all creatures by humanity (created as *imago Dei*) was stymied by the violent quest for autonomy and control recorded in Genesis 3—11, God chose Abraham and his descendants to bring blessing to the nations in order to restore humanity to its original vocation. But as God's elect, Israel was a dismal failure. Whether the impediments were external and military or internal and ethical, Israel never accomplished the purpose for which it had been chosen. Time and again God sent his appointed agents of plot resolution, beginning with Moses, continuing through the judges and the Davidic kings to a long list of prophets. These all shared a common calling: to restore the people of Israel to *their* calling of bringing blessing to the nations, thus restoring all human beings to *their* calling of mediating God's blessing to the earth and all its creatures.

From the perspective of the biblical metanarrative, none of God's elect, with the possible exception of Moses, had been successful. Indeed, by the first century, Israel was oppressed by the external, military threat of Roman occupation, which was compounded by the internal threat of a holiness ideology that had come to dominate Israelite consciousness. In one manifestation, this ideology was equivalent to an internalized "Babylonian" sense of national identity, which resulted in Israel positioning itself in a stance of self-righteous opposition as the elect, holy nation vis-à-vis the unclean, degraded Romans (along with all Gentiles). And although idolatry (that is, cult images) had been effectively eradicated from Israelite religion by the first century, the cultic manifestation of the holiness ideology served to disqualify many of the poor and marginalized within Israel from access to God and full benefits of the covenant (since they were unclean), thereby reproducing, without the necessity of a system of images, the very control-disempowerment dialectic of ancient Near Eastern religion.[60]

By the first century, then, the story was once more at a dead end. Given this massive plot conflict, this human stubbornness which had thwarted God's narrative purposes, how was the Author of the story to proceed? How could God possibly unravel the plot which had been so tied up in knots? And the short answer, of course, is that God did this through Jesus, in particular, through his death on a cross. It is crucial to note, however, that the act of Jesus which accomplishes plot resolution is the *precise opposite* of the act (or set of actions) which brought plot conflict in the first place (and which continues to maintain this conflict throughout the biblical story). Whereas it is the violent misuse of the human power of *imago Dei* that interrupts God's purposes in history, it is the compassionate, ultimately self-sacrificial, use of this same power that unravels plot conflict and sets the biblical story decisively on the track of resolution and fulfillment. Whereas sin and death entered the world through human disobedience, says Paul in Romans 5:12-21, so forgiveness and life are available through the obedience of Jesus. Jesus is thus the second Adam, who enacts the reversal of Adam's primal sin. And as the one who fulfills the role Adam forfeited by disobedience, Jesus is the paradigmatic human being, manifesting the fullness of God's image and glory (2 Cor 4:4-6; Col 1:15; Heb 1:3).

But Jesus can also be considered a second Abel, since he was, like Abel, a victim of human violence. The life of Jesus was rendered futile, brutally snuffed out on a Roman cross, an imperial instrument of torture and execution. And Jesus is indeed compared with Abel in the book of Hebrews, in the chapter immediately following the list of heroes of faith where it is mentioned that "Abel still speaks" (11:4). But the comparison is actually more of a contrast, for we are told that the blood of Jesus "speaks a better word than the blood of Abel" (Heb 12:24).

What is this word, and why is it better? Perhaps the place to start is by noting that, unlike Abel, Jesus voluntarily chose death. The New Testament is clear that Jesus willingly became a victim of human violence. In the words of the ancient hymn which Paul quotes in Philippians 2:

Although he was in the form of God,
  he did not consider equality with God
  something to be used for his own advantage,
but emptied himself,
  taking the very nature of a servant,
  being made in human likeness.
And being found in human form,
  he humbled himself
and became obedient to death—
  even death on a cross. (vv. 6-8)[61]

In this, Jesus fulfills the vocation of the servant of Yahweh as articulated in the book of Isaiah, especially chapters 42—53. In these prophetic texts, written during Babylonian exile, when Israel's dreams of nationalistic triumph had been dashed, we see the clearest restatement in the Old Testament of Israel's original vocation to be a blessing to the nations (Is 42:6-7; 49:6). But combined with this restatement is another theme, one that is essentially undeveloped in Scripture up to that point (although it is anticipated here and there in isolated texts). This is the theme of vicarious suffering, the insight that in order to accomplish God's will in history, thus bringing resolution to the story of the world, God's elect servant will have to suffer on behalf of others (Is 52:13—53:12). It is by bearing their evil, by becoming *hebel* on their behalf, that the servant of Yahweh will effect the redemption of Israel, and therefore the redemption of the nations, and ultimately of the entire cosmos.

This is something Abel's death did not accomplish. Although Abel's faith may speak volumes for those with ears to hear, anticipating as it does the coming eschatological reversal of *hebel*, the blood of Jesus speaks a better word than Abel's precisely because it was efficacious in *accomplishing* this reversal. The dialectic of idolatry is thus matched by the paradox of redemption. If it is true that the autonomous grasping at power and glory results in futility, ultimately thwarting God's plans to bring blessing to the world, then it is also true, Scripture proclaims, that the voluntary assumption of the futility of death on behalf of the world results in the reversal of the world's futility, thus its liberation and glory. And as testimony to this liberation, as a foretaste of this glory, Jesus has been raised from the dead. His resurrection, his reversal from futility to glory, is the "firstfruits" of a rich and extravagant harvest of blessing that is to come (1 Cor 15:20-23).

The paradox of this reversal is the resolute focus of the New Testament's portrayal of Jesus. It spans his birth as the king of the Jews in a lowly stable attended by barnyard animals and shepherds (Lk 2:1-20), to his Messianic enthronement or glorification on a cross.[62] Jesus consistently utilized his agency and power as *imago Dei* for the benefit of the needy and powerless, even to the point of death on their behalf, with the result that he was vindicated by God and raised from death into glory. This vindication is summarized in the second half of the early hymn that Paul cites in Philippians 2:

> Therefore God exalted him to the highest place
> > and gave him the name that is above every name,
> that at the name of Jesus every knee should bow,
> > in heaven and on earth and under the earth,
> and every tongue confess that Jesus Christ is Lord,
> > to the glory of God the Father. (vv. 9-11)

This paradox of redemption is also at the heart of the vivid picture of Jesus in Revelation 5 as the Lion of Judah, the conquering Davidic king, who turns out to be the Lamb who was slain. It is this slain Lamb who alone is worthy to open the scroll of world history, to unravel the plot of the biblical story and usher in the new age of the fulfillment of God's purposes.[63]

### Humanity Renewed in the Image of God

Although the New Testament regards this act of Jesus as uniquely effecting the redemption of the world in a once-for-all manner, there is a sense in which it is also an exemplary model for us to follow. Thus Paul cites the hymn about Jesus' self-emptying and submission to the cross precisely as a norm for Christians: "Let the same mind be in you that was in Christ Jesus" (Phil 2:5).[64] Because he knew the meaning of true kingship, Jesus resisted the popular acclamation of the crowds who wanted to make him king, and he resolutely walked the road to the cross to accomplish redemption. He also gathered a community of disciples and instructed them concerning the normative use of power. Alluding to the pervasive ancient Near Eastern model of kingship, which Israel had from the beginning unthinkingly bought into, Jesus explained that his followers were to exercise power not as the Gentiles did, lording it over one another, but in serving each other, "for even the Son of Man came not to be served but to serve, and to give his life a ransom for many" (Mk 10:42-45).[65] The *imago Dei* as the right use of power is thus equivalent to *imitatio Christi* (the imitation of Christ).

But Jesus did more than gather a community of disciples to model an alternative view of power. He commissioned them to go into all the world as his witnesses, making disciples of all nations. The original disciples were, in effect, the remnant of elect Israel, called by the Messiah to complete Israel's vocation to the nations which had never been fulfilled. This is the point of the great commission in Matthew 28 and parallel texts.[66] It is testimony to the obedience and faithfulness of that first band of Jesus followers that a Jewish sect acclaiming Jesus as Messiah was transformed into a multiethnic, international community of faith which the New Testament regards as the new humanity, renewed in the image of God. And Paul significantly connects the renewal of the image in the early church with this community's ethnic and social inclusiveness. Referring to the new way of life of this redeemed people, a way of life modeled on Jesus, he says:

> You have put on the new humanity, which is being renewed in knowledge in the image of its Creator. Here there is no Greek or Jew, circumcised or uncircumcised, barbarian, Scythian, slave or free, but Christ is all, and is in all. (Col 3:10-11)[67]

The very existence of the early church thus signals the fulfillment of Abraham's calling to bless all nations, a blessing which brings about the restoration of the image of God in the human race. But this fulfillment, the New Testament recognizes, is far from complete. Thus Colossians 3 does not portray the renewal of the image as a *fait accompli*, but as a continuing process ("which is being renewed").

This distinction between the already and not yet of the renewal of the image is congruent with the differing ways in which 1 Peter 2 and Revelation 5 cite the classic Old Testament text about Israel's election (Ex 19:6) to describe the vocation of the church. First Peter describes the Christian community as aliens and sojourners in the Roman empire, faced by the constant threat of persecution, hence the letter is permeated by references to the necessity of imitating Christ's suffering as a witness to the world. It is thus in the context of a continuing mission that 1 Peter 2 understands the church as inheriting the election and vocation of Israel: "But you are a chosen people, a royal priesthood, a holy nation, a people belonging to God, that you may declare the praises of him who called you out of darkness into his wonderful light" (1 Pet 2:9).

The situation is significantly different in Revelation 5, which portrays the consummation of the biblical story, with plot conflict finally resolved. There, the conquering Lion who is the Lamb that was slain is addressed with these words: "You are worthy to take the scroll and to open its seals, because you were slain, and with your blood you purchased for God people from every tribe and language and people and nation. You have made them to be a kingdom of priests to serve our

God, and they will reign on the earth" (Rev 5:9-10).

This interpretation of the Exodus 19 election text is not simply identical with that found in 1 Peter. Whereas 1 Peter 2 focuses on the church's vocation of witness to the nations in the midst of history, Revelation 5 focuses on the new humanity's eschatological rule of the earth.[68] This is precisely the distinction between election and *imago Dei* that we have discussed earlier. It is the present historical mission of God's elect to impact the nations with the gospel, even by their suffering (1 Pet 2), for the ultimate purpose of restoring human beings to their original calling of ruling the earth as God's image (Rev 5). And, in the nature of the case, this royal-priestly *imago Dei* mediating God's blessings to the nonhuman creation will be the church, the renewed humanity ingathered from all the nations. Thus the biblical story will have come full circle (or perhaps we should say full spiral), moving from God's original narrative intent, through the plot conflict of human disobedience and the counter-mission of God's servants sent to unravel this conflict, to the final implementation and fulfillment of God's purposes for creation.

### Dancing in the Dragon's Jaws

What ties together this entire spiral trajectory from Genesis to Revelation is the consistent biblical insight that humans are, from the beginning, throughout history, and at the end of the age, both *gifted* by God with a royal-priestly status and dignity (implying access to the divine presence and genuine agency and power in the world) and *called* by God actively to represent his rule as Creator and Redeemer by the manner in which they use their power.[69] This view of humanity as both gifted and called by God constitutes a radical, liberating alternative to the dehumanizing alternatives for human identity available to us, whether in the ancient Near East or in our contemporary context.

Contrary to the ideal of autonomous dragon slayer, the self as gift implies that we neither construct ourselves nor effect our redemption by overcoming evil. On the contrary, our identity as human beings and as redeemed people is the gracious gift of our Creator and Redeemer, who has provided for us a creational home and a normative, redemptive story in which to dwell and be nurtured. But the self as gift also addresses our experience of powerlessness and fragmentation, since with identity comes agency. Contrary to the disempowered sense that we are motes in the dragon's jaws, mere effects, constructed by the multiple, often oppressive worlds and stories we inhabit, the Scriptures grant us a vision of empowered agents, delegated genuine authority and stewardship in the earth, able even to impact and affect

God's metanarrative of redemption by our actions.

But with the gift comes a calling to stewardship and to love; with identity and agency comes responsibility. Contrary to the self as autonomous dragon slayer, there are limits placed on our agency and power. We are answerable to God, responsible to our Creator and Redeemer for the way in which we exercise our power vis-à-vis other human beings and the nonhuman creation. And this responsible calling challenges also our sense of entrapment in the dragon's jaws, since God actually seems to expect us to exercise our power in the world. God's redeemed people have been called from servile passivity before the oppressive and futile gods of the age and pressed into active service as ambassadors of an alternative kingdom, called to embody and image God's own compassionate use of power to empower others.

Instead of passively mirroring the oppressive formations of the culture around us, we have the high calling of mirroring God's love in and to the culture in which we live. But a mirror, though a traditional symbol for the *imago Dei*, is too flat and too passive to capture the full-orbed, embodied character of the human calling to be God's royal-priestly representatives in creation and history. A more adequate symbol might be the *prism*. Humanity created in God's image—and the church as the renewed *imago Dei*—is empowered to be God's multifaceted prism in the world, reflecting and refracting God's brilliant light into a rainbow of cultural activity and historical action that scintillates with the glory of the Spirit and manifests Christ's reign. As God's gifted and called image-bearers on earth, the church is empowered to function as the body of Christ, continuing his mission of manifesting God's presence and scattering God's dazzling light abroad to a world and to people clamped in the jaws of a dragon. And the teeth need redemption too.

Instead of bearing the imprints of the dragon's jaws, "conformed to the world" as Paul puts it in Romans 12:2, we are called to be active ambassadors of God's kingdom on earth, agents of God's joyful rule that is surely coming. And instead of struggling to overcome the dragon by the exercise of our autonomous power, a struggle which simply perpetuates suffering and oppression, it is our privilege to announce the Day of the Lord, when God will take care of the dragon once and for all and restore creation to what it was meant to be!

The biblical vision of humanity thus calls into question the equally oppressive alternatives of impotence and autonomy. It shatters the false mirrors of victim and tyrant. And as the shards fall to the ground, maybe—just maybe—if we look with the eyes of faith we'll catch a glimpse of ourselves as we were meant to be, neither impotent motes nor defiant dragon slayers, but a redeemed humanity dancing with joy even in the dragon's jaws. We can catch that glimpse because One has danced before us, a dance of empowered suffering on a cross, which paradoxically overcame the dragon when a direct attack could not. Even now, if we look "just beyond the range of normal sight" we might see with the eyes of faith the Lord of the Dance, "this glittering joker," as songwriter Bruce Cockburn describes him, "dancing in the dragon's jaws."[70]

# 7/Reality Isn't What It's Meant to Be

**M**ostly Harmless *is the fifth book in Douglas Adams's* increasingly inaccurately titled Hitchhiker's Guide to the Galaxy Trilogy. In this novel we again meet Arthur Dent, something of a cosmic nomad, wandering through a homeless and apparently meaningless universe. Arthur doesn't like things this way. Somehow he knows that this reality isn't what it's meant to be. So he travels to the planet Hawalius, famous for its population of oracles, seers and soothsayers. On this planet he meets a prophet who places before him what on Hawalius is common knowledge:

You cannot see what I see because you see what you see. You cannot know what I know because you know what you know. What I see and what I know cannot be added to what you see and what you know because they are not of the same kind. Neither can it replace what you see and what you know, because that would be to replace you yourself. Everything you see or hear or experience in any way at all is specific to you. You create a universe by perceiving it, so everything in the universe you perceive is specific to you.[1]

For some reason, this piece of Hawalian wisdom doesn't do much for Arthur. Knowing the uniqueness of his own cognitive functioning and being assured that his perceiving abilities could create a universe does not address Arthur's problem, which is that his universe (self-created or not) is not what it ought to be. Indeed, this advice could only make things worse. If the universe is created by one's own perception of it, then any experience of the universe being awry is essentially the fault of the perceiver. So Arthur's malaise is of his own making.

The narrator, however, will not leave Arthur (or us) here. The story gets picked up a few pages later, and we get a glimpse of Arthur's deepest longings.

> He so much wanted to be home. He so much wanted his own home world, the actual Earth he had grown up on, not to have been demolished. He so much wanted none of this to have happened. He so much wanted that when he opened his eyes again he would be standing on the doorstep of his little cottage in the west country of England, that the sun would be shining over the green hills, the post van would be going up the lane, the daffodils would be blooming in the garden, and in the distance the pub would be opening for lunch.[2]

While the prophet offers Arthur assurances of his omnicompetence to create his own unique and specific world by means of his perception, Arthur longs for a commonly shared world—the "actual Earth," complete with familiar hills, postal vans, daffodils and pubs. He longs for home.

Arthur's homelessness, though construed in terms of the science-fiction genre, echoes the postmodern condition. Postmodern a/theologian Mark Taylor describes the postmodern self as a "wanderer," a "drifter," "attached to no home" and "always suspicious of stopping, staying and dwelling." This "rootless and homeless" self is no more than a "careless wanderer" yearning for neither "completion" nor "fulfillment" and therefore is not unhappy.[3] All of this sounds like Arthur Dent, except that Arthur is tired of the wandering, desperately seeks completion, is profoundly unhappy and wants to go home. The only problem is that it seems that there is no way back for Arthur. The question is whether there is any way back for postmodern culture.

In earlier chapters of this book we have had occasion to meet another homeless wanderer with sci-fi connections—Trudy the bag lady. She asks herself whether she is crazy or not and in so doing she raises the question for all of us. Are we all crazy? Are we all homeless bag ladies? Is there any way that we can do a "reality check"? Or is any "reality" we could check our constructions against itself merely a construction?

Throughout chapter two we developed the postmodern answer to the question

Where are we? We are in a world of our own construction. And while that answer has animated and driven the experiment in history known as "modernity" for around half a millennium, filling modern culture with self-confidence and pride, in a postmodern context this answer often leaves us with dread and a paralyzing anxiety. While modern culture was self-assured in its control of the world and taming of nature in order to make a human home, postmodern culture is plagued by a profound homelessness.[4]

## Omnipotent World Constructors Without a Home

When Peter Berger and Thomas Luckmann first introduced the notion of social constructions of reality, they described the way in which people constructed the world as a home to inhabit. In this way, social constructions of reality function in a manner analogous to worldviews.[5] Human beings do not perceive the world as their home apart from constructing (or construing) it as such. The problem is that once we become aware that our sense of being-at-home in the world is a construal, not a given, that sense of being-at-home is stripped away from us. The result is a sense of cosmic homelessness.[6] To use Berger's terms, once we notice that the sacred canopy is a cultural product, not a gift of the gods, that canopy can no longer provide protection.[7] Or to use worldview language, once we know that we live our lives, do our science and construct our culture in terms of some sort of overarching worldview and admit that this worldview was not divinely handed to us but constructed over time by a particular community within a particular tradition, the power of that worldview is, at least initially, diminished.

As we have seen in chapters two and four, this problem is deepened in postmodern critique. Postmodern authors like Lyotard, Derrida, Foucault and Eagleton go beyond the language of social construction to describe our relation to the world in terms of metanarratives and totalizing ways of thinking that are inherently violent.[8] From the perspective of these postmodern authors, not only is the world socially constructed, but it is constructed in violent ways that invariably oppress the marginal while ideologically legitimating those with the most world-constructing power.

When we add to this critique the voice of the environmental movement, we meet the argument that not only is the modern worldview a particularly violent way in which to construct reality, it has also defiled the house in which we live through degrading and destroying the natural environment.[9]

It is therefore appropriate to describe postmodernity as a culture of radical homelessness. We can no longer be at home in the world: first, because we recognize that any notion of the world as home is merely a social construction; second, because we are racked with guilt and embarrassment about the violence of our social construction vis-à-vis other people in the world; and third, because the very environment in which we live is now polluted to the point where it is becoming inhospitable to us and even a threat to any sense of humans remaining at home in this world. Bruce Cockburn is right—the notion of home has become little more than a "sweet fantasia," not a reality of safety and love.

In this chapter we return to the first worldview question: Where are we? Employing certain central ideas from the last chapter (especially the relation of gift and call) we want to inquire, What kind of a world must this be in order for a view of the self as a communal agent of stewardship to be cogent? If we are called to be stewards, servants of the Creator, then we need to know something about the world in which we exercise this stewardship. How does our answer to the Who are we? question lead to an answer to the Where are we? question in a way which leaves behind the imperialistic and violent way of being in the world that has characterized the modern project?

Christopher Lasch has insightfully noted that "identity has become uncertain and problematical not because people no longer occupy fixed social stations . . . but because they no longer inhabit a world that exists independently of themselves."[10] We have seen that a radical constructivism is, in fact, not really *post*modern at all, but an expression of hypermodernity—the ultimate success of the Baconian project. A truly postmodern answer to the Who are we? question must abandon the heroic pretensions of autonomous world construction in favor of a more humble, covenantal and communal understanding of the self as steward. But such an anthropology is literally groundless without a world of a certain sort in which to exercise that stewardship. In the Bible that world is described as *creation*. Creation is the biblical answer to the question, Where are we?

In this chapter we will (1) contrast a biblical view of creation as an extravagant and eloquent gift of the Creator with the mute "nature" construed by both modern and postmodern anthropocentrism, (2) develop the theme of the goodness of creation over against the aggressive mastery of both realism and hyperreality, (3) investigate how the biblical story addresses postmodern homelessness and (4) address questions of anomie in the light of a covenantal understanding of creation order.

But we have seen that the postmodern critique of realism is not simply a matter of questioning the independent reality of the world. The issue goes beyond matters of ontology—What is the world like?—to take aim at the epistemological presumptions of an aggressive realism that is totalizing in character. Therefore we must also address, if only in a beginning way, (5) the epistemological questions that have arisen with the death of realism. We propose that some form of creational and covenantal epistemology is a Christian alternative to both the naive, rationalistic realism of modernity and the radical perspectivalism or constructivism of postmodernity.

## Creation as Extravagant and Eloquent Gift

We have seen that in a postmodern context no explanation, orientation, metanarrative, worldview or totality scheme can be absolute. And Walter Truett Anderson notes that "once we let go of absolutes, nobody gets to have a position that is anything more than a position. Nobody gets to speak for God, nobody gets to speak for American values, nobody gets to speak for nature."[11] Many people respond to this kind of claim with horror. Allan Bloom is typical in his famous assertion that this kind of relativism will result in the closing of the American mind.[12] The difference between Bloom and Anderson is not really that great, however. While they certainly disagree about whether anyone gets to speak for American values, God and nature—Bloom being rather confident that the Western intellectual tradition has done this quite well and Anderson saying that we need to listen to other voices which will relativize our own contribution—they are in fundamental agreement that if *anyone* gets to speak for God and nature, it is certainly neither God nor nature that gets a voice.[13] It doesn't seem to matter all that much whether one is a modernist or postmodernist when it comes to this issue. Neither believes that God and nature get to speak for themselves!

In *Crossing the Postmodern Divide,* Albert Borgmann claims that the "postmodern theorists have discredited ethnocentrism and logocentrism so zealously that they have failed to see their own anthropocentrism," and then asks, "Why reject a priori the very possibility that things may speak to us in their own right?"[14] Borgmann argues that what has been deconstructed in postmodernity is not *reality* but the arrogant assault upon reality by autonomous humanity. In place of this kind of aggressive realism he offers us a postmodern realism that attends to what he terms "the eloquence of reality." The aggressive realism of modernity has silenced creation: "Rivers are muted when they are dammed; prairies are silenced when they are stripped for coal; mountains become torpid when they are logged."[15] And postmodern concerns for hearing the voice of the other have not been extended to the nonhuman other.[16] But without such a hearing of the voice of the other, there can be no response to the other's cry and no learning from the other's wisdom.

It is precisely such a responsiveness and a hearing of cries that characterizes the biblical worldview. The Scriptures name the world in which we live—indeed, name the very being of all reality—"creation." And a good name for the relationship between the Creator and creation is "covenant."[17]

The great Jewish philosopher Martin Buber once said, "In the beginning is the relation."[18] This is a profound insight into the covenantal nature of the world. At its most fundamental level, the biblical worldview understands the world, and all creatures within the world, to stand in a relationship of covenant to the Creator. The very act of creation is covenantal insofar as it is characterized by a relationship of responsiveness. The Creator calls the creation into being by means of the creative word, and the creation, in its very being, is a response to that call.[19]

But mere call and response is not enough to characterize the world as covenantal. More is needed because in the Scriptures covenant (*bᵉrît*) refers to a binding relationship rooted in a commitment that carries with it promises and obligations. Indeed, it is precisely the binding character of covenant that gives it the quality of constancy or durability. We can see such a binding commitment in the God/creation relationship. Not only is the creation bound to the Creator via the specific stipulations of the relationship of God to human beings (as image bearers), but we discover in the biblical story that the Creator is bound to the creation as well. This becomes explicit after the flood when we first meet the language of covenant:

> I now establish my covenant with you and with your descendants after you and *with every living creature that was with you . . . every living creature on earth.* I establish my covenant with you: Never again will all life be cut off by the waters of a flood; never again will there be a flood to destroy the earth. (Gen 9:9-11)

Throughout this passage (vv. 9-17) God says no less than seven times that the covenant is not simply with Noah and his descendants, but with the very creation. And the sign of this covenant is the bow in the sky. This is a symbol of a literal bow (as in bow and arrow) and therefore functions as a self-imprecatory oath. This sign is saying that God is bound to the creational covenantal partners in such a way that if God should break the covenant, then let the arrow fly—straight into the heart of God![20]

We see from this passage that the very being of creation is rooted and grounded in the covenantal relationship with the Creator.[21] Walter Brueggemann describes covenant as "the deep and pervasive affirmation that our lives in all aspects depend upon our relatedness to this other One who retains initiative in our lives (sovereignty) and who wills more good for us than we do for ourselves (graciousness)."[22] Another way to say this is that covenant reminds us of the fundamental gift character of creational life. Our life is gifted to us, it is something we receive from a covenant partner who, for no apparent reason apart from wanting to love us, called us into being.[23]

Throughout the Scriptures, one of the most characteristic things said about God is that he is love, and that he relates to his creation with *ḥesed*—which is translated as unfailing love, steadfast love, or faithfulness. Different from modern contracts which are binding because of legal arrangements, God's covenantal relationships are bound together in love. And it is precisely this love that characterizes the Creator-creation covenantal relationship. The very psalmist who proclaims that "by the word of Yahweh were the heavens made. . . . For he spoke, and it came to be; he commanded, and it stood firm" (Ps 33:6, 9) describes that world with the words "the earth is full of his unfailing love *[ḥesed]*" (v. 5). In other words, God's love not only is at the root of the divine decision to create the world (answering the question *why* God created) but also describes the most fundamental character of reality (*what* God created). Creation is wrought by the extravagant generosity of God's love.[24] It is, therefore, not trite to respond to Descartes's famous dictum *cogito ergo sum* (I think, therefore I am) with a more biblical *sum amatus ergo sum* (I am loved, therefore I am). The former results in a spirituality and ethos of self-created heroism and aggressive realism. The latter engenders a spirituality and ethos of thankful stewardship and fundamental kinship with all of creation.

Such a kinship, in which we experience our life and the life of all of creation as rooted in the very same love of God and co-responsive to this love, is not possible, however, without listening to the voice of creatures that are other than human. It is this theme of creational otherness that remains lost in a postmodern culture that has proven itself to be as anthropocentrically myopic as modernity ever was. Thomas Berry describes our culture as creationally autistic. He says, "Emotionally, we cannot get out of our confinement, nor can we let the outer world flow into our own beings. We cannot hear the voices or speak in response."[25]

In a biblical worldview, however, nonhuman creatures are not mute, mechanistic objects given simply for human analysis and manipulation. Rather, all creatures are viewed as subjects, responsive to their Creator and to each other.[26] Not only are all creatures seen to be servants of their Creator,[27] radically dependent upon God for their very life and daily renewal,[28] revelatory of God[29] and appropriate witnesses to covenantal renewal ceremonies,[30] but all creatures are also invited to sing praise to their Creator.[31] Just as Jesus tells the Pharisees during the Palm Sunday entry into Jerusalem that if his disciples' loud hosannas are silenced then even "the stones will cry out" (Lk 19:40), so also does David sing during the festivities surrounding the return of the ark of the covenant that "the trees of the forest will sing, they will sing for joy before Yahweh, for he comes to judge the earth" (1 Chron 16:33).

This connection between the trees' singing and God's judgment is also found in Psalm 96:10-13:

> Say among the nations, "Yahweh reigns."
>> The world is firmly established, it cannot be moved;
>> he will judge the peoples with equity.
> Let the heavens rejoice, let the earth be glad;
>> let the sea resound, and all that is in it;
>> let the fields be jubilant, and everything in them.
> Then all the trees of the forest will sing for joy;
>> they will sing before Yahweh, for he comes,
>> he comes to judge the earth.
> He will judge the world in righteousness
>> and the peoples in his truth.

The announcement that Yahweh reigns is heard as good news by all of creation. Indeed, the rule of the Creator issues forth in a rearticulation of the very language of creation. "Let there be," said the Creator. When that Creator reestablishes his sovereign rule over creation, "let there be" is spoken again. "*Let* the heavens rejoice, *let* the earth be glad . . . *let* the fields be jubilant." Let it be that the creation is set free to sing its praise. *Then,* in concert with the rest of creation and in response to the judgment of God that sets things right in this creation, the trees of the forest will sing for joy.

A truly postmodern appreciation of otherness that would abandon all attempts at Promethean mastery must be able to hear the voices of the trees, fields, earth and heaven as they sing their praise. But it must also be able to listen to that very same creation as it groans and weeps in travail. Like its human cousins, the rest of creation knows both joy and sorrow. And it is only when we can hear the lament of the creation that we can be called by its voice to covenantal responsibility. Jeremiah and Hosea describe the land as mourning.[32] Leviticus speaks of the land "vomiting out" its idolatrous inhabitants (Lev 18:24-28). Ezekiel is sent to prophesy to the mountains of Israel, with the full expectation that they will indeed be able to "hear the word of the LORD" (see Ezek 36:1-16). And Paul brings all of these biblical themes to a head when he writes of the creation eagerly longing for the revealing of the children of God in which it will be set free from its present bondage. Indeed, Paul says, "We know that the whole creation has been groaning in labor pains until now" (Rom 8:22 NRSV). The question is, Can we hear those groans? Can we, in fundamental solidarity with all of creation, join in this longing for redemption with the trees, fields, animals and galaxies? If we cannot, then Paul would say that we are fundamentally out of touch not just with the deepest longings of creation but also with our own deepest longings and, indeed, the deepest longings of the Holy Spirit. For the passage goes on to say, "And not only the creation, but we ourselves, who have the first fruits of the Spirit, groan inwardly while we wait for adoption, the redemption of our bodies. . . . Likewise the Spirit helps us in our weakness; for we do not know how to pray as we ought, but that very Spirit intercedes with sighs too deep for words" (Rom 8:23, 26 NRSV). The Spirit of God, portrayed here with the feminine imagery of childbirth, participates in the very same groanings as do the creation and human beings. If we cannot hear the pained voice of creation longing for its redemption we will also be deaf to the voice of the Spirit of God as she joins in this chorus of groaning.[33]

But perhaps a postmodernist would respond to this whole portrayal of a covenantal, responsive, dynamic creation as a valiant construction to avoid the pitfalls of anthropocentrism. It may well provide us with a worldview that gives us a sense of being more fully open to the voice of the other, but it is still a construct. It is still an imaginative product of a particular community's religious tradition and should not be mistaken for a description of the way the world really is. Indeed, making such an assumption would mean we had fallen back into a form of naive realism! Or perhaps this imaginary postmodern dialogue partner would cite Richard Rorty's argument that any attempt to say something about reality beyond our subjective interpretation of that reality is "merely incantatory," "chanting one of a number of equally baffling words."[34] How might we respond to this?

Perhaps the easiest thing to say would be "Let the incantation begin!" Is this language of creation singing, praising, groaning and mourning a matter of chanting a number of baffling words? Well, in a sense, yes. But whether we experience these words as baffling or not depends on whether they open up the world to us in a way that will allow us to truly hear the otherness of creation. If Rorty still finds this language baffling, then perhaps he simply doesn't "have the ears to hear." For our part, we are willing to take the risk of this incantation. Our cultural autism has gone on long enough; the postmodern project of hearing the voice of the marginal requires the ears to hear the voice of that which we have most violently marginalized, namely the nonhuman creation itself.[35] Is such language incantatory? Of course it is, and that is its most grounding power. This is incantatory language in the sense that we are not attempting to convince anyone of its scientific veracity (more on that later)—that kind of argumentation has been rightly discredited by postmodernity as a façade. Rather, we are confessing what we believe to be true.[36]

In a postmodern world in which any worldview is discarded as a modernist luxury and whose ethos is characterized by a carnivalesque cacophony in which *no one's* voice finally gets heard, we are employing biblical language to convey a worldview and ethos that can bring healing. We offer this biblical vision of a covenantal creation, wrought by the overwhelming generosity of God's love and eloquent in its songs of praise and groans of sorrow, in critique of the mechanistic worldview of modernity, in opposition to any anthropocentric mastery and exploitation of the world (whether that be in the industrialization of modernity or the hyperreality of postmodernity), and in fulfillment of the important postmodern sentiment of wanting to hear the voice of the marginalized other.

This is a worldview that insists upon attending to the *given.* This is not just another way to bolster up an oppressive metaphysics of presence. The given is not there for our mastery but is offered to us as an invitation to covenantal responsibility.[37] Christian literary critic Roger Lundin has wisely noted that "those who cannot discern grace in the given are unable to express gratitude for what they have received."[38] A biblical view of creation engenders precisely such a gratitude. We receive the world as a gift.

**The Goodness of Creation Versus an Ontology of Violence**
A worldview that insists upon listening to the voice of creation, attending to the given and receiving the world as a gift must be grounded in the primordial goodness of that creation. If we are to respond creatively to the concern of postmodern authors that we end the violence against the marginal, that we end terror, then our starting point must be a *good* creation. But we must also investigate the deepest roots of this violence. Is this violence simply an unfortunate byproduct of modernity's unique form of mastery, or does it have deeper roots?

Let's put the question another way. Why do we feel that the world needs to be mastered by us? Why do we feel that the world is such a threat? While we cannot even begin to answer such a question in all of its complexity here, there is at least one dimension of this issue that we need to take note of. A common theme that runs through much of Western thought is the notion that the world is fundamentally a threatening chaos that must be ordered. John Milbank calls this an "ontology of violence." This is "a reading of the world which assumes the priority of force and tells how this force is best managed and confirmed by counter-force."[39] Whether it is the Babylonian god Marduk doing battle with the sea-goddess of chaos, Francis Bacon's "knowledge as power," or postmodernity's hyperreal reconstruction of the given in our own image, the theme remains the same. There is something fundamentally wrong, deficient and threatening about reality, and it must be tamed, controlled, ordered or reconstructed in order for it to be inhabitable. We will return to some of these themes in a later section of this chapter, but it is important to note at this stage of the discussion that in this underlying ontology of violence (and that is a better name for it than the deconstructionist's metaphysics of presence), evil, violence and threat are woven into the very fabric of reality. Evil is equiprimordial with good.

If this is true, if we must answer the Where are we? question by saying that we are in a world that is as equally chaotic and evil as it is coherent and good, then there is simply no way for the violence to end. Violence becomes ontologically necessary. Without the ordering violence that keeps the forces of violent disorder (chaos) at bay, there would be no reality. We would be, literally, nowhere. Indeed, if the world is a matter of wresting order (or cosmos) out of the hands of chaos, then, says Venezuelan theologian Pedro Trigo, "violence is original, it is primordial." Trigo goes on to describe this worldview: "Chaos comes before cosmos, and abides at its heart still; therefore, it cannot be transposed." Indeed, within this worldview, "violence is sacred."[40]

The only way that we can even begin to imagine an ending to the terror is to begin with a vision of the primordial goodness of creation.[41] Consequently, Trigo perceptively notes that rather than a struggle with primordial chaos, "Yahweh's creative action proceeds from an invincible love."[42] Rather than beginning with a conflict amongst the gods, the Scriptures begin with the effortless, joyous calling forth of creation by a sovereign Creator who enters into a relationship of intimacy with his creatures.[43] Therefore, creatureliness qua creatureliness is good. The creation exists, as we have seen, by virtue of the extravagant love of the Creator, not out of any necessity, and certainly not out of any battle that God engaged in with evil. This means that a biblical worldview will grant no ontological standing or priority to evil or violence.[44] Indeed, violence is seen, in this worldview, as an illegitimate intruder into God's good creation. In contrast to an ontology of violence, then, the Scriptures begin with an ontology of peace.[45] This is not, however, the peace of an imposed homogeneity. That would just be violence all over again. Rather, the biblical worldview perceives in the world a wonderful variety of different *kinds* of creatures living together in fundamental harmony. Within this worldview, coherence and peace ontologically precede fragmentation and chaos. Before there is the cacophony of Babel, there is the creational symphony described in the Garden.

Such an understanding of a good creation that manifests a gloriously complex diversity can affirm what Milbank calls "harmonic peace" without recourse to any totalizing reason that will impose any particular definition on that peace. Milbank says, "Peace no longer depends upon the reduction to the self-identical, but is the *sociality* of harmonic difference."[46] This is a very important point. The world knows difference, and resists any and all reductionistic attempts to erase difference. Men are not women, ethics is not economics, art is not pure emotion, personal identity cannot be reduced to genetics, and cells are not merely bundles of atoms.[47] But difference and diversity occur within a larger context of creational cohesion and unity.[48] There is, therefore, a *sociality* of difference. And well there should be, if the world is the creation of the covenantal God. Creation, in all of its diversity and difference, is characterized—at its most foundational roots—by relationships of sociality. All of creation is ecologically interrelated and together is called to sing praise to its Creator God.

A biblical worldview does not just begin with a vision of harmony and peace, it also ends there. As we have seen in earlier chapters, the biblical metanarrative tells the story of creation, fall, redemption and consummation. And consummation, in the Scriptures, is always a matter of the restoration of all of creation. Biblical hope is hope that creational mourning will be turned to joy, groaning will give way to songs of praise. This is why Ezekiel offers a "covenant of peace" that is a vision of creational harmony (34:25-30), Hosea promises a covenant with the animals and birds in which creation will engage in a mutual and fruitful responsiveness (2:14-23), and Isaiah proclaims that the wilderness will bloom, the mountains and the hills will burst into song and the trees will clap their hands (55:12-13). Walter Brueggemann captures the spirit of these prophecies well:

> *Imagine a world,* no longer a closed arena of limited resources and fixed patterns of domination, no longer caught in endless destructive power struggles, but able to recall that lyrical day of creation when the morning stars sang for joy, a world no longer bent on hostility, but under God's presence as a place where creatures

"no longer hurt or destroy."[49]

Such a world is at the heart of the best of postmodern dreams. But this world is literally unimaginable without that prior affirmation of the fundamental goodness of creation. Only a memory and vision of a good creation, we contend, can enable us to imagine that the violence will finally end.

Can this vision of a good creation also be an answer to our postmodern homelessness? To this question we now turn.

### Creation, Exile and Home

Arthur Dent feels homeless in a universe that he can reconstruct simply by means of his own perception. Paradoxically, social constructions of reality have precisely the task of making the natural environment into a home for us. If this is the case, then one would think that Arthur really should heed the wisdom of the Hawalian prophet and get over his sense of aimlessness and displacement in the universe by looking at things differently.

Trudy the bag lady figures that reality is no more than a collective hunch. The problem is that her hunch doesn't jive that well with that of the rest of the world. That's why she is crazy and everyone else is sane. That's also why she is homeless. To be at-home in this world boils down to sharing the collective hunch of the majority. But who gets to determine what the majority will take to be reality? Who gets to say what *home* really is? Or, to use Trudy's terms, which hunch about reality will keep the crowd under control? Whose collective hunch gets to rule? The answer is that it is the three-piece business-suit view of reality that rules.[50] It is those with the most economic, technological and political power that will hegemonically define reality. And they will be at-home in this reality of their own making, leaving anyone who views things differently to be designated as crazy and homeless.

In a postmodern world we are all homeless. Arthur Dent and Trudy the bag lady come to represent all of us. The postmodern worldview crisis has left us not only with a profound anxiety but also with a sense of betrayal and dispossession. Our modernist dreams have become nightmares, and it feels like our Western inheritance of world leadership, progress, economic growth, moral superiority and a well-controlled, safe environment has been stripped away, leaving us as homeless nomads in a postmodern desert, exiled from the only home we have known.[51]

It is precisely when we experience ourselves as exiles, displaced and uprooted, that the biblical story can speak most eloquently to us of being at home in a secure creation. The most powerful biblical language of coming home is articulated in the context of either wilderness wanderings or exile. Such language speaks words of healing and hope in a postmodern age.

In the Scriptures, wilderness is Israel's primary and most radical memory of homelessness and threat. The wilderness is referred to as a "howling waste" (Deut 32:10), echoing the "formless void" *(tōhû wābōhû)* of Genesis 1:2.[52] This is a place that Jeremiah describes as "not sown" (Jer 2:2). The radical opposite of the Garden, and contrary to the Creator's intention of a fruit-bearing creation, this place is seedless. In the biblical story, wilderness cannot be home because it does not provide the necessary culture-forming resources to make it a home. One cannot "be fruitful and multiply" (Gen 1:28) in the wilderness, because in such a wasteland there is nothing to "till and keep" (Gen 2:15). Stewardship, as the loving and careful management of creation, is not possible in the wilderness. The wilderness is preeminently the place where it seems impossible to fulfill our *calling* to be God's image-bearing agents in the creation. And precisely for this reason it becomes a place where Israel is reawakened to the *gift* character of the world. Walter Brueggemann perceptively notes that "wilderness is not managed land . . . but is gifted land."[53]

The story of the manna and quail in Exodus 16 illustrates our point well. Faced with starvation in the wilderness, the Israelites begin to be nostalgic about Egypt. They complain to Moses, "If only we had died by Yahweh's hand in Egypt! There we sat around pots of meat and ate all the food we wanted, but you have brought us out into this desert to starve this entire assembly to death" (Ex 16:3). In Egypt things were managed well. Indeed, we could say that Pharaoh's royal ideology hegemonically controlled the world in such a way that a well-constructed home was established. Even the Jewish slaves of the empire could appreciate the fact that, all of their oppression notwithstanding, there still was food at the end of a day of impossible brick quotas. Being marginalized by a totalizing power is at least better than finding oneself completely without resources in a wilderness of death.

Yahweh, however, does not think so. Totalizing, hegemonic rule is not a viable option for this God. Satiation under the terms of injustice and oppression is not acceptable. Such a response to the *call* to stewardship is fundamentally against life; it is anticreational, subverting the goodness of this creation.[54] And so the story tells us of how God overthrows this hegemonic power and takes his people into the wilderness (Ex 1—15). But what then? Is wilderness starvation really preferable to oppressive satiation?

Yahweh's response is to provide sustenance in the wilderness—the gift of manna and quail (Ex 16). In this story we are surprised to learn that food security—the security of daily bread and meat—is ultimately dependent not upon our management, our constructions or our control of the creation, but upon our receiving this security as a gift from the hand of God. Wilderness becomes a place of sustenance. It is precisely in a context of marginality, where constructions are impossible that there is a renewed opportunity for gift reception. And this story goes on to make sure that Israel gets the point by insisting that the manna must not be stored up for the next day. Israel must live totally dependent upon the life-giving resources of its God.

This does not mean, however, that wilderness becomes the final destiny of Israel. While the wilderness experience teaches the people of Israel anew that their security and sense of being at home in this world must be rooted in the reception of the creation as a radically contingent gift, nonetheless, in the biblical worldview, they cannot be at home simply on the basis of gift reception. There is still a call inherent in every gift.[55]

The connection of gift and call becomes clear when Israel enters the Promised Land. On the boundary of wilderness and land, as they are about to enter, the Israelites pause on the plains of Moab. And the book of Deuteronomy records for us the question Israel must face before taking possession of the land. It is the question of memory versus forgetfulness. Once you are no longer dependent on daily manna and quail but are responding to your call to care for and manage the land, will you *remember* that this land is the gift of the covenant God? Or will you *forget* that this is covenant land and begin to exercise autonomous and hegemonic rule over it?[56]

Deuteronomy makes it clear that Israel must not presume on God's gift of land. The text emphasizes the contingent character of being landed, or receiving the inheritance. A gift given can be a gift lost. Israel must therefore find its sense of being at-home in the creation by means of obedient listening to its covenant God.[57] And Israel can secure itself in the land only if it engages in a stewardship of the land, attending to its covenantal responsibility both to the land itself (granting it sabbath rest, thereby facilitating its creational praise) and to the most vulnerable inhabitants of the land—the poor.[58] Indeed, the text says, "Follow justice and justice alone, *so that* you may live and possess the land that Yahweh your God is giving you" (Deut 16:20). You can be at home in this world, and you can engage in homebuilding tasks, but that homebuilding must be directed to justice, to a hearing of the voice of the other and to a setting of the captives free. If you attempt to make this world a home of ideological control and self-service, then, says Deuteronomy, you will again find yourself homeless, subject to the hegemonic whims of someone else.

This, of course, is precisely what happened. Israel got a king "such as all the other nations have" (1 Sam 8:5) and proceeded to establish a culture like the nations. This royal culture not only ignored the pleas of the poor, engaged in violent oppression and forgot the covenantal character of the land and its inhabitants, it also did what all hegemonic rule attempts to do—it made a home for God! The rule of Solomon, especially his building of a temple for Yahweh, has been justifiably described as "the paganization of Israel."[59] Beyond anything as abstract as assuming a "metaphysics of presence," Solomon, and the royal tradition that followed him, ideologically legitimated his hegemonic rule by means of a domestication of the Presence. By building a house—a domicile—for God, Solomon attempted to domesticate God, using the divine Presence as the ultimate and final legitimation of his own rule. This is the way that temple and palace related throughout the ancient Near East, and Israel was no different. The house of God legitimates the house of the king, and both can be securely at-home in the world.

The prophetic tradition is an impassioned protest *against* this arrangement, *against* this way of being at-home in the world, and *for* a return to covenant. Rooted in the story of the exodus God, the prophets declare that God will not be domesticated by the temple. Rather, the covenant God will, in fact, abandon the temple, leave his house and take Israel into exile. The message to those who have become secure yet numb and apathetic is that they will once again be stripped of their homes and cast into homelessness. This is the fate of those who manage the land and construct their homes without covenantal listening, who have forgotten that land is to be managed as a gift.[60]

Exile is a return to the wilderness. It is an experience of radical land loss and therefore a fundamental experience of homelessness. Once again Israel finds itself in a situation in which there is no room for homemaking. All of its royal constructions have been deconstructed, and it must now live under the obviously successful rule of Babylonian constructions of reality. And once again, it is precisely in such a situation that a radical word of hope and homecoming can be heard anew.

A prophetic imagination perceives in history radical reversals.[61] The secure and landed royal court will become landless exiles. Those who are at-home in their constructions will be homeless. The self-blessed will be cursed. But those who are cursed will also experience blessing. Those who are thrust into a barren homelessness will settle down and bear fruit. Jeremiah counsels the exiles in Babylon to make that exilic situation into home, to "build houses and settle down; plant gardens and eat what they produce. . . . Increase in number there; do not decrease" (Jer 29:5, 6). Brueggemann comments:

> The assurance is that what had seemed homelessness is for now a legitimate home. What had seemed barren exile is fruitful garden. What had seemed alienation is for now a place of binding interaction. His very word redefined a place for placeless Israel. The assurance is that the landless are not wordless. He speaks just when the silence of God seemed permanent. Exile is the place for a history-initiating word.[62]

Where there is covenantal word and a listening to that word, there human beings can experience life as home in creation. Home is granted to us by the very word of God that called the creation to be and continues to sustain it. Home construction apart from that word will always result in homelessness. Listening to that word empowers us to build houses, be at-home and experience fruitfulness even in the barrenness of an exilic situation.

But exile is never the final word of this covenant God. That is why the prophets (even Jeremiah) envision a world beyond exile, beyond landlessness.[63] They envision homecoming. Isaiah 40 to 55 is perhaps the most evocative literature of homecoming in the whole Bible.[64] Rooted in a radical faith in Yahweh as the Creator God who sent his people (and accompanied them) into exile, Isaiah proclaims that the word of God will do a new thing (42:9; 43:19; 48:6) and will not return empty (55:11).

> Thus says God, Yahweh,
>> who created the heavens and stretched them out,
>> who spread out the earth and what comes from it,
> who gives breath to the people upon it
>> and spirit to those who walk in it:
> I am Yahweh, I have called you in righteousness,
>> I have taken you by the hand and kept you;
> I have given you as a covenant to the people,
>> a light to the nations,
>> to open the eyes that are blind,
> to bring out the prisoners from the dungeon,
>> from the prison those who sit in darkness. (42:5-7 NRSV)

This is powerful and evocative language for a God whose people are still in exile. Rather than simply presenting them with the rhetoric of ultimate victory over their oppressors, this God promises them a renewal of their servant vocation: they will be a covenant to the people and a light to the nations. This is, after all, not a local deity but the Creator God speaking here. This God is concerned with all of creation and therefore all of the nations. Homecoming, then, must not be a return to a self-secure royal ideology, yet another attempt at building a home with even higher protective walls. Rather, homecoming for Isaiah is a matter of renewed covenant. And covenants are always for healing and ministry. Notice that the text does not say that Yahweh will make a covenant *with* Israel, but rather that Yahweh will *give* Israel to *be* a covenant to the peoples. The very existence of the people of God, their return home, is to be of service to others.[65] Such an open, hospitable, serving home is the only kind worth having. Indeed, without such an understanding of covenantal service, all of our homebuilding efforts will result in homelessness.

A recurring theme throughout biblical literature, especially at times of historical rescue and return, is the reign of Yahweh. Moses and Miriam conclude the triumphal "Song of the Sea" with the words "Yahweh will reign forever and ever" (Ex 15:18), and the good news of Isaiah to the exiles comes to a crashing crescendo when the runner blurts out his breathless message, "Your God reigns" (52:7). In the first story, the rule of Yahweh is the reason for liberation. In the second story, the reign of God leads to homecoming.[66]

Jesus stands firmly in this tradition when he comes into Galilee proclaiming, "The time has come. . . . The kingdom of God is near. Repent and believe the good news!" (Mk 1:15). He comes as another prophet of homecoming—for where the kingdom is, there the subjects will find their home and protection. And he comes to a situation that is still fundamentally one of exile. Israel remains under the rule of a powerful empire, inhibited in fulfilling its call to be steward of creation because the land is subject to Roman rule. In this context Jesus joined the chorus of so many others proclaiming the end of exile and the radical inversion of history. But his proclamation calls for no heroic military action, no grasping of national liberation and no autonomous construction of an alternative social order.[67] Rather, he stands in the prophetic tradition of radical inversion:

> For those who want to save their life will lose it, and those who lose their life for my sake, and for the sake of the gospel, will save it. (Mk 8:35 NRSV).
>
> Whoever wants to be first must be last of all and servant of all. (Mk 9:35 NRSV)
>
> You know that among the Gentiles those whom they recognize as their rulers lord it over them, and their great ones are tyrants over them. But it is not so among you; but whoever wishes to become great among you must be your servant, and whoever wishes to be first among you must be slave of all. For the

Son of Man came not to be served but to serve, and to give his life a ransom for many. (Mk 10:42-44 NRSV)

Herein Jesus rejects "the world of grasping" and affirms "the world of gift."[68] He comes as the agent of the kingdom of God, dispensing the gifts of the kingdom to those who have been dispossessed. His ministry of healing, exorcism, table fellowship and teaching restored the broken, set free the oppressed, welcomed the outcast and taught a new pathway home. This was the path of the cross, of sacrificial suffering on behalf of another. Those who grasp their life, who attempt to take back their home by force,[69] will lose their life and remain homeless. The way back home, says Jesus, the way beyond this present exile, is the way of the cross.

This world cannot be our home when we seek to secure it as such. Home is a gift to be received. This gift is still offered to us in a postmodern context populated by disappointed, wandering, homeless nomads. Grasping the gift will invariably result in its loss. Receiving the gift and heeding its call to suffering service can provide us with a profound sense of home even in the midst of exile and animate our lives with a hope of a final restoration, a final and joyous homecoming.

This discussion of the way in which a biblical worldview addresses postmodern homelessness brings us back to a problem that we have repeatedly noted in our description of postmodernity—the problem of anomie. Homes are places where a certain familiar order has been constructed. That order allows the inhabitants of the household to feel secure and comfortable. Culture forming, we have seen, is the business of homebuilding on a broad societal level. Widespread anomie is experienced when we come to realize that the order that we have constructed is just that—a construction, not the way things are structured in the universe. And this anomie—this loss of *nomos*—is deepened when we realize that our constructed social order is not just particular and limited but also exclusivist and violent.

In this section we have noted that a certain kind of totalizing praxis results in homelessness and, following the Scriptures, we have advocated an alternative praxis of suffering love as a path back home. Such a praxis of suffering love addresses postmodern anomie in a way that is radically different from the constructivist's vacillation between an arbitrary imposition of order (from industrialism to hyperreality) and a wild Dionysian embrace of the flux of anomie. The difference lies in the biblical affirmation of creation order as a gift that issues forth in a call.

## Creation Order, Cultural Ordering and Postmodern Anomie

The biblical view of creation order speaks directly to a postmodern context of anxious anomie in which we feel dislocated, worldless and homeless.[70] Indeed, throughout this chapter we have argued that it is precisely because the creation is called, directed and ordered that it is possible to be at-home here. A biblical understanding of creation order roots us in a moral universe in which there is normative direction for human life; it tells us that parting from such direction results in nothing less than death. There are "orders, limits and boundaries within which humanness is possible and beyond these there can only be trouble."[71] Indeed, this worldview is bold enough to assert that "there is an ordered quality to life that will not be mocked,"[72] and this (we are bold enough to claim) is good news in a postmodern culture. In a disintegrating, fragmenting world we need a vision of order— of integrality and coherence. And in the Scriptures such integrality and coherence is named *shalom.*[73]

Although throughout this book we have addressed the problem of false, hegemonic and totalizing order, it is crucial to note that order is not per se evil. Indeed, in the face of chaos, shalom is experienced *as order.* When Israel is confronted with the chaos of life under the imperial rule of Egypt or Babylon, what is desperately needed is a revelation of the sovereign God who orders all creation and who therefore deposes and topples over all pretentious and idolatrous claims to sovereignty. At first glance, however, it would not seem that chaos was really the threat in either Egypt or Babylon. These were, after all, highly ordered and controlled societies. But order and chaos are terms that we use to judge the character of certain situations. And the Scriptures tend to view these situations from below. So what the Egyptian pharaoh or Babylonian emperor calls order, Yahweh calls chaos, because oppressed Israelites experience this order *as chaos.* This is why these empires are so often identified with Rahab and Leviathan, the sea-monsters of chaos.[74] In this literature, chaos is not formless anarchy but repressively ordered power.[75] This appears to be an ordering of creation, but it is in fact a masquerade, a false representation.

One of the central characteristics of imperial order is that it is a construct of a royal ideology and must be cruelly imposed upon its subjects. Biblical creation order breaks through this kind of ideology by insisting that creation order is not a construction of kings and emperors, nor does it serve to legitimate such imperial arrangements. Rather the order of creation comes to us as a *gift* from the hand of a gracious God who brings about the liberation of people laboring under the weight of imperially oppressive order. Such a claim flies in the face of not only ancient Near Eastern emperors but also late modernity. Creation order is not, ultimately, a product of our social construction of reality. Nor is a shalom-filled ordering of life an accomplishment of human technique. Creation order is a gift of a good, wise and loving Creator.

With every gift, however, there is also a task. As we have seen, gift always comes with a call. While an order is quite literally *given* to life, we are also called *to give* order to life. Such an ordering of life is constitutive to human culture-forming. And to a very large degree, the issues before us in developing a Christian perspective in a postmodern culture are at the intersection of order-as-given and order-as-task. If we only notice the given, indeed gift, character of creation's order, thereby ignoring our ordering role in the world, then we will likely succumb to the temptation of an authoritarian and absolutistic realism. We will identify our own worldview and cultural praxis so closely with the given order of the world that we will be closed to all other perspectives. The result is precisely the self-protective, myopic and aggressive worldview that postmodern authors perceive in modernity. If, however, we only attend to the reality-constructing activity of ordering our own world, then regardless of how much goodwill we have, and regardless of how much we want to avoid totalizing violence, our efforts will lack creational integrity and direction. Indeed, without recognizing that order is a gift, it is likely that we will end up with competing tribes with nothing to appeal to beyond their own tribally defined "realities." Paradoxically, the cultural-historical result will be the same. Tribal particularism is just as prone to totalizing violence as is absolutistic realism. Witness the tribal warfare that plagues our world! Given the perverse self-justifying brokenness of fallen humanity, either constructing order apart from *gift* or a supposed submission to the order of things apart from taking seriously our *call* to order-construction will end up in the same violent place.

Perhaps that is the rub. We are talking about engaging in the task of cultural ordering in a fallen world. And that is the ultimate source of our disorientation. "Order" language and the language of our "social constructions of reality" is inextricably language of legitimation. That which is orderly and which we have constructed is legitimate. That which is disorderly and doesn't fit our constructions is illegitimate. Expressed pain is seldom orderly. We need only think of racial riots in places like Los Angeles and other North American cities to see that this is true. Indeed, one only needs to think of one's last domestic quarrel to see that this is true. The question that confronts all notions of order is, What do we do with pain? In a programmatic essay on the shape of Old Testament theology, Brueggemann says, "What we make of pain [and pain-bearers] is perhaps the most telling factor for the question of life and the nature of our faith."[76]

It is telling, therefore, that one of the defining characteristics of the imperial creation orders of the ancient Near East is that they ruled pain out of order. When the Hebrew supervisors complained to Pharaoh that his brick quotas were unjust, he accused them of being lazy (Ex 5:15-18). Pharaoh didn't hear the cry of the Israelites groaning under their oppression because he had no ears to hear such crying within the constructs of his own world. Neither were Babylonian emperors renowned for their compassionate response to the pain of their vanquished and enslaved peoples: slavery was the real goal of humans in service of the gods and their imperial image-bearers. The pain of the oppressed was disregarded or censored because if it was acknowledged it would bring into question the legitimacy of the empire and the creation order that that empire was erected upon. The expressed pain of the other brings into question our totalizing, excluding constructions of reality. This remains the case in our time. Brueggemann puts it this way: "Where pain is not embraced, critical uneasiness about every crushing orthodoxy is banished. It is certain that, where there is the legitimation of structure without the voice of pain embraced, there will be oppression without compassion."[77]

In postmodern terms such legitimation of structure without embracing the voice of pain is what totalization is all about. And it is indeed a deadly temptation to Western culture in general and Christianity in particular.

When we talk about order legitimation and the embrace of pain we invariably find ourselves talking about the *character* of order. Specifically, what kind of an order *could* embrace pain? Only a redemptive order. This does not mean an order violently imposed in order to bring redemption from a primordial chaos, but a creation order oriented toward shalom. In radical contrast to all notions of an ordered universe that either legitimate or ignore pain and brokenness, the biblical worldview conceives of a creation ordered toward healing, restoration and justice. This is a very strange order indeed. In fact, it often seems more like a turning of the world upside down. God's order accomplishes radical inversions of everything that we thought was well-ordered by setting captives free, changing tears to laughter and laughter to tears, exalting the poor and bringing down the rich. Before such a redemptive order pain always has legitimate complaint. And the biblical understanding of our earth as full of the love of a just and righteous God leads us to understand that this is a covenantal creation order in which God is available for complaint. Therefore, any humanly constructed order that is a covenantal response to the gift of this order of justice and righteousness must be equally concerned with the complaint of those in pain.

A covenantal creation order is dialogic in character, not the monologue of the order-giver to the subjects of order. Since the relationship is one of covenant partnership, the troubles of one partner impinge upon the other. Unlike his Babylonian and Egyptian rivals, Yahweh is involved in the pain of his people. In the psalms of lament, God is implicated in our disorientation. In a time of troubles, the biblical God does not remain trouble free.[78] Only in a relationship of covenantal partnership could people be so bold as to rise above docile submissiveness and raise a voice of protest before the throne of God. Lament gives voice to the pain of a world that does not seem to be very well ordered at all. Lament refuses to acquiesce to the chaos that goes under the name of order. Indeed, lament arises out of the profound sense of a lack of order, lack of justice and lack of integrity. It legitimately asks God to intervene historically to bring about a renewal of shalom.

And it can ask for such intervention, often with tears, wailing and a loud voice, because this God is always in the fray, always in the midst of our historical troubles. This God is always with us. If the place where we are is a place of pain, then this God will be with us in the only way that can help—that is, compassionately sharing our passion throughout the history of creation and especially in the events of the Passion Week. But this also means that the embrace of pain must inform and guide our constructions of shalom-bringing order in this fallen world. Just as our home-building must be for the sake of a ministry of hospitality and healing, so must we construct our praxis in response to the call of a covenantal God who deals with our pain by bearing it.

Since part of that praxis is our active knowledge of the world, the question arises, What are the implications of the view of creation we have been developing for the problematics of postmodern constructivist epistemology? To this we now turn.

### Epistemological Stewardship

This chapter began with the wisdom of a Hawaiian prophet, "You create a universe by perceiving it."[79] While this may seem a tad simplistic, it is not that different from certain themes in postmodern epistemology. Linda Hutcheon summarizes the post-modern problem well: "It is not that representation now dominates or effaces the referent, but rather that it now self-consciously acknowledges its existence as representation—that is, as interpreting (indeed creating) its referent, not as offering direct and immediate access to it."[80] The recognition that we have no immediate access to reality apart from our representation of that reality, that is, apart from a cultural discourse and worldview, should not be problematic to Christians.

The problem comes with the parenthetical remark "indeed creating." In what sense do our representations of reality amount to creating the referent? And if we create the referent, how is it that we do not thereby dominate it? Or, to put the question differently, once we grant the epistemological point that we relate to the world, know it, make a home in it and order it according to our particular and historically conditioned social constructions, what then is the epistemological and moral status of those constructions? Is there any way that they can be corrected? If so, how? Do we create the referent pure and simple, with no remainder? Or does the world—the *other*—have a voice? Does it get to speak back to us? Can the referent correct our representation of it? These are epistemological questions that deserve a whole volume (or volumes) of their own. But our discussion of a Christian appraisal of postmodernity would be gravely deficient if we did not attempt to address them. What follows is not a full-blown epistemology but a sketch of a possible approach. We suggest that the relationship between gift and call that we have been explicating throughout the last two chapters may shed light on the relationship between the *givenness* of the world and our epistemological *response* to that world.

We should begin by clarifying the epistemological problem. In chapter two we told the story of the three umpires debating the nature of their calls at a baseball game. Are there balls and strikes and the ump calls them the way they are (the first umpire)? Or are there balls and strikes and the ump calls them they way he sees them (the second umpire)? Or must we give up on the notion that the umpire's calls *refer* to actual pitches at all and conclude that they "ain't nothin' " until the ump calls them (the third umpire)? As we have seen, the debate between the first and the third umpire is between a naive realism which insists that there is an objective reality out there that human reason and observation has secure access to (usually by means of the scientific method)[81] and a radical constructivism that insists that reality is socially constructed and there is no way to get behind or beyond such constructions to the "thing itself." For naive realism the central epistemological problem is getting the facts straight and convincing others of the veracity of one's conclusions. For the constructivist, however, any hope of simply getting the facts straight and being "objective" is quickly deconstructed as a totalizing procedure. The constructivist is more aware of the incommensurability of our various social constructions of reality. The best that the constructivist can hope for is a laid-back pluralism that can allow us all to live in peaceful coexistence because there is no point getting too worked up about competing truth claims (unless, of course, those truth claims serve to marginalize or do violence to anyone who does not share them).

We suggest that a Christian epistemology should be able to find a way beyond this impasse. Believing that the world has a givenness that is ontologically prior to our knowing it and that this givenness comes to us as a *gift* of the extravagant love of the Creator makes us want to acknowledge the moment of truth in the realist claim. Contrary to Hawalian wisdom, our perceptions do not create the universe. But we are *called* to epistemological responsibility in response to this gift. Involved in the call to image God in the creation as careful and loving stewards is the call to know this world. And the only way that we can know the world is, as the constructivist insists, via our representation of the world, our worldview, our perspective. Therefore, we must not lose the moment of truth in constructivism. Knowing is always perspectival.[82] The question will be, how can we responsibly form a worldview that will represent the world in a way that appropriately responds to its givenness?

Another way that we could set up the postmodern problem would be to ask, Is there an alternative to both the naive realist's metaphysics of presence that myopically assumes that reality is unproblematically present to the knower with the best (read: scientific) epistemological tools and the radical constructivist's metaphysics of absence that despairs of the givenness of reality ever disclosing itself to us? A number of diverse Christian scholars have advocated *critical realism* as a way beyond this impasse.[83]

Biblical scholar N. T. Wright describes critical realism as "a way of describing the process of 'knowing' that acknowledges the *reality of the thing known, as something other than the knower* (hence 'realism'), while also fully acknowledging that the only access we have to this reality lies along the spiralling path of *appropriate dialogue or conversation between the knower and the thing known* (hence 'critical').... Knowledge, in other words, although in principle concerning realities independent of the knower, is never itself independent of the knower."[84] In a similar way to the second ump, the critical realist recognizes that any description of the pitch, indeed any judgment of the pitch, depends on the relationship between his or her perspective on the pitch and the pitch itself.

Langdon Gilkey gets at the same thing by talking about the relationship between the *constructive* and *responsive* nature of human knowing. He argues that "the human response to the reality encountered is structured, conceived, and articulated in a human and hence a cultural mode of symbolic discourse. The response is in that sense relative, a perspective on what is there, a *responding construction* of consciousness or spirit."[85] Understanding human knowing as a matter of a responding construction is central to Gilkey's understanding of critical realism: "By 'critical realism' is meant the view that experience and knowing are a response to an external world but also a response in human signs, symbols, categories, i.e., in human language."[86]

In a similar way to Wright and Gilkey, we think that an appropriate epistemology must account for the mediated dialogue between the known and knower. We hesitate, however, to embrace the nomenclature of "critical realism." Our problem with critical realism is that such an epistemological framework still carries too many overtones of a realism that has proven to be bankrupt and has legitimately been deconstructed by postmodern thought. "Critical realism" could be a cover for a chastised, more humble (kinder and gentler) realism. But as a realism it seems to still hide a pretentious aspiration to "get reality right." "If only we are sufficiently self-critical," the critical realist seems implicitly to be saying, "then we will finally get to the thing itself." Such an aspiration, however, is epistemologically impossible to realize.[87] Indeed, it rests upon the conviction that a final, universally true perspective can be achieved. But more important, in the light of a biblical understanding of reality, such an aspiration is undesirable because it invariably (if unwittingly) ends up in a totalizing stance that is idolatrous in character. Simply put, critical realism does not seem sufficiently to fill the requirements of epistemological stewardship.

Therefore, while we honor the intentions of Christian critical realists like Wright and Gilkey as they attempt to steer a course between naive realism and radical constructivism, we propose a covenantal epistemology of gift and call to be more faithful to a biblical worldview and more appropriate for our times. Or perhaps we could describe our position as epistemological stewardship. Knowing is a constitutive element of our call to be loving stewards of the gift of creation. Because we confess that we live in a creation that we receive as a gift, a Christian epistemology begins with the ontological affirmation that our knowing is of real referents that, in an important respect, stand outside of our representations. But rather than buying into the modernist "myth of the given" which justifies an arrogant epistemology of final control and mastery, we confess that the world is "given" as a gift of the extravagant love of God. Moreover, this creation is eloquent. Creation is not composed of inert objects simply awaiting our objective analysis and control. Rather, in this covenantal worldview, all of creation is subjective, all of creation speaks. The task of human knowing, in all of its forms, is to translate that creational glossolalia into human terms. James Olthuis summarizes the biblical worldview well when he writes: "Life has a certain evocative quality, a certain connectedness about it, a dynamic, an intention, a direction, a presence, a meaning. And we answer its call. Listening . . . is where it begins."[88]

An epistemology intent on listening to our covenantal partners (God and the rest of creation) will decidedly *not* silence the voice of the other. Wright puts it well: "To know is to be in relation with the known, which means that the 'knower' must be open to the possibility of the 'known' being other than had been expected or even desired, and must be prepared to respond accordingly, not merely to observe from a distance."[89] This means that our translation of creational glossolalia can be wrong, and we should be able to expect reality itself to correct us, if we are only willing to listen.[90]

This is a relational epistemology, rooted in a covenantal understanding of the world. It is an epistemology committed to respecting the other, attending to how the other discloses itself to us. Indeed, this is an epistemology of stewardship. Pedro Trigo says,

> There are paths that lead to life, and paths that lead to death. One must choose. The paths must be managed. They must be straightened out. This is a serious business. Lives are at stake, our own and others'. *But all of this must be done without mutilating reality. Reality must be respected for what it is.*[91]

Managing epistemological paths, with respect for what is, is what epistemological stewardship is all about. In response to the gift of creation, we are called as stewards to a knowing that opens up the creation in all of its integrity and enhances its disclosure. Rather than engaging the real world as masters, we are invited to be image-bearing rulers.[92] Our knowing does not create or integrate reality. Rather, we respond to a created and integrated reality in a way that either honors and promotes that integration or dishonors it. Creation, in its integral wholeness, is given to us as a gift. We are called to reciprocate the Creator's love in our epistemological stewardship of this gift. Wright describes such an epistemology of love beautifully when he says, "The lover affirms the reality and the otherness of the beloved. Love does not seek to collapse the beloved in terms of itself." In a relational and stewardly epistemology, " 'love' will mean 'attention': the readiness to let the other *be* the other, the willingness to grow and change in oneself in relation to the other."[93]

This means that this is a dynamic, processive epistemology. We must totally abandon any lingering aspirations of epistemological arrival, of having finally got it right.

Indeed, any worldview that has the kind of counterideological dimensions that we have discerned in the Scriptures in chapter five will be deeply suspicious of any kind of self-assured naive realism. The biblical worldview engenders an open-ended, counterideological epistemology not out of any overstated respect for the critical capacities of reason but out of a profound regard for both the finite and the fallen character of our epistemological context.[94] Because we are finite, our knowing is always limited, fallible and particular. We know from a particular perspective or worldview that can function both to open the world up to us and to close it down. The matter of epistemological closedness attends to the fallen character of human knowing. Postmodern suspicions about the violent and homogenizing nature of all epistemological totality claims are well founded. We *do* tend to construct perspectives, worldviews and metanarratives that erase difference and marginalize whatever does not fit. And therefore, a Christian epistemology will be profoundly suspicious of all totalizing epistemological claims precisely because it recognizes the situated particularity of all finite knowing and the universal brokenness of all human subjects. This means that there can be no final closure in any human knowing. All knowing is provisional, open to correction, redirection and deepening.

A covenantal epistemology of stewardship must therefore take account of human sin. Any discussion of stewardship must acknowledge the brokenness of the world and the perversion of the *imago Dei* by idolatry. As Bruce Cockburn sings,

Way out on the rim of the galaxy
The gifts of the Lord lie torn
Into whose charge the gifts were given
Have made it a curse for so many to be born.[95]

The gifts lie torn. The given is broken. Those to whom the gift has been entrusted have broken covenant and the gift has been transposed into an oppressive given. The mandate to epistemological stewardship has been distorted into the totalizing and controlling pretensions of Babel. And the results have been devastating. For Derrida, the symbol of Babel, subject to God's judgment, "does not merely figure the irreducible multiplicity of tongues; it exhibits an incompletion, the impossibility of finishing, of totalizing."[96] In these terms, the tower of Babel is not a statement about whether there can be a unity of truth; it is rather a radical critique of the pretensions of human totalizing constructions. Epistemologically, Babel symbolizes human knowing (and culture construction) *outside of covenant*. Like the account of the fall in Genesis 3, this story tells us that seeking autonomously to be "like God," outside of covenantal partnership and obedience—pursuing the *task* of knowing outside of the context of *gift*—is always a self-defeating grab at mastery.

In the aftermath of such epistemological self-destruction we are called to be stewards of redemption. Covenants are for healing. And this means that we need not just an epistemological stewardship but a *transformational* and healing epistemology. When the "gifts of the Lord lie torn" human knowers are called to an epistemological commitment to redemption. That which is known is not only founded in the creative love of God but also enveloped in the redemptive love of God. God is in the process of making "all things new" (Rev 21:5).[97] Therefore, our knowing of all things must be attuned not just to the way things are but to the way that they will be, to the way they were meant to be. Over against postmodern masturbatory language games, this kind of transformational epistemological stewardship attempts to construct an alternative consciousness, an alternative worldview that will bear fruit of healing in the creation.

Perhaps the best way to characterize this epistemology in contrast to the naive realist or constructivist worldviews is by comparing how each deals with the question of whether we can be epistemologically at-home in the world. The naive realist assumes that we are at-home. This epistemology knows the lay of the land, has everything under control and is committed to keeping things pretty much the way they are. The constructivist, however, knows that all we have is the façade of a home—a façade that we have constructed and that is eminently deconstructable. This perspective despairs of ever being at-home in the world. An epistemology of healing stewardship, however, is a sojourning epistemology—one that is on the way home. Such an epistemology knows that truth is stranger than it used to be precisely because reality isn't what it's meant to be. While naive realism is a self-deluded dream and radical constructivism perpetuates the myth of autonomous control, epistemological stewardship seeks to hear the groanings of creation and listen to the voices of creational praise. And in response to the voices of creation, epistemological stewardship engages in the task of constructing a world in which the sound of creational groans decreases and the voices of praise increase. That is, we are called to epistemological homebuilding. But for now we see through a glass darkly. Then we will see face to face (see 1 Cor 13:12). And then we will receive the world as our home from the hand of the One who comes to make all things new—the One who goes to prepare a place for us.

# 8/The Hope
# of Our
# Times

T he modern project is in radical decline. Like the tower of Babel described in Genesis 11, modernity is coming to a grinding halt, its ideals unraveling, its accomplishments incomplete. And in the wake of modernity's demise we find ourselves enmeshed in a confusion of tongues, a bewildering cacophony of local agendas and perspectives. We live in a post-Babel situation of tribal warfare, cultural disintegration and homelessness, where the self is under siege.

Now that we have examined not only the growing crisis of modernity (chapter one) and key features of the emerging postmodern worldview (chapters two through four), but also the contours of a biblical grounded vision (chapters five through seven), it is our task in this chapter to look to the future. What hope is there for our culture and for the church? Given the massive crisis of our times, we are compelled to ask, with the Babylonian exiles, "How then shall we live?" At issue is the matter of our praxis.

### How Then Shall We Live?

Some (even in the name of the Christian faith) would have us embrace without reservation the postmodern carnival, encouraging us to celebrate heterogeneity and radical pluralism. But this embrace, we have argued, is ultimately vacuous and can provide no real guidance in our postmodern crisis. In its abandoned surrender to the postmodern spirit this response ultimately fails to take the crisis seriously. Simply celebrating heterogeneity fails to recognize the profound tragedy of our times.[1]

Others resist the postmodern turn and yearn for a return to the good old days before things began to get confused. Rather than abandon the traditions of the past, these people dig in their heels and attempt to hold the line against postmodern disintegration. This is a stance of retrenchment, insisting that the past traditions are fundamentally sound. Many Christians also yearn for a return, if not to modernity exactly, then to the "faith of our fathers," the "old-time gospel," or to "traditional family values," which are supposed to offer us a timeless remedy for all our ills.[2]

But any faith which claims to be timeless is simply unaware of its own contextual character, and in seeking to transcend (even escape) the problems of the present many Christians simply enshrine and absolutize some supposed golden age in the historical past. But every age is essentially ambiguous, and much of what passes for Christianity today is really an admixture of genuine faith with modern (especially American) ideals. Thus going back is in itself not a true solution; it is, as Derrida would put it, "pharmacological."[3] This medicine could just as well prove to be a poison, deepening rather than healing the present malaise. Just as Israel after exile could not simply go back to its prior life in the land, to the status quo of temple, monarchy and guaranteed security, so we are not looking for a naive return to some modern or premodern Christian ideal. Neither a Dionysian embrace of chaos nor a fearful imposition of a prior orientation will do. We need to come through our disorientation to a reorientation, a return to our biblical roots, that propels us forward to grapple with life in a postmodern culture. Rejecting both postmodern abandonment and a myopic conservative retrenchment, we desire what Paul Ricoeur called a "second naiveté," a renewed encounter with the historic Christian faith that takes seriously where we have come historically.[4] It is only this sort of reorientation that will be able to provide us with genuine hope and critical guidance as we move into the twenty-first century.

### Indwelling the Biblical Story

As the *re* of reorientation indicates, there is a sense in which we must go back. Our entire exposition of the biblical worldview has made clear our belief that without a renewed rooting in the Scriptures Christians will have nothing to say to postmodernity and no basis for living *as Christians* in a postmodern culture. So the first and indispensable step we need to take is to immerse ourselves in the Bible as the nonnegotiable, canonical foundation of our faith. "The church has no business more pressing," asserts Walter Brueggemann, "than the reappropriation of its memory in its full power and authenticity."[5] And this memory is encoded paradigmatically in the Bible.

But this reappropriation is considerably harder than it seems. We are, each one of us, inextricably members of a variety of social groups and communities, embedded in assorted traditions and stories, many of which are extrabiblical or quasibiblical at best. Having been decisively shaped by a variety of cultural factors, not the least of which is modernity, how do we then gain significant access to a distinctively biblical way of life, one shaped by the vision of the Scriptures?

According to the model that has been dominant for centuries, it was the task of the interpreter to *correlate* the essential message of the Bible with the contemporary cultural situation in which we live. Whether this is viewed as a branch of theology called "apologetics" or "contextualization," or is simply understood to be the core theological or hermeneutical task, the underlying—and unstated—assumption is the same.[6] The interpreter of the Christian faith is pictured as somehow standing *outside* both the Christian faith and the contemporary context in order to magisterially correlate the two. But this is a profoundly *modernist* conception which naively ignores the fact that there is no neutral place to stand outside of a culturally encoded narrative. Interpretation, we have come to realize, is intrinsically tradition-dependent.[7]

We therefore require a more honest—and more postmodern—understanding of what it means to live out of the Christian faith with authenticity in our contemporary culture. Indeed, we need a way of thinking about the practical implications of our faith that is consonant with the Bible itself. Instead of standing outside the biblical story in order to interpret and apply it to our lives, we need, as Lesslie Newbigin puts it, to "indwell" or "inhabit" this story in such a way that it becomes our normative "plausibility structure."[8] First of all, we need to indwell the story, to so live inside it that it becomes *our* story. This is simply the meaning of faith. Biblical faith is not abstract, contextless or timeless but is a personal and communal response to what God has done in the story.[9]

That this is not mere subjectivism is evident from an intriguing passage in the book of Deuteronomy in which Moses makes what is, on the surface, a simple historical error. In rearticulating the Ten Commandments to the second generation of Israelites, who were quite definitely *not* present when the commandments were originally given, Moses asserts:

Hear, O Israel, the decrees and laws I declare in your hearing today. Learn them and be sure to follow them. Yahweh our God made a covenant with us at Horeb. *It was not with our fathers that Yahweh made this covenant, but with us, with all of us who are alive here today.* Yahweh spoke to *you* face to face out of the fire on the mountain. (Deut 5:1-4)

Is Moses going senile? Has he simply forgotten whom he is speaking to? Or, on the contrary, does this text indicate a profound inner-biblical methodology or hermeneutic for reading Scripture? Indwelling the biblical story, we would suggest, means living with the text in such a way that we come to experience the story as fundamentally about us. *We* are the people whom God liberated from Egypt and led through the Red Sea; *we* are the people languishing in exile and crying out for release; *we* are the disciples whom Jesus rebuked for misunderstanding his mission and to whom he appeared after his resurrection; *we* are the newly formed church who received the outpouring of the Spirit at Pentecost.

But not only do we need to indwell the story, we need to indwell it precisely as canonical and normative. Brueggemann is eloquent on this point:

This text does not require "interpretation" or "application" so that it can be brought near our experience and circumstance. Rather, the text is so powerful and compelling, so passionate and uncompromising in its anguish and hope, that it requires we submit our experience to it and thereby reenter our experience on new terms, namely the terms of the text. The text does not need to be *applied* to our situation. Rather, our situation needs to be *submitted* to the text for a fresh discernment. . . . In every generation, this text subverts all our old readings of reality and forces us to a new, dangerous, obedient reading.[10]

It is important to note that the canonical power of the biblical text lies not simply in its ideas or story line but in its character *as text*. Whereas Alasdair MacIntyre has observed that, in general, the only way to acquire fluency as an insider in a tradition is by immersion in the classic, paradigmatic texts of that tradition,[11] Brueggemann emphasizes the "odd angularity" of the biblical text in particular.[12] The Bible seems to be full of stories that don't fit, that seem to subvert, or at least be in tension with, our modern consciousness. This angularity can easily be smoothed out by reducing the text to a series of generalized theological ideas. But the transformative power of the Scriptures is precisely their ability to challenge us by the odd things they actually assert and narrate about God, the world and ourselves. Textual specificity is thus of the essence for a canonical approach to the Scriptures. It will not do to take a course in theology and then blithely assume that we have "mastered" what the Bible has to say. The odd angularity of the biblical text constantly challenges any theological formulations, even the most well-intentioned (including the ones in this book), and especially any that claim to have mastered the Scriptures.

### Texts of Terror

The trouble is that, if we were honest, we would have to admit that there are many biblical texts that we find difficult to take as normative. Indeed, there are passages in Scripture that we find downright offensive. Not only does the Old Testament seem to justify the mass destruction of innocent people in holy war (at God's command), but it assumes, as if unproblematic, slavery and polygamy, not to mention a pervasive patriarchal social order in which women are effectively marginalized. The New Testament too seems to accept, within limits, slavery and patriarchy.

Many Christians, of course, are taught very early that one should never articulate one's discomfort with, much less objection to, a biblical text. No matter what we think of the passage in question, we are to simply suppress our honest response and submit to the text as authoritative. But this is quite literally impossible. It is analogous to the desire for the good old days before the crisis of postmodernity. Once you become aware, however, through actual engagement with the text of Scripture, of problems with the text, you can't simply fall back on a naive assertion of biblical authority. Indeed, in our experience, those who assert most forcefully an unquestioning submission to biblical authority are precisely those who avoid the odd angularity of the actual text of Scripture and refuse to struggle with our postmodern disorientation. They remain in the relative safety of well-entrenched "orthodox" theological abstractions. But the Bible often shatters what we take to be orthodoxy. And perhaps it is in orthodoxy-shattering biblical texts that we will find resources for a genuine postmodern reorientation.

A classic example of "angular" texts are those marginal stories of violence and brutality against women that are preserved for us in the Bible. Although many feminist biblical scholars have highlighted such stories, Phyllis Trible's careful literary-rhetorical studies of four "texts of terror" from the Old Testament are especially poignant.[13] What is particularly admirable about Trible is that she has both a profound trust in the God of the Scriptures and a deep respect for the specificity of scriptural texts.[14] Her studies of the self-serving banishment of Hagar by Abraham and Sarah (Gen 16 and 21), the rape of Tamar by her brother Amnon (2 Sam

13), the death by gang rape, then dismemberment, of an unnamed concubine (Judg 19) and Jephthah's sacrifice of his daughter to fulfill a vow to God (Judg 11) all articulate dimensions of the biblical story that we would rather not countenance. By careful exegesis of the four texts in question Trible shows that here, at least, the Scripture records stories of violence that are unassimilated in terms of the larger metanarrative. It is not just that acts of violence are perpetrated against women, but that this violence is either explicitly or tacitly approved of by other characters in the story, by the story's narrator or the editor of the biblical book in which the story occurs, or by later biblical commentators on the story.

Take the two rapes that Trible discusses. David is "furious" at what has been done to his daughter (2 Sam 13:21), yet it is significant that while he mourns the revenge killing of the rapist (2 Sam 13:37), the text is silent on his mourning the victim. Indeed, he does nothing to redress the crime against Tamar. In the case of the unnamed concubine, although her common-law husband and the congregation of Israelite males condemn the terrible act of gang rape (Judg 19:30; 20:4-12), it is telling that not only did her husband give her to the rapists to protect himself (19:25) but he expected her to "get up," having been left on the doorstep after the night of violence, because *he* was ready to travel (19:28). Further, instead of mourning her death (which may have been caused by the ensuing travel) he further violates her by dismembering her body and sending it throughout Israel as a call to arms, to exact revenge. This callousness, combined with the fact that the hospitality extended to her husband did not cover either the concubine or the householder's virgin daughter (indeed, he offers both to the rapists; 19:23-24), indicates that the affront taken by both husband and Israel did not have much to do with concern for the plight of the woman. In both rapes (of the unnamed concubine and Tamar), what is condemned is the affront to male power-holders and not to the "inferior" women under their authority. The result is that while we as readers may sense that these stories introduce some sort of plot conflict into the redemptive metanarrative of Scripture, conflict by which the essential thrust of the larger story has gotten stuck, this plot conflict does not seem to be recognized *in the biblical text.*

To illustrate this point, the texts Trible highlights may be contrasted effectively with the Genesis 38 story of Tamar, who is judged righteous by the narrator and by a character within the story (Judah) for deceptively subverting the social rules of the day (including sexual mores) to fulfill family obligations.[15] Specifically, the widowed Tamar poses as a shrine prostitute in order to become pregnant by Judah, who had not fulfilled his legal obligation of providing a husband for her from among his sons so that she might have children. Both the explicit judgment in the text ("you are more righteous than I") and the placement of the episode in Genesis 38 are significant. Although it has long been recognized that Genesis 38 interrupts the extended story of Joseph's dizzying rise to power in Egypt (Gen 37—50), this is neither inexplicable nor the result of sloppy editorial work in the composition of the book of Genesis but an intentional arrangement in which a marginal story of a woman's struggle in patriarchal society serves as a counterpoint to a man's rags-to-riches success story in the Egyptian royal court (Joseph certainly would not have risen to the position that he did had he been a woman). Although this explanation does not exhaust the function of the Tamar story, the story does seem to serve as a warning against superficial and self-serving readings of Joseph's success.[16]

The four stories of terror Trible brings to our attention, however, have no such commendable purpose, at least none discernible from attention to the texts in question.[17] They thus force us to ask whether we were too quick in chapter five to speak of the counterideological or antitotalizing character of the biblical metanarrative. Don't these texts of terror testify to the metanarrative's own totalizing blindness to the oppression and suffering of others, indeed to its own contribution to this suffering? But this is no longer, as it was in chapter five, simply a postmodern objection coming from the outside; it is a problem we will have to address for ourselves, as Christians, if the Scriptures are actually to function as normative for us. The question therefore arises as to what options are open to us when we encounter such problem texts in the biblical canon. And note, these texts are not just problematic to our contemporary sensibilities; they stand in significant tension with the overwhelming ethical thrust of the biblical story.

We have already mentioned the traditional approach of claiming that since the Bible is the Word of God we should simply swallow our objections and submit to the text's authority. Or, without being quite so hard-edged, one could employ a variety of hermeneutical moves to put the problem on the back burner, so to speak. Thus it is commonly asserted that these sorts of problems do not really exist *in Scripture*, but only in *our understanding* of the text. Therefore, we are to hold our objections in abeyance and assert unqualified acceptance of biblical authority.

It is of course possible to take the opposite tack and simply write the Bible off as subethical and oppressive, consequently abandoning the faith altogether. Alternatively, one could take the half measure of holding to some form of faith but refuse to ground this faith in something as untrustworthy as the Bible.

In our opinion, none of these approaches is satisfactory. Apart from the fact that a facile assertion of the Bible's authority often drives sensitive readers of Scripture to abandon either their faith or their trust in the Bible as canonical, none of the above approaches asks the important question *why* these unassimilated texts of terror were included in the canon of Scripture.

## Canonical Pluralism

Why, in a story line of God's mighty deeds of redemption—evident in the exodus, when God heard his people's cry of oppression in Egypt, and supremely in Jesus, when he acted decisively to set creation free—do we find tragic stories of violence and brutality in which the protagonists (or victims) do *not* experience God's redemption or liberation? Indeed, in these stories the victims often experience violence at the very hands of those who represent the dominant story line. Why does "the total literature of the Bible, with its strange, undisciplined inclusiveness," as Walter Brueggemann puts it,[18] contain not simply the "grand recital" of God's saving deeds (what we have called the metanarrative) but also stories and voices from the margins that do not sit well with the metanarrative? That is, whereas God indeed responded to his people's cry for help in delivering them from Egyptian bondage, the Scriptures record other cries to which God has *not* responded (like Psalms 39 and 88) and other episodes in Israel's history in which there has been neither deliverance nor resolution of plot tension (the texts of terror).

Brueggemann suggests that such texts were preserved in the larger biblical witness precisely as a dissenting, counter-experience to Israel's credo or grand recital of God's mighty acts. He notes:

It is important that in the memory and writings of Israel, those texts and experiences have not been lost or censored entirely. They continue to arise "from below," forcing their ways into the normative world and into the canonical recital, declaring that the legitimated recital is partly false because it is partial.[19]

They function, in other words, as an inner-biblical critique of any totalizing or triumphalistic reading of the metanarrative.

Such critique is actually quite pervasive in Scripture, once our eyes are opened to it. Besides the function of the Tamar episode in the story of Joseph's rise to power, we could cite Isaiah 56:3-5, which explicitly encourages, in a later context, exactly what earlier Mosaic legislation had prohibited. Whereas Deuteronomy 23:1 declared in no uncertain terms that eunuchs were not allowed to participate in temple worship since they were unclean, Isaiah tells eunuchs that they are accepted by Yahweh so long as they keep Sabbath.

Then there is the case of Jeremiah and Psalm 78. This lengthy storytelling psalm celebrates God's election of Judah, the southern kingdom, and the Jerusalem temple (located in the south). Judah's election is sharply contrasted with God's rejection of Ephraim, the northern kingdom, a rejection illustrated by the Philistines' destruction of the northern shrine at Shiloh. The prophet Jeremiah, however, turns the contrast into a comparison in his famous temple sermon in Jeremiah 7. There he draws a vivid parallel between the fall of Shiloh centuries before and the imminent destruction of the Jerusalem temple at the hands of the Babylonians, thus challenging Judah's smug and self-serving understanding of election and of the temple's inviolability. Simply stated, Jeremiah 7 corrects an ideological reading of Psalm 78.

But whereas these examples of inner-biblical critique are explicit and intentional by either prophets or narrators, the function of texts of terror to subvert or call into question ideological uses of the metanarrative seems to transcend *authorial* intentionality. To what, then, can we attribute the strange canonical pluralism of the Bible that preserves marginal voices of pain and oppression along with the grand narrative of God's redemption? Could there be a larger, overarching *canonical* intentionality, evidence of the guiding hand of the Spirit who inspires not just the authorship of texts but also the canonical process itself?[20]

If, as we argued in chapter five, Israel's sensitivity to suffering (which arose from their founding exodus experience) became central to the recital of God's mighty deeds, it is likely that the recital became over time simply a traditional, stylized formulation of faith, removed from the experience of pain that gave rise to it. In that case, the narrative would not necessarily foster sensitivity to suffering and oppression but might well come to function ideologically, to legitimate oppression. If so, what counterideological resources are there for inner-biblical correction beyond those we suggested in chapter five? We want to propose that beyond the exilic shaping of the Pentateuch to exclude land possession from the foundational story and to ground that story in God's creational purposes, such critical resources are found in the minority voices of resistance and dissent which are included in the biblical canon. These voices echo the cry of pain at the heart of Israel's exodus experience, thus evoking a primal biblical memory of suffering and oppression, and in so doing they have the potential to call into question violent and abusive uses of the biblical story. In their angularity, in their difference and heterogeneity, these voices "insist that the recital must be opened for new acts of rescue and transformation."[21] In their articulation of pain and terror, they serve to keep the story open.

### An Unfinished Drama

We do well to attend to Trible's work on the texts of terror to see how this counterideological dynamic actually works. Having sensitively and poignantly opened up the stories in question so that we might resonate with the pain of the victims, Trible ends each chapter in *Texts of Terror* with a remarkably similar strategy. At the end of her study of the Sarah/Hagar story, she writes: "All we who are heirs of Sarah and Abraham, by flesh and spirit, must answer for the terror in Hagar's story. To neglect the theological challenge she presents is to falsify faith."[22] This challenge is echoed by her comment at the end of her study of the rape of Tamar that "in answering the question, Israel is found wanting—*and so are we.*"[23] With the end of her third chapter, her focus becomes more explicit. Having discussed the imperatives with which the story of the unnamed woman in Judges 19 concludes ("Direct your heart to her, take counsel, and speak"[24]), and five responses to these imperatives within Scripture (which she judges to be morally inadequate), Trible comments: "From their ancient setting, these imperatives move into the present, challenging us to answer anew. Thus, the sixth response awaits the readers of the story."[25]

Trible's strategy, it seems, is to highlight, through her exegesis of each text, the implicit plot conflict or tension which each episode of terror introduces into the larger redemptive story the Bible tells, using this plot conflict to call the reader to participate in what we might call narrative resolution. The story in each case, as Trible exegetes it, *cries out* for resolution. This is literally the case in Trible's final chapter, which ends not with an explicit call for action but with Trible's own memorial lament for Jephthah's slain daughter—thus concluding her entire book on a heightened note of plot tension. Far from bringing closure, this final lament serves rhetorically to awaken a passionate desire for justice and compassion on behalf of the marginal, propelling the reader toward enacting plot resolution.

But this is a resolution that occurs—if it occurs at all—*outside* the parameters of the biblical text. And this is entirely consistent with the Christian confession that the Bible is not a self-enclosed book of theoretical ideas but a covenantal text which calls for our response to the God revealed therein.[26] Both Paul D. Hanson and N. T. Wright have linked our response to the biblical text specifically to its status as a narrative, resulting in the notion of the Bible as a *drama* requiring enactment.[27]

Hanson likens the Bible to the "foundational chapters" in the "spiritual autobiography" of God's people, chapters which recount the story of God's dealings with our ancestors in the faith (Israel and the early church), thus providing orientation for our lives in the present.[28] The church does not thereby, Hanson cautions, become "an archive where members can study records about ancient happenings, or an institution committed to perpetuating structures of a bygone age, but rather a community called by God to participate in an *ongoing* drama."[29] Far from being a closed book about a story that has ended, the Bible authorizes our faithful enactment of the Author's purposes precisely in order to continue the story across the pages of history.

Similar to Hanson's notion is Wright's imaginative construal of the Bible as an unfinished dramatic script. By adapting his analysis slightly, we could portray the biblical metanarrative as composed of a drama in six acts, each with a multiplicity of scenes. If creation consists in Act I, where the Author's plot intentions are initially revealed, Act II would be the fall, the first major incursion of plot tension or conflict into the story. The remainder of the metanarrative, which consists in the often torturous route to the resolution of this tension, could be divided into four further acts. If Act III is the story of Israel and Act IV the story of Jesus (the decisive, pivotal act, which begins to unravel the plot conflict at its deepest roots), then Act V would be the story of the church, and the sixth and final act would be the eschaton or consummation, in which the Author's narrative purposes are finally realized.[30]

What is unusual about the biblical drama, Wright notes, is that the script breaks off in the midst of the fifth act, resulting in a sizable gap or lacuna between Act V, scene 1 (the story of the early church), and the climactic finale of the story in Act VI. While there are hints here and there of how the story will end (most notably in Rev 21—22), there is no clear line leading from the break in Act V to the conclusion of the drama.

The situation would be analogous, suggests Wright, to the discovery of an unfinished stage play by Shakespeare. Suppose the script of such a play were discovered, with such vivid characters and crescendo of plot excitement that it was agreed the play ought to be staged. How would that be done? Although ending the performance abruptly in the middle of Act V would be unsatisfactory, it would also be inappropriate to simply add a completed fifth act to the *script*, since that would freeze the play into a form Shakespeare might not approve of.

> Better, it might be felt, to give the key parts to highly trained, sensitive and experienced Shakespearean actors, who would immerse themselves in the first four acts, and in the language and culture of Shakespeare and his time, *and who would then be told to work out a fifth act for themselves.*[31]

The actors, in other words, would have to improvise an ending. But not just any ending would do. It would have to be consistent with the script so far and further the author's plot intentions, insofar as these are discernible from careful study of the (incomplete) script. Although there would, of course, be disagreement—even among trained Shakespearean actors—about whether this or that improvisation was more appropriate, the extant script would function as a nonnegotiable given, a touchstone for evaluating various improvisations. This means that while not just any improvisation would do, there would be room for a range of different interpretations of the play.

### Christian Living as Faithful Improvisation

We believe that this is a particularly fruitful model for thinking about the nature of biblical authority, that is, about how the Bible authorizes the church's praxis. Like the experienced Shakespearean actors immersing themselves in the script, Christians need to indwell the biblical drama by serious, passionate study of the Scriptures. This indwelling requires us to become intimately familiar with the biblical text in order to gain a deep, intuitive sense of the story's dramatic movement and the Author's plot intentions. Like the Shakespearean troupe, the purpose of this indwelling would be to ground faithful improvisation.

The church's praxis or "performance" must be faithful to the thrust, momentum and direction of the biblical story. Any action (whether that be adopting a moral stance, responding to postmodernity or making cultural-political decisions) that is inappropriate to this story (for example, sexual promiscuity, entrenched denial of the force of the postmodern critique or rabid cultural-political nationalism) must be judged in the light of the story.

But if our praxis is to be faithful to the story, this requires taking the risk of improvisation that is creative, innovative and flexible.[32] It is important that our performance not simply repeat verbatim earlier passages from the biblical script. That would not be faithfulness for the simple reason that these earlier passages are not a script intended for our performance in a postmodern world but are the record or transcript of past performances of God's people. While we can see how our ancestors in the faith responded to God with varying degrees of faithfulness in a variety of circumstances, much of our difficulty in living as Christians today is that the concrete shape of our lives in the world is quite literally unscripted.

Of course we know *that* we are to maintain faithful, committed relationships, even in the midst of a culture of convenience. We know *that* we are to practice justice and economic stewardship, even in a society of power grabs and unlimited consumption. The trouble is that *how* we are to embody these admirable goals is not specified. The Bible is neither strictly a script for us to enact nor a rule book or repository of timeless truths into which we can dip when we need guidance. Whereas a script would prescribe exactly what we should do and say, leaving us very little freedom, rules and timeless truths would be too general and abstract to be of real help in the day-to-day business of living.

This does not mean that we have no guidance for our improvisation. Apart from the canonical givenness of Scripture as the authoritative story in terms of which we are to read our lives, we have access to the Author of the story. Whereas we would be on our own in interpreting the hypothetical unfinished play by Shakespeare, since the author is dead and gone, the Author of the biblical drama has sent his Spirit to be our compassionate and empowering dramatic Director and Acting Coach, who helps us to discern what would be faithful improvisation in our own time. And recognizing that such historical-cultural improvisation is a fearful, anxiety-producing matter, God sends the Spirit precisely as a Comforter (Jn 14:16-17, 25-27).

But there is another reason that verbatim repetition of the extant script is inappropriate. Apart from the fact that repeating past acts of the drama means the abdication of our calling to contribute to narrative resolution in the present, unthinking repetition of the script runs the risk of perpetuating precisely the sort of oppression and violence that we are called to counter by our enactment of God's redemptive purposes in our own time. There is a sense, then, in which genuine faithfulness to the authority of Scripture means that we must go not only beyond the biblical text but sometimes even *against* the text.

This becomes clear when we consider how Trible treats the texts of terror. "Truly, to speak for this woman," says Trible (referring to the abused woman in Judges 19), "is to interpret against the narrator, plot, other characters, and the biblical tradition because they have shown her neither compassion nor attention."[33] Instead, she explains, we must "direct our hearts to that most uncompromising of all biblical commands, speaking the word not to others but to ourselves: Repent. Repent."[34] It is intriguing that Trible here appeals to what she takes to be normative dimensions of the biblical text (namely the minority voices of dissent and the prophetic call to repentance) in order to call into question other, violent and abusive dimensions of the text.

Trible thus embodies a profound indwelling of the biblical metanarrative. It is not an indwelling that would have us submit blindly to the text, acting out an ancient script of violence and abuse. Rather, it is an indwelling that takes seriously the character of Scripture *as a narrative.* That is, it takes seriously the fact that while the story the Bible tells is guided by God's overarching purposes, the story is full of dead ends, plot conflict and narrative tension, which are *not* normative but interrupt plot fulfillment and go against God's purposes. Faithful improvisation thus does not mean blind submission to every text of Scripture but the enactment of God's redemptive purposes through discernment of the thrust of the entire metanarrative.

It is of course possible to object to this approach to Scripture as embodying a "canon within the canon," since we obviously discriminate in some way between biblical texts. However, this is not a matter of mere preference, as if we were simply being subjective in the pejorative sense of the term. The fact is that there are difficult, even offensive, texts in Scripture with which many Christians have serious ethical problems. The issue is what we are to do about this if we desire to root our faith in the Scriptures as normative and canonical.

We believe that the notion of *narrative* has the merit of taking seriously not only these problematic, even offensive, biblical texts (while letting them stand as offensive) but also the divine inspiration and canonical status of Scripture.[35] If our approach is still deemed inadequate, then it is up to the reader to formulate an alternative and more adequate proposal that also takes seriously the narrative character of the text.

### A Counterideological *Phronēsis*

Our approach to the Bible's authority also has the merit of taking seriously the integrity of the reader and the covenantal nature of the reader's relationship with the Author of the drama. God's authority is not that of an implacable tyrant who demands blind obedience. On the contrary, this is the loving Creator of the universe who cares intimately about his creation and who desires to see all creatures flourish. This is the Redeemer who delivered his people from slavery in Egypt and who entered history supremely in Jesus to liberate creation from the bondage of sin and death. This is the Author of an unfinished drama who invites us to participate in a genuinely open future in which we can indeed make a difference, as we implement in new, even unforeseen circumstances the plot resolution that Jesus initiated through his death and resurrection.

Did we ever imagine that this sort of God would require blind obedience to his Word, whether given directly to prophets of old or encoded in the text of Scripture (which 2 Pet 1:19 describes as "the word of the prophets made more certain")? On the contrary, there is ample record within the Bible of God's faithful servants who voiced their honest disagreement with God's ways, who called God to task and questioned his justice. From Abraham's objection to God's plan to destroy Sodom and Gomorrah, since there might be righteous people living there (Gen 18), and Moses' argument with God about his decision to destroy Israel, from which God "repents" (Ex 32), to Jeremiah's frank doubts about the righteousness and dependability of the One who called him to be a prophet (Jer 20), we are confronted both with people of faith who are allowed to be honest in their relationship with God and with a God who can handle this honesty. The psalms of lament (such as 13, 22, 39, 88 and 130, to name just a few) likewise provide models for faithful dissent and resistance to God. We also have recorded the anguished prayers of Jesus in Gethsemane ("Take this cup from me," Mk 14:36) and on the cross ("My God, my God, why have you forsaken me?" Mk 15:34).[36] In all of these biblical examples we find the honest articulation of pain, doubt and questioning *in the context of a faithful, covenantal relationship with God.* Indeed, the purpose of this honest articulation is precisely to maintain the relationship. It is dissent in the service of faithfulness. In real life, the alternative to such gritty honesty is not blind obedience but typically the ending of the relationship, a falling away from faith.

This suggests that besides the distinctive counterideological thrust of the biblical metanarrative, there is a distinctive *phronēsis* or mode of thinking about, indwelling and processing this metanarrative which is congruent with its counterideological character. If claiming to stand outside both the biblical text and our contemporary context in order to correlate the two concedes too much to a modernist understanding of the ego as autonomous (that is, rejecting any authority outside of oneself), blind submission to the text treats Scripture (and God, its Author) as heteronomous (that is, as a tyrannical authority to be imposed from the outside). The Bible instead models an alternative, dialogical or covenantal paradigm, which allows us to wrestle trustingly with God—and with the text of Scripture—as we seek to discern and embody the Author's will and enact his purposes in our lives.

Not only does this model of indwelling and processing Scripture respect and honor human freedom and integrity, but it takes seriously the fact that human life is itself narratively shaped. Just as the biblical metanarrative moves toward resolution through a long, often difficult route of dead ends and subplots, so in the story of our lives we do not arrive quickly or once-and-for-all at our destination. The God who created us and understands us intimately allows us room in the journey of life to work through the issues at our own pace. This compassionate and humane manner of processing the biblical metanarrative is an important prerequisite to a faithful living out of the Scriptures.

It is, moreover, consistent with the metanarrative's antitotalizing thrust. This leads us to propose that alongside the *sensitivity to suffering* that pervades the biblical story and the story's rootage in the *creational intent* of the Author (as we argued in chapter five), there might be a third counterideological or antitotalizing dimension of Scripture that bears consideration. This third dimension might best be summarized as the *open-endedness* of the biblical text. This open-endedness is evident not only in the explicit inner-biblical critique of earlier totalizing readings of the metanarrative and the inclusion of marginal voices of dissent in the larger canonical literature, but also in the Author's gracious invitation to us to play a significant role in the biblical drama by contributing to plot resolution in a future that is genuinely unscripted.

### Beyond Babel to Pentecost

Although faithful improvisation is certainly a privileged role for humanity in the biblical drama, implying that we can impact the drama, furthering or stymieing plot resolution, it also serves to relativize any person's or any group's claim to have control of the story line. Indeed, whenever anyone attempts to control the plot, thus bringing premature closure to the story—as the builders of the tower of Babel did—God opens up the story once again by exercising his own role as sovereign Participant in this drama. Throughout the biblical story—at Babel, in Egypt, during the exile and most supremely in the crucifixion and resurrection of Jesus—God is constantly transforming apparent tragic endings into radically new beginnings. Because of God's entry into the story—thus putting himself at risk—weeping is turned to dancing, sorrow gives way to joy, funerals are transformed into festivals and death is conquered by resurrection. In each instance, the story line that seemed to have run into a dead end is reopened and people who thought that it was all over are invited to enter the drama as meaningful participants and to indwell it anew through their faithful improvisation. As Abraham was called by God to make a new beginning after the chaotic collapse of the tower of Babel, so it is that after the demise of modernity, in the midst of a time of paralyzing and numbing disorientation, the church is called to a praxis of empowering passion and reorientation.

We began this book and this chapter by likening the whole historical project of modernity to the building of the tower of Babel. Babel can function as a symbol of modern autonomous world construction. Let us engage in the social construction of reality, said the architects of modernity, and let us do so in such a way to exalt human glory. Let us build a tower from which we can get a God's-eye view of the world. And let us build a homogenized, centralized culture, a global culture hegemonically unified in service of the gods of scientism, technicism and economism. Let us proclaim to the world the gospel of autonomous progress!

But modernity, like Babel, has faltered and is about to topple. The homogeneity of the modern worldview has fragmented into tribalism, gender wars, racial tension, ethnic cleansing and widespread cultural confusion. The sacred canopy of the progress myth that gave us a normative historical orientation is ripped to shreds, and we are left with the tatters of disorientation and anomie. The shared language of Enlightenment rationality, technical efficiency and economic growth has been drowned out by the deafening cacophony of the postmodern carnival. And like the builders of Babel, we experience the human family as profoundly scattered in its diversity and are fundamentally unable to hear with compassion the voice of the other.

How did all of this happen? On the most ultimate level we need to confess that the cultural pain and confusion of postmodern culture is the doing of God. Just as God confused the speech of the tower builders and scattered the tower dwellers in Genesis 11:7-8, so he has brought judgment upon the arrogant culture of modernity.

But God is not concerned with judgment only for its own sake. On the contrary, God brings the story of Babel to a close in order to open up a new path for the human story. That path leads from Babel through Abraham and the story of Israel with the exodus, monarchy, exile and return, to its denouement in Jesus Christ. That denouement, however, is not the end of the story. For after Jesus comes the church, born on the day of Pentecost. We are now in the fifth act of the biblical drama, and Christ's ministry—indeed, his very presence—continues through the church, his body. At Pentecost we see not only the birth of the church and the inauguration of Act V but also a further, significant step in plot resolution of the conflict that was introduced into the story line at Babel.

The curse of Babel—like the curse of modernity—is twofold. First, human language is confused so that people cannot "hear" each other anymore (Gen 11:7).[37] Postmodernists would say that the totalizing voice of modernity marginalizes and refuses to listen to all other voices. But postmodernity, with its discordant cacophony of competing voices, may itself be seen as the outworking of the failed modern project. The story of Babel would then teach us, as Michael Oakeshott puts it, that the penalty for trying to see the world from God's perspective is a "chaos of conflicting ideals, the disruption of a common life."[38] The second curse of Babel is that human community is fragmented and scattered. And while this scattering is in judgment upon an autonomous attempt at establishing unity, it also enforces God's original creational intent that we multiply and fill the earth, thus diffusing an oppressive concentration of human power. Hence Jacques Derrida explains that the story of Babel, exposed to God's deconstruction, "does not merely figure the irreducible multiplicity of tongues; it exhibits an incompletion, the impossibility of finishing, of totalizing."[39]

Both of the curses of Babel were redressed at Pentecost. Those present that day in Jerusalem were assembled from the furthest reaches of the Jewish diaspora. They were a scattered, broken and confused people. The people of the covenant had for five hundred years been living under the domination of one empire after another (Assyria, Babylon, Persia, Greece, Rome). Their hopes and dreams of national restoration had been dashed again and again. The promise to Abraham (renewed in Isaiah 42) that they would be a light and blessing to the nations must sometimes have seemed to be a pipe dream. Far from being a light, they were hardly a smoldering stump. Far from being a blessing, they were essentially an abject and servile people. Like us at the end of modernity, they experienced disorientation and fundamental confusion. Indeed, they experienced their lives as if they were still in exile.[40]

It is in this context that Act IV of the biblical drama (the story of Jesus) gives birth to Act V (the story of the church). On the day of Pentecost, as the Spirit began to work a new creation and form a new people, the Jews of the diaspora experienced a radically new ingathering. And this ingathering was accomplished precisely through a new "hearing." According to the second chapter of Acts, the focus of the day was not only on the ability of the disciples to speak in the tongues of the gathering crowd (as some have emphasized), but, more importantly, on the ability of the crowd to hear anew (see Acts 2:6, 8, 11, 14, 37). Indeed, this scattered group of people became a community as they heard about God's deeds of power (v. 11) in the story of Jesus (vv. 22-36). In other words, hearing anew the story of how God is busy redeeming the world breaks down old barriers. It empowers those who enter this story through repentance (vv. 37-47) to begin to live out of the story. Pentecost not only brings significant plot resolution to the story of Babel, it also opens up the whole drama for the fifth act.

In a postmodern context we need first to ask the Spirit to open our ears so that we can hear. Postmodernists are right: the voices of the marginalized, of those who have been left outside the story line that has been dominant in the West, need to be heard. And we have suggested in chapter seven that the anguished voice of the earth itself must be heard as well. But we need to hear anew not so we can appropriate these voices for our own agenda, nor to conspire toward some sort of God's-eye view of the world, which would simply perpetuate the Babel error of autonomy. Rather, we need to be able to hear each other and the whole creation that we might join together in fulfilling the story of redemption.

### Prophecy, Visions and Dreams

But hearing is not enough. Simply hearing the voices of the other, especially if these are multiple and conflicting voices crying out in pain, can leave us lost in a discordant cacophony, a stifling heterogeneity, a paralyzing plurality. An overwhelmed hearing can bring the story to a halt. The story can continue only if there is also something to *say*. It is clear that the newly formed church at Pentecost had a message. Sensing the clear connection of what was transpiring that day in Jerusalem to the overall biblical story, Peter cites the prophet Joel:

> In the last days, God says,
>    I will pour out my Spirit on all people.
> Your sons and daughters will prophesy,
>    your young men will see visions,
>    your old men will dream dreams.
> Even on my slaves, both men and women,
>    I will pour out my Spirit in those days,
>    and they will prophesy. (Acts 2:17-18)[41]

Peter applied these ancient words to his own time as he addressed the crowd in Jerusalem. Though this prophecy began to be fulfilled that Pentecost morning some two thousand years ago, in a significant sense it still remains to be fulfilled. Joel's radically inclusive vision of women and slaves prophesying has only begun to be realized even at the end of the twentieth century. The need for Spirit-inspired prophecy, visions and dreams continues throughout Act V and is especially heightened during times of cultural crisis. Postmodernity is precisely a time of such crisis.

Genuine prophetic visions and dreams were in short supply not only in the first century but also in our own. The false prophecy of modernity, grounded in scientific reason and technical efficiency, has disintegrated into language games and hyper-reality. The idealized vision of progressive modernization and global harmony has degenerated into violent and deadly tribalism. And the utopian dream of a world of economic affluence has become a grim nightmare of economic contraction, mass poverty, systemic inequity and environmental collapse.

Having experienced our own diaspora, a postmodern scattering, we can rejoin the biblical story as the early church did only if we too have prophetic discernment of where we have come from and where we are, an alternative vision that will animate our praxis and a dream of a new order that will captivate our imaginations.

In our context of cultural confusion, the church needs a prophetic ministry that will "nurture, nourish, and evoke a consciousness and perception alternative to the consciousness and perception of the dominant culture around us."[42] Continuing the story is impossible without prophetic discernment that uncovers and dismantles the idolatries of past and present and points forward to a new path of faithful improvisation. Such prophecy is deeply rooted in the biblical story and sheds light on our historical path. In a carnivalesque world of multiple constructions of reality that are put on the market for sale and consumption, a prophetic vision offers the gospel neither as a product nor as for sale. The good news of the gospel, the reopening of the human story, is received as a gift of the sovereign God and offered to all takers for free. And the reception of that gift transforms our reality from a series of postmodern theater pieces or sideshows into the ongoing drama of God's redemption of the world.

But that prophetic reading of the world also requires a vision that will animate our praxis if it is to be proven true in everyday life. This is a vision that can dare to receive life as a gift for responsible and grateful stewardship rather than as mere material for our autonomous construction. Concretely, this vision will engender an economics of care rather than exploitation, of enough rather than insatiable greed,[43] an ethos of listening to the voices of creation rather than mere prediction and control,[44] an environmental ethic of loving and wise development rather than an aggressive lifestyle of global toxification, waste, extinction and degradation.[45]

This is a vision of life that will replace the decentered, multiphrenic self of postmodernity with a biblical understanding of the self as empowered and responsible agent in community. This is precisely what we see on the day of Pentecost. The Spirit widens the margins of who can participate fully in the community (women and slaves are now included), and when this group of people devote themselves (Acts 2:42) to fellowship, breaking of bread, prayer and the apostles' teaching (that is, to deepening their understanding of the biblical story) the result is that "all the believers were together and had everything in common. Selling their possessions and goods, they gave to anyone as he had need" (vv. 44-45). The Spirit thus forms a scattered people into a community.[46] And it is only in community that we are empowered to believe and live out an alternative vision, one that the rest of the world regards as either illusory or a cute pious convention. Marginalized by a rampant consumerist approach to life, the Spirit-formed community strives to be a living, covenantal alternative to both the worn-out worldview of modernity and the fragmentation of postmodern times.[47]

This prophetic community, indwelling the biblical story and animated by a biblical vision of life, is also a place where we can dare to dream dreams of newness. Pentecost serves to remind us anew that no historical dead ends are final in God's scheme of things. The story of redemption can be opened up again—even after modernity—and a new dream of God's redemptive purposes can be imagined. But imagination and dreams are dangerous things. We have had enough experience of dreams being dashed on the cold rocks of reality or of their frightful transposition into nightmares. The Spirit of God, however, enables us to risk dreams of an alternative world that can capture our imaginations and thereby liberate us from the constrictions of the dominant culture. It is only when we can imagine the world to be different from the way it is that we can be empowered to embody this alternative reality which is God's kingdom and resist this present nightmare of brokenness, disorientation and confusion.

A liberated imagination is a prerequisite for facing the future. Consequently, we need to ask ourselves some honest questions. Can we *imagine* a politics of justice and compassion in place of the present global politics of oppression and economic idolatry?[48] Dare we *imagine* an economics of equality and care in place of the dominant economics of affluence and poverty? Can we *imagine* what would happen if we began to nurture our children with a prophetic vision and with biblical dreams? Can we *imagine* our work life to be at one with our worship—an act of service and praise, rather than a grim necessity or a means to an affluent lifestyle? Can we *imagine* a society which has broken through its morbid preoccupation with death and instead truly affirms life, both at the fetal stage and in all of its dimensions? Is a relationship of friendship, instead of exploitation, with the rest of the creation *imaginable*? Is it *imaginable* that the mass media could be an agent of awakened social, cultural and spiritual renewal, rather than the one thing that most numbs us into cultural complacency and sleep? And is our imagination open enough to conceive of a business enterprise that is characterized by stewardship, environmental responsibility and real serviceability, rather than profits, pollution and the production and marketing of superfluous consumer goods? If we cannot have such a liberated imagination and cannot countenance such radical dreams, then the story remains closed for us and we have no hope.[49]

These dreams, this vision of life and this prophetic discernment are not, however, for the private consumption of a localized and secluded community of faith. The story of Pentecost does not legitimate Christian tribalism. The drama of the great deeds of God that transformed those first Pentecost believers and that continues to transform us today is not a local tale, the private domain or idiosyncratic convention of this particular band of Jesus-followers. It is nothing less than the metanarrative of God's redemptive plan for the world. Consequently, those who follow Jesus and are anointed by the Holy Spirit have the audacity to proclaim *this* story as *the* light of the world. And that is why the rest of the book of Acts tells of how the early Christian community scatters throughout the Roman empire, not in confusion, as at Babel, but in order to proclaim the metanarrative of world redemption. This particular marginal community thus goes into the world with a message of universal importance.

## Beyond Pentecost

But the church's mission to proclaim the message does not mean that the story is over. This mission does not consist simply in retelling the story up to that point over and over again. Rather, the newly formed community of Jesus-followers is set on the challenging path of continuing to live out the story. The first challenge that the early church had to face was that of ethnic boundaries. Who could be in this community (that is, who could gain entry into the story?) and on what conditions? Specifically, could Gentiles—that is, newcomers, who had no roots in the covenant story of God and Israel—indwell this story, and if so, on what grounds? The early Christian community continued to struggle with this problem throughout much of the New Testament. Like us, they had no script. They had to improvise faithfully. How could they discern the path of the Spirit for this new situation?

At the Jerusalem Council (in Acts 15) we see the church struggle with this issue. Both their decision and their methodology—the way they come to their decision— are instructive. First, they listen to the stories of what the Spirit has been doing among the Gentiles (vv. 4, 7-12), and then they reflect on the biblical story and how it will guide them in assessing and responding to the stories they have been hearing (vv. 15-18). They attempt to be both faithful to the biblical tradition and sensitive to a new reality in their midst. And out of this mix, they improvise. Their radical conclusion is that Gentiles no longer need to be circumcised, though they do need to follow certain dietary laws, including abstaining from meat offered to idols (vv.

19-20). Interestingly, this does not settle the issue once and for all in the New Testament. Not only do we have continued debate over the necessity of circumcision (see, for example, 1 Cor 7:17-20; Gal 5:6; Col 2:11), but Paul seems to relativize the question of meat offered to idols in 1 Corinthians 8. In this passage he basically says that meat offered to idols is a nonissue, though the "stronger" members of the community who know that such meat is acceptable for consumption should be sensitive to their "weaker" brothers and sisters who still have qualms about such things.

Thus the story continues. Under the direction of the Spirit and equipped with prophecy, visions and dreams, the community moves forward to act out this unfinished drama. Just as the early Christians had to grapple with what initially seemed to many of them to be an unacceptable distortion of God's good order for the world—namely, that Gentiles, uncircumcised and with unclean food in their bellies, could be grafted into the covenant people—so we have to struggle today with issues that seem just as difficult to us.

Could it be that the dominant voice of the Western world (including that of the Western church) must now be quiet long enough to listen to the voices of others? Could it be that the era of Western dominance of the world is over? Could it be that our future will necessarily be one of economic contraction, not growth? Might it be the case that the very foundations of Western culture are weak and we must engage in a painful process of dismantling and rebuilding again? Might it be that the assumed normality of human conquest of nature needs to be abandoned for a model of covenantal partnership? Are there dimensions of the church's thought and practice that continue to legitimate patriarchy and keep women in an unbiblical and subservient position?

All of these are difficult questions. We ought not to ignore them. But neither should we simply succumb to every shifting wind of cultural life that comes our way. Rather, we must, in solidarity with God's people throughout the ages, struggle with these questions, attempting to discern paths of life in the midst of our confusion. This is, admittedly, a risky undertaking, fraught with danger. But it is required by nothing less than faithfulness to the Scriptures. As an open-ended canonical drama inviting us on a journey of improvisation, the Bible is a dangerous book.

### The Risk of Discipleship
At the beginning of the film *The Neverending Story*, a young boy named Bastian finds himself in an old bookstore, inquiring of the bookstore owner about a special book that he has noticed.

"What's that book about?" asks Bastian.

"Oh, this is something *special,*" says the bookstore owner.

"Well, what is it?"

"Look, your books are safe," the owner says. "By reading them you get to become Tarzan, or Robinson Crusoe."

"But that's what I like about them," replies Bastian.

"Ah, but afterwards you get to be a little boy again."

"What do you mean?" asks Bastian.

"Listen," says the man. "Have you ever been Captain Nemo, trapped inside your submarine while the giant squid is attacking you?"

"Yes," says Bastian.

"Weren't you afraid you couldn't escape?"

"But it's only a *story!*"

"That's what I'm talking about," says the man. "The ones *you* read are safe."

"And this one isn't?"[50]

The biblical story that we have been exploring throughout chapters five through eight is not safe. We cannot read this story without being caught up in its drama. We cannot claim to have genuinely understood the Bible without taking the risk of improvisation. Our times are also dangerous. Old worldviews, and the cultural and political empires that have been erected upon them, do not die peacefully.

Our desire has been to invite you, the reader, into the plot of the biblical story, to indwell it as your own. Our prayer has been that in so doing you will find the resources to live a life of faithful, yet risky, discipleship in a postmodern world. We are convinced that without such faithful indwelling and improvisation the church will fail to respond redemptively to our cultural malaise.

And we know that we can risk such faithful improvisation because the Spirit of God accompanies us along the way, reminding us of the story and shedding light on our path. And should we make mistakes—even slip and fall—we also know that this Spirit is a Comforter and that "we have an advocate with the Father, Jesus Christ the righteous" (1 Jn 2:1 NRSV).

# Notes

### Chapter 1: The Crisis of Our Times

[1] It is important to add that the film's perspective was more ambivalent and less bald-faced than this description. Columbus is portrayed as a tragic hero. He is a creative man, bristling with hope, who pushes the boundaries of the dominant worldview of the late medieval period only to witness (and to some degree participate in) the cruel conquest of both the aboriginal inhabitants and the natural resources of what clearly appears to him to be a paradise.

[2] This issue has received significant attention in the popular press. For example, see the cover article for *Time* on October 19, 1992, "To Be Themselves," p. 16. Also relevant are J. N. Wilford, "Discovering Columbus," *The New York Times Magazine*, November 8, 1991, and (from a Christian perspective) David Batstone, "Rape, Revelation and Repentance," *Third Way*, May 1992. For a retelling of Christian missionary activity in North America from a Native American perspective, see George E. Tinker, *Missionary Conquests: The Gospel and Native American Cultural Genocide* (Philadelphia: Fortress, 1993).

[3] Indeed, the complexity of this debate ought not be underestimated. Much of the argument centers on how we evaluate both the aboriginal cultures that predate 1492 and the European tradition that "conquered" those peoples. For a defense of the more Eurocentric interpretation see James Axtell, *Beyond 1492: Encounters in Colonial North America* (New York: Oxford University Press, 1992); Robert B. Edgerton, *Sick Societies: Challenging the Myth of Primitive Harmony* (New York: Free Press, 1992); and Robert Royal, *1492 and All That* (Washington, D.C.: Ethics and Public Policy Center, 1992). A more guilty conscience is discernible in Kirkpatrick Sale, *The Conquest of Paradise: Christopher Columbus and the Columbian Legacy* (New York: Knopf, 1990); David E. Stannard, *American Holocaust: Columbus and the Conquest of the New World* (New York: Oxford University Press, 1992); and the collection of articles edited by Alvin J. Josephy, *America in 1492: The World of Indian Peoples Before the Arrival of Columbus* (New York: Knopf, 1991).

[4] *Discovery* has been replaced by the more politically correct terms *encounter* and *arrival*. See Wilcomb E. Washburn, "Columbus: On and off the Reservation," *National Review*, October 5, 1992, pp. 55-57.

⁵Albert Borgmann, *Crossing the Postmodern Divide* (Chicago: University of Chicago Press, 1992), p. 22.

⁶Ibid., p. 20.

⁷Ibid., p. 48.

⁸Brian J. Walsh and J. Richard Middleton, *The Transforming Vision: Shaping a Christian World View* (Downers Grove, Ill.: InterVarsity Press, 1984), chap. 2.

⁹Charles Sanford describes Columbus as motivated by the hope of recovering the lost Eden in *Quest for Paradise: Europe and the American Moral Imagination* (Urbana: University of Illinois Press, 1961), p. 39.

¹⁰David Suzuki hosted a series of profound television shows on the Canadian Broadcasting Corporation entitled *A Planet for the Taking* that explored the environmental, ethical, scientific and cultural implications of this answer to the first worldview question.

¹¹It is instructive to note that in Richard Middleton's home country of Jamaica the Columbus story is told primarily in terms of the extermination of the aboriginal peoples of the West Indies and the advent of the slave trade. See, for example, Caribbean high-school textbooks like Clinton V. Black, *History of Jamaica*, 3rd ed. (London: Collins, 1965), and Eric Williams, *From Columbus to Castro: The History of the Caribbean 1492-1969* (New York: Random House, 1984).

¹²One disturbing example of such divisiveness was the debate in Oregon concerning Measure 9. This measure, added to the ballot of the 1992 U.S. presidential election, proposed to write into the Oregon constitution a moral condemnation of homosexuality. The campaigns for and against this measure were characterized by bitterness, fear, hatred, violence and even murder.

¹³For a summary of the debate see James Atlas, "Ferment in Higher Education," *Dialogue* 2 (1989): 21-27. An African-American perspective in this debate can be easily seen in the contention of Henry Louis Gates Jr. that "the high canon of Western masterpieces represents . . . an order in which my people were subjugated, the voiceless, the invisible, the unrepresented and the unrepresentable." Cited by Kenneth Gergen, *The Saturated Self: Dilemmas of Identity in Contemporary Life* (New York: Basic Books, 1991), p. 125.

¹⁴A recent exhibition on Africa at the Royal Ontario Museum in Toronto was constantly subject to protests from the black community, who felt that their story was being told in a latently racist and blatantly paternalistic way. In 1992 the museum began to live down this negative reputation by presenting an exhibit collected and curated by native people. In fact this show, "Fluffs and Feathers: An Exhibit on the Symbols of Indianness," illustrates the postmodern hearing of other voices as well as the Columbus controversy does.

¹⁵See Robert Unger, *The Critical Legal Studies Movement* (Cambridge, Mass.: Harvard University Press, 1986). For a conservative response to this movement see Robert Bork, *The Tempting of America* (New York: Free Press, 1990). The reader will recall that Bork was the Reagan nominee to the Supreme Court who was denied confirmation by the Senate.

¹⁶Gergen, *The Saturated Self*, p. 7.

¹⁷See Walsh and Middleton, *The Transforming Vision*, chap. 8.

¹⁸Richard Rorty is concerned that any kind of periodization attempts "to describe every part of a culture as suddenly swerving off in the same new direction at approximately the same time." *Essays on Heidegger and Others* (Cambridge: Cambridge University Press, 1991), p. 1. What we attempt here, however, is at one level not so ambitious, yet at another level it is

more ambitious. We are not trying to paint a monolithic picture of Western culture that ignores various alternative worldviews and communities within that culture. Indeed, as Christians, we believe that a radically biblical faith and many of the historical expressions of that faith in the last 500 years cannot be accommodated by any monolithic understanding of modernity. But our portrayal is more ambitious because it attempts to plumb the spiritual depths of what has in fact been a dominant (and dominating!) cultural project. Such spiritual depths are what Paul Tillich called the "religious substance" of a culture. See Tillich's *Theology of Culture* (London: Oxford University Press, 1959), and *Systematic Theology*, vol. 3 (Chicago: University of Chicago Press, 1963), esp. pp. 57-61.

[19]John Dewey, *Reconstruction in Philosophy* (New York: Henry Holt, 1929), pp. 47-49.

[20]On the issue of gender-biased language, we agree with feminist authors who insist that the modern worldview is inherently patriarchal. Rosemary Radford Ruether, for example, has insightfully shown how Western anthropocentrism (that is, human centeredness) has consistently taken the form of androcentrism (that is, male centeredness). See *To Change the World: Christology and Cultural Criticism* (New York: Crossroad, 1983), p. 60.

[21]We have explored the themes of autonomy and self-salvation in the modern worldview in *The Transforming Vision*, chaps. 8 and 9.

[22]Bob Goudzwaard, *Capitalism and Progress: A Diagnosis of Western Society*, trans. Josina Van Nuis Zylstra (Toronto: Wedge/Grand Rapids, Mich.: Eerdmans, 1979), p. xxiii. This is the best study of the progress motif in Western culture written from a Christian perspective.

[23]Christopher Dawson, *Progress and Religion: An Historical Inquiry* (New York: Sheed & Ward, 1938), p. 3. Beyond Dawson and Goudzwaard already cited, one could also consult J. B. Bury, *The Idea of Progress: An Inquiry into Its Origin and Growth* (London: Macmillan, 1920), p. 4; Karl Lowith, *Meaning in History* (Chicago: University of Chicago Press, 1949), p. 96; Reinhold Niebuhr, *The Nature and Destiny of Man* (New York: Charles Scribner's Sons, 1943), 2:164, and Reinhold Niebuhr, *Faith and History* (New York: Charles Scribner's Sons, 1949), pp. 94-95. More recently one can find such an interpretation of progress in Jeremy Rifkin, *Time Wars: The Primary Conflict in Human History* (New York: Simon & Schuster, 1987), chap. 10. For a comprehensive discussion see Christopher Lasch, *The True and Only Heaven: Progress and Its Critics* (New York: W. W. Norton, 1991).

[24]See Langdon Gilkey, *Society and the Sacred: Toward a Theology of Culture in Decline* (New York: Seabury, 1981), pp. 23-24.

[25]The quotation from Genesis 11:4 is the authors' rendering. Although Genesis 11 clearly intends to depict what is a fundamentally human, international aspiration, it seems to have been modeled specifically on ancient Babylonian civilization, which in biblical times epitomized this aspiration. Indeed, Babylon becomes in the Bible something of a paradigm or prototype of autonomous culture. See the extended prophetic critique of Babylon in Isaiah 13—14 and 47 and Jeremiah 50—51 and the use of similar language for a later "Babylon" in Revelation 18. (See 1 Pet 5:13 for another symbolic use of "Babylon.") Walter Brueggemann has provided a particularly sensitive exegesis of the Babel story in his commentary *Genesis* (Atlanta: John Knox, 1982), pp. 97-104.

[26]For more detailed analysis of the role of Francis Bacon in casting the vision of modernity, see Walsh and Middleton, *The Transforming Vision*, chap. 8. For an in-depth discussion of the scientific revolution see Richard Foster Jones, *Ancients and Moderns: A Study of the Rise of the Scientific Movement in Seventeenth Century England* (New York: Dover, 1982).

²⁷For a fascinating, in-depth portrayal of this period, see Carl L. Becker, *The Heavenly City of the Eighteenth-Century Philosophers* (New Haven, Conn.: Yale University Press, 1932).

²⁸One of the most succinct analyses of the historical factors in the developing worldview of the eighteenth century may be found in Goudzwaard, *Capitalism and Progress*, esp. chap. 6, "The Industrial Revolution and Its Consequences."

²⁹On the origin and development of the market economy, see Robert L. Heilbroner's classic study "The Economic Revolution," chap. 2 in *The Worldly Philosophers: The Lives, Times and Ideas of the Great Economic Thinkers*, rev. ed. (New York: Simon & Schuster, 1961).

³⁰For the texts of Prince Albert's speech and Queen Victoria's diary, see Charles Harvard Gibbs-Smith, *The Great Exhibition of 1851* (London: HM Stationery Office, 1950). We are indebted for these references and for the *Times* article to *Introduction to a Christian Worldview*, ed. Jon Chaplin (London: Open Christian College, 1986), pp. 6-8, which is an excellent course manual on the Christian worldview.

³¹In his famous *Sketch for a Historical Picture of the Progress of the Human Mind*, trans. J. Barraclough (London: Weidenfeld and Nicolson, 1955; from the French original, 1795), the Marquis de Condorcet (1743-1794) gave voice to Enlightenment confidence when he predicted the inevitable "perfectionnement de l'homme."

³²Futurist Tom Sine argues that every culture and every worldview has a stock of images of the preferred future. The images employed by modernity tend to be economic. Modernity's preferred future is a future of increased consumption. All other subsidiary images derive from that central one. See Tom Sine, *Wild Hope: Crises Facing the Human Community on the Threshold of the 21st Century* (Dallas: Word, 1991), p. 210.

³³Brian Walsh has also discussed the progress myth in *Subversive Christianity: Imaging God in a Dangerous Time* (1992; reprint, Seattle, Wash.: Alta Vista College Press, 1994), esp. chap. 2, and *Who Turned Out the Lights? The Light of the Gospel in a Post-Enlightenment Culture*, an inaugural lecture (Toronto: Institute for Christian Studies, 1989).

³⁴Gilkey, *Society and the Sacred*, pp. 23-24. Emphasis ours.

³⁵Bruce Cockburn, "Candy Man's Gone," © 1983 Golden Mountain Music Corp. From the album *The Trouble with Normal*.

³⁶Once again from Cockburn's song "Candy Man's Gone." In *The Transforming Vision*, chap. 8, we discussed how the historical division in Western culture between the sacred and the secular allowed Francis Bacon to separate Christian salvation from his proposal of a humanistic scientific utopia. In chapters 6 and 7 we analyzed at some length both the problems inherent in this division (which we term worldview "dualism") and the historical development of this dualism from classical times until the modern era.

³⁷We have described modernity this way in *The Transforming Vision*, chap. 9. On the notion of this false trinity, see Bob Goudzwaard, "Our Gods Have Failed Us," chap. 2 in *Aid for the Overdeveloped West* (Toronto: Wedge, 1975), esp. p. 16. On the relation of what we have called *scientism* and *technicism* see Egbert Schuurman, *Reflections on the Technological Society*, trans. H. Van Dyke and L. Teneyenhuis (Toronto: Wedge, 1977), and Stephen V. Monsma, ed., *Responsible Technology* (Grand Rapids, Mich.: Eerdmans, 1986), chap. 6. Also helpful are Jacques Ellul's classic text *The Technological Society*, trans. J. Wilkinson (New York: Knopf, 1964); Langdon Winner, *The Whale and the Reactor: A Search for Limits in an Age of High Technology* (Chicago: University of Chicago Press, 1986); and George Grant, *Technology and Empire: Perspectives on North America* (Toronto: Anansi, 1969).

[38]Perhaps the best introduction to this intellectual/cultural movement is William Barrett's *Irrational Man: A Study in Existential Philosophy* (Garden City, N.Y.: Doubleday/Anchor Books, 1958). The classic anthology of this movement is Walter Kaufmann's *Existentialism from Dostoevsky to Sartre*, rev. ed. (New York: New American Library, 1975).

[39]In a rather famous essay, Francis Fukuyama argued that the demise of the Soviet Union represented the "end of history" because the clear victory of liberal democratic capitalism would bring to a close the ideological development of the race. In Hegelian terms, the Idea of pure spirit (or *Geist*) has been realized. See his "The End of History?" *The National Interest*, Summer 1989, pp. 3-18. Walsh has criticized Fukuyama's position at length in *Subversive Christianity*, chap. 3, arguing that the ending of the Soviet empire is simply an advance warning of the ending of the American empire. Both empires are rooted in the worldview of modernity that is presently in decline. A similar argument can be found in Thomas C. Oden, *Two Worlds: Notes on the Death of Modernity in America and Russia* (Downers Grove, Ill.: InterVarsity Press, 1992). We will address Fukuyama's position further in chapter four.

[40]Jane Flax, *Thinking Fragments: Psychoanalysis, Feminism and Postmodernism in the Contemporary World* (Berkeley: University of California Press, 1990), p. 5.

[41]This is the way the editors of the journal *Precis* describe the culture of advanced capitalist societies (vol. 6, 1989). Quoted in David Harvey, *The Condition of Postmodernism: An Enquiry into the Origins of Cultural Change* (Oxford: Basil Blackwell, 1989), p. 39.

[42]*Catch-22.* © 1979 by Paramount Pictures Corp. Based on the novel by Joseph Heller.

[43]Gilkey, *Society and the Sacred*, p. xi. We employed this metaphor also in *The Transforming Vision*, p. 142. Gilkey describes the crisis of modernity also as a "time of troubles," a notion he borrows from Arnold Toynbee, *A Study of History*, 7 vols. (London: Oxford University Press, 1934-1961), 1:53 and 4:1-5. Gilkey also employs this metaphor in "Theology for a Time of Troubles: How My Mind Has Changed," *Christian Century* 98 (April 29, 1981): 474-80. For further discussion of Gilkey's understanding of this "time of troubles," see Brian J. Walsh, *Langdon Gilkey: Theologian for a Culture in Decline* (Lanham, Md.: University Press of America, 1992), chap. 3.

[44]See Friedrich Nietzsche's famous parable of the madman (*The Gay Science*, aphorism 125) for a vivid prophetic description in the nineteenth century of the coming crisis of modernity. Using the image of a planet severed from its sun to portray modern autonomy (= the death of God), Nietzsche foreshadows our description of the crisis in terms of the bitter cold of anomie. See *The Gay Science: With a Prelude in Rhymes and an Appendix of Songs*, trans. Walter Kaufmann (New York: Random House, 1974), pp. 181-82.

[45]See Peter L. Berger, *The Sacred Canopy: Elements of a Sociological Theory of Religion* (Garden City, N.Y.: Doubleday, 1967); Richard John Neuhaus, *The Naked Public Square* (Grand Rapids, Mich.: Eerdmans, 1984).

[46]Clifford Geertz, *The Interpretation of Cultures* (New York: Basic Books, 1973), p. 99.

[47]Susan Littwin, *The Postponed Generation: Why American Youth Are Growing Up Later* (New York: Morrow, 1986).

[48]An insightful discussion of this psychology of fear as it is manifest in one North American city, namely Toronto, is found in David MacFarlane's article "High Anxiety," *Toronto*, October 1988.

[49]Langdon Gilkey, *Reaping the Whirlwind: A Christian Interpretation of History* (New York: Seabury, 1976), p. 16.

[50]This cynicism was evident in the overwhelming rejection of the Canadian constitutional accord in the October 1992 referendum and in the odd role and surprising support that Ross Perot enjoyed in the U.S. presidential campaign of that year.

[51]Jeremy Rifkin with Ted Howard, *The Emerging Order: God in the Age of Scarcity* (New York: Putnam's Sons, 1979), p. 212.

[52]Robert Hughes, "The Fraying of America," *Time* 139, no. 5 (1992).

[53]This was a much-repeated refrain heard from all three U.S. presidential candidates in 1992 and a dominant theme in both the Republican and Democratic conventions of that year. At a certain point a sensitive observer might conclude that "the lady doth protest too much" (Shakespeare).

[54]A line from the Indigo Girls' song "Prince of Darkness," written by Emily Saliers. From the album *Indigo Girls,* © 1988 Godhap Music (BMI).

[55]Cockburn, "Candy Man's Gone."

[56]"Broken Wheel," from the album *Inner City Front,* © 1981 Golden Mountain Music Corp. We have analyzed the postmodern, yet hopeful, character of this song at some length in "Theology at the Rim of a Broken Wheel: Bruce Cockburn and Christian Faith in a Postmodern World," *Grail* 9, no. 2 (1993): 15-39.

### Chapter 2: Reality Isn't What It Used to Be

[1]From the title of Walter Truett Anderson's book *Reality Isn't What It Used to Be: Theatrical Politics, Ready-to-Wear Religion, Global Myths, Primitive Chic and Other Wonders of the Postmodern World* (San Francisco: Harper & Row, 1990).

[2]Jane Wagner, *The Search for Signs of Intelligent Life in the Universe* (New York: Harper & Row, 1985), p. 18. The play, written by Wagner, is acted by Tomlin, who has become in effect the play's coauthor by the joint development of the script at the workshop stage.

[3]Anderson, *Reality Isn't What It Used to Be,* p. 75.

[4]Ibid., p. 19.

[5]N. T. Wright describes this postmodern epistemology as a form of phenomenalism: all I can really be sure of are the phenomena, my own sensory experiences, not anything external to which those sensory experiences correspond. The result is solipsism; private reality is all there is. See part 2, the methodological section, of Wright's book *The New Testament and the People of God* (London: SPCK/Minneapolis: Augsburg/Fortress, 1992), esp. pp. 33-35, 51-53. This is volume 1 of Wright's projected five-volume New Testament theology entitled *Christian Origins and the Question of God.*

[6]Richard Rorty, "Pragmatism and Philosophy," in *After Philosophy: End or Transformation?* ed. Kenneth Baynes, James Bohman and Thomas McCarthy (Cambridge, Mass.: MIT Press, 1987), p. 57. Rorty has this phrase in italics in his text.

[7]See part 1 of Brian J. Walsh and J. Richard Middleton, *The Transforming Vision: Shaping a Christian World View* (Downers Grove, Ill: InterVarsity Press, 1984).

[8]For further discussion of *worldview* in relation to Christian higher education see Brian J. Walsh's article "Worldviews, Modernity and the Task of Christian College Education," *Faculty Dialogue* 18 (Fall 1992): 13-35.

[9]The recognition of the perspectival character of human knowing has revolutionized the philosophy of science. For example, see Thomas Kuhn, *The Structure of Scientific Revolutions,* rev. ed. (Chicago: University of Chicago Press, 1962); Mary Gerhart and Allan Russell, *Meta-*

*phoric Process: The Creation of Scientific and Religious Understanding* (Fort Worth: Texas Christian University Press, 1984); Ian Barbour, *Myths, Models and Paradigms: A Comparative Study in Science and Religion* (New York: Harper & Row, 1974); John Greene, *Science, Ideology and World View: Essays in the History of Evolutionary Ideas* (Berkeley: University of California Press, 1981); and Michael Polanyi, *The Tacit Dimension* (Garden City, N.Y.: Doubleday, 1966). From a more explicitly Christian perspective see Del Ratzsch, *Philosophy of Science: The Natural Sciences in Christian Perspective* (Downers Grove, Ill.: InterVarsity Press, 1986); Nicholas Wolterstorff, *Reason Within the Bounds of Religion*, 2nd ed. (Grand Rapids, Mich.: Eerdmans, 1984); James Sire, *Discipleship of the Mind* (Downers Grove, Ill.: InterVarsity Press, 1990); Langdon Gilkey, *Religion and the Scientific Future* (New York: Harper & Row, 1970); and Walsh and Middleton, *The Transforming Vision*, chaps. 11 and 12.

[10]Rorty, "Pragmatism and Philosophy," p. 60.

[11]Richard Rorty, *Philosophy and the Mirror of Nature* (Princeton, N.J.: Princeton University Press, 1979), p. 325. As the title suggests, Rorty is concerned to debunk the classic notion of the human mind functioning as a mirror of nature. If there is any "mirroring" going on in human knowing, then the postmodernist is suspicious that it is a conjuring trick.

[12]Playing with the title of Alasdair MacIntyre's book *Whose Justice? Which Rationality?* (Notre Dame, Ind.: University of Notre Dame Press, 1988).

[13]For a helpful introduction to deconstructionist philosophy see Linda Hutcheon, *The Politics of Postmodernism* (London: Routledge, 1989), esp. chap. 2.

[14]Derrida first used the term regarding Edmund Husserl's phenomenology of consciousness. See especially *Speech and Phenomena*, trans. David Allison (Evanston, Ill.: Northwestern University Press, 1972), and *Edmund Husserl's Origin of Geometry: An Introduction*, trans. John P. Leavy (Stony Brook, N.Y.: Nicholas Hays, 1978).

[15]Peter Berger and Thomas Luckmann, *The Social Construction of Reality* (Garden City, N.Y.: Doubleday, 1967), p. 89. In *The Sacred Canopy: Elements of a Sociological Theory of Religion* (Garden City, N.Y.: Doubleday, 1967), chap. 4, Peter Berger describes alienation as forgetting that this world was and continues to be coproduced by humans. He says, "Men then live in the world they themselves have made as if they were fated to do so by powers that are quite independent of their own world-constructing enterprises" (p. 95). The irony of Berger's career is that his later insistence that capitalism needs no legitimation because it has the "normative power of facticty" on its side falls into precisely the alienated reification he warned against twenty years earlier. See his *The Capitalist Revolution* (New York: Basic Books, 1986), pp. 207-8. We are indebted to a former student, Iskandar Saher, for bringing this to our attention in his master's thesis at the Institute for Christian Studies, Toronto.

[16]Jane Flax, *Thinking Fragments: Psychoanalysis, Feminism and Postmodernism in the Contemporary West* (Berkeley: University of California Press, 1990), p. 34.

[17]From René Descartes, *Discourse on Method*, chap. 6. See *Essential Works of Descartes*, trans. Lowell Bair (New York: Bantam, 1961), p. 37.

[18]Jacques Derrida, "Violence and Metaphysics: An Essay on the Thought of Emmanuel Levinas," in *Writing and Difference*, trans. Alan Bass (Chicago: University of Chicago Press, 1978), p. 91. Although Derrida is at this point explaining Levinas's thought, he is in agreement with the judgment.

[19]This is Albert Borgmann's description. See *Crossing the Postmodern Divide* (Chicago: University of Chicago Press, 1992), p. 27.

²⁰The classic discussion of totalization is found in Emmanuel Levinas, *Totality and Infinity: An Essay on Exteriority*, trans. Alphonso Lingis (Pittsburgh: Duquesne University Press, 1969). This is a very dense and complex philosophical text, but see pp. 17-18 of the introduction by John Wild for a succinct summary of what Levinas means by "totalization."

²¹James H. Olthuis, "A Cold and Comfortless Hermeneutic or a Warm and Trembling Hermeneutic: A Conversation with John D. Caputo," *Christian Scholar's Review* 19, no. 4 (1990): 351. This is an important article which attempts to articulate Christian sympathies with, yet ultimate divergence from, a philosophy of deconstruction.

²²Kenneth J. Gergen, *The Saturated Self: Dilemmas of Identity in Contemporary Life* (New York: Basic Books, 1991), p. 252.

²³Jean-François Lyotard, *The Postmodern Condition: A Report on Knowledge, Theory and History of Literature*, trans. Geoff Bennington and Brian Massumi (Minneapolis: University of Minnesota Press, 1984), p. 81.

²⁴This theme is summed up well by Gary J. Percesepe in his article "The Unbearable Lightness of Being Postmodern," *Christian Scholar's Review* 20, no. 2 (1990): 118-35.

²⁵Hutcheon, *The Politics of Postmodernism*, p. 2. The expression "made by us not given to us" is a variation of Richard Rorty's famous statement that truth/reality is "made not found."

²⁶Jane Flax says that the postmodern condition creates "a most uncomfortable form of intellectual vertigo to which appropriate responses are not clear" (*Thinking Fragments*, p. 6).

²⁷Berger, *The Sacred Canopy*, p. 22.

²⁸Clifford Geertz, *The Interpretation of Cultures* (New York: Basic Books, 1973), p. 89.

²⁹For an insightful catalog of the geopolitical, environmental, technological and economic crises that we presently face, see Tom Sine, *Wild Hope: Crises Facing the Human Community on the Threshold of the 21st Century* (Dallas: Word, 1991), pt. 1.

³⁰From "Awakening from Modernity," *Times Literary Supplement*, February 20, 1987. Cited by David Harvey in *The Condition of Postmodernity: An Enquiry into the Origins of Cultural Change* (Oxford: Basil Blackwell, 1989), p. 9.

³¹Deconstruction is, admittedly, a very complex philosophical movement which often intentionally couches its insights in obscure, even obtuse formulations. The obscurity of deconstructionist writing is so renowned it has led to the following joke: "What do you get when you cross a Mafioso with a deconstructionist?" Answer: "You get an offer you can't understand." Yet since deconstruction articulates philosophically what is a widespread and growing sentiment about reality, it is important for Christians to grapple creatively with its basic tenets. Hence our somewhat lengthy analysis.

For a lucid interpretation of why Derrida in particular is so obscure, see Richard Rorty, "From Ironist Theory to Private Allusions: Derrida," chap. 6 in *Contingency, Irony and Solidarity* (Cambridge: Cambridge University Press, 1988), pp. 122-37.

³²We first noticed this ad in the 1982 "Careers Supplement" to *The Varsity*, the campus paper at the University of Toronto. A version of the ad, always with the same headline, ran in Canadian campus papers throughout the 1980s.

³³The title of a song from U2 on the album *Achtung Baby*. © 1991 U2 Admin. by Chappell & Co.

³⁴Borgmann, *Crossing the Postmodern Divide*, p. 93.

³⁵Jean Baudrillard, *Simulations*, trans. Paul Foss, Paul Patton and Philip Beitchman (New York: Semiotext, 1983). Linda Hutcheon describes Baudrillard's argument in terms of the way in

which the mass media have neutralized reality by stages: "First they *reflected* it; then they *masked* and perverted it; next they had to *mask its absence;* and finally they produced instead the *simulacrum* of the real, the destruction of meaning and of all relation to reality" (*The Politics of Postmodernism,* p. 33).

[36]Harvey, *The Condition of Postmodernity,* p. 289. See also the discussion of Baudrillard in Steven Best and Douglas Kellner, *Postmodern Theory: Critical Interrogations* (New York: Guilford, 1991), chap. 4.

[37]See Baudrillard, *Simulations,* pp. 23-26.

[38]Borgmann, *Crossing the Postmodern Divide,* p. 94.

[39]We could say that *hyper*reality soon becomes *hypo*reality. The ultrareal is experienced as subreal.

[40]Cited by Gergen, *The Saturated Self,* p. 204.

[41]Anderson, *Reality Isn't What It Used to Be,* p. 12.

[42]Ibid., p. 165.

[43]Ibid., p. 166. Anderson has the word *intellectual* in italics in the above quote. Perhaps we could say that Reagan's politics represented a lingering modern *content* presented in a decidedly postmodern *form.* The question is whether such content can be sustained when encompassed by a form that fundamentally subverts it. Political cynicism seems an inevitable result. Anderson describes the Reagan administration as a public relations outfit that took over the country (p. 168).

[44]Tim Robbins's 1992 film *Bob Roberts* is a wonderful and biting parody of precisely this kind of theatricality.

[45]The Christian philosopher Herman Dooyeweerd has discussed the implicit tension between what he calls the "science ideal" and the "personality ideal" (or the nature/freedom dialectic) in modern thought. See his *Roots of Western Culture,* trans. John Kraay, ed. Mark Vander Vennen and Bernard Zylstra (Toronto: Wedge, 1979).

[46]Richard Rorty, *Objectivity, Relativism and Truth* (Cambridge: Cambridge University Press, 1991), p. 33, esp. n. 16. See the essays in part 1 for his critique of the Cartesian ideal and in part 2 for his defense of the Baconian ideal.

[47]It is important to note that Derrida and other deconstructionists reject *both* the Cartesian and Baconian ideals. But this radical philosophical position is not characteristic of "postmodern" culture. On this question Rorty is more representative of our times.

[48]Films within films and stories within stories are common postmodern devices. In this film, Hutcheon says that "real and reel life mingle in self-conscious irony" (*The Politics of Postmodernism,* p. 109).

[49]Borgmann, *Crossing the Postmodern Divide,* p. 90. On p. 97 he goes on to say, "We cannot finally, he [Allen] suggests, be citizens both of the hyperreal universe and of the real world."

[50]Gergen, *The Saturated Self,* p. 193. Mark C. Taylor also employs the metaphor of carnival in *Erring: A Postmodern A/theology* (Chicago: University of Chicago Press, 1984), beginning at p. 160, as did Nathan A. Scott Jr. in his 1986 presidential address to the American Academy of Religion, "The House of Intellect in an Age of Carnival: Some Hermeneutical Reflections," *Journal of the American Academy of Religion* 55, no. 1 (1987): 3-19. Both are dependent upon the Russian literary critic Mikhail Bakhtin's book *Rabelais and His World,* trans. H. Iswolsky (Cambridge, Mass.: MIT Press, 1968).

[51]See *The Communist Manifesto,* trans. Samuel More (Chicago: Henry Regnery, 1954), p. 20.

Marx's comments, published in 1848, were part of his argument in the first chapter of the *Communist Manifesto* that capitalism (read: modernity) was a "revolutionary" force that had desacralized and disenchanted (we could say naturalized) the medieval and Renaissance worlds. On the influence of Marx's famous phrase see Marshall Berman, *All That Is Solid Melts into Air* (New York: Penguin, 1988).

[52]One of the theologians who jumped on the Enlightenment bandwagon and attempted to produce a "secular theology" adapted to a postreligious civilization was Harvey Cox. See his *The Secular City: Urbanization and Secularization in Theological Perspective* (New York: Macmillan, 1965). Cox later retracted his views in *Religion and the Secular City: Toward a Postmodern Theology* (New York: Simon & Schuster, 1989).

[53]Anderson, *Reality Isn't What It Used to Be*, p. 188. Actually it might be argued that a similar situation existed in ancient Greco-Roman culture, with its rampant polytheism and plethora of competing mystery religions and guilds. In this respect, it is significant that many postmodern thinkers glorify the pluralism of ancient pagan times as a model for contemporary postmodernity.

[54]Berger, *The Sacred Canopy*, p. 138. The emphasis is Berger's. In Canada, the commodification of religious belief has been well documented by the social scientific work of Reginald Bibby. See his *Fragmented Gods: The Poverty and Potential of Religion in Canada* (Toronto: Irwin, 1987). For an important analysis of postmodern consumerism see David Lyon, *Postmodernity* (Minneapolis: University of Minnesota Press/Buckingham, U.K.: Open University Press, 1994), chap. 4.

[55]Liberalism is thus a totalizing vision of life that attempts to control, marginalize or placate difference within strictly defined bounds. This accounts for the history of Western democratic marginalization of religious, ethnic or ideological groups that would challenge the status quo.

[56]For a critique of liberal notions of tolerance and the public-private dichotomy, see Brian Walsh, "Liberal Tyranny," *Third Way* 15, no. 6 (1992): 26-30; Paul Marshall, "Liberalism, Pluralism and Christianity: A Reconceptualization," *Fides et Historia* 23, no. 3 (1989): 4-17; and Lesslie Newbigin, *The Gospel in a Pluralist Society* (Grand Rapids, Mich.: Eerdmans/Geneva: WCC, 1989), chaps. 1 and 2.

[57]Our thanks to David Lyon of Queens University in Kingston, Ontario, for this phrase. Lyon cited an interview with Giovanni Vattimo for the characterization of the postmodern spirit in this way at an informal presentation to the Canadian Evangelical Theological Association in June 1993. For Vattimo's valorization of heterogeneity see his *The Transparent Society* (Cambridge, U.K.: Polity, 1992).

[58]Such a spirit permeates the writings of Mark C. Taylor. See his *Erring: A Postmodern A/theology* and *Deconstructing Theology*, AAR Studies in Religion 28 (New York: Crossroad/Chico, Calif.: Scholars, 1982), esp. the final essay, "GNICART/TRACING: *Inter Alios.*" Brian J. Walsh provides a critical review of this book in *Christian Scholar's Review* 23, no. 3 (1984).

[59]The Hebrew *bābel* used in Genesis 11 is the same word used throughout the Old Testament for Babylon, whether referring to the entire imperial civilization or to its capital city. Babylon as a symbol of all cultural formation that is opposed to God is employed apocalyptically in Revelation 18.

[60]Brian Walsh has explored the theme of mourning further in *Subversive Christianity: Imaging God in a Dangerous Time* (1992; reprint, Seattle, Wash.: Alta Vista College Press, 1994), esp.

chap. 3, "Waiting for a Miracle: Christian Grief at the End of History." In the second part of a programmatic article on Old Testament theology, Walter Brueggemann describes the "embrace of pain" as central to a biblical worldview. See his "A Shape for Old Testament Theology, II: Embrace of Pain," *Catholic Biblical Quarterly* 47, no. 3 (1985): 395-415.

### Chapter 3: The Decentered Self

[1]Jane Wagner, *The Search for Signs of Intelligent Life in the Universe* (New York: Harper & Row, 1985), p. 15.

[2]We have discussed the modernist understanding of human autonomy at greater length in *The Transforming Vision: Shaping a Christian World View* (Downers Grove, Ill.: InterVarsity Press, 1984), pp. 118-26.

[3]Ernst Cassirer, *The Individual and Cosmos in Renaissance Philosophy*, trans. Mario Domandi (New York: Harper & Row, 1963), p. 95. For further discussion of the Promethean reinterpretation of Adam see Cameron Whybrow, *The Bible, Baconianism and Mastery over Nature: The Old Testament and Its Modern Misreading* (New York: Peter Lang, 1991), esp. pt. 3. Robert Heilbroner also views modernity as animated by a Promethean spirit in *An Inquiry into the Human Prospect* (New York: W. W. Norton, 1974). For a critique of Heilbroner's analysis see Langdon Gilkey, *Reaping the Whirlwind: A Christian Interpretation of History* (New York: Seabury, 1976), pp. 79-90, and "Robert Heilbroner's Vision of History," *Zygon* 19 (September 1975): 215-33.

[4]Cassirer, *Individual and Cosmos*, p. 96.

[5]Giovanni Pico della Mirandola, *Oration on the Dignity of Man*, trans. A Robert Caponigri (Chicago: Henry Regnery, 1965). The following quotations are from pp. 7-8.

[6]Again, the exclusive language throughout these pages is intentional. Many feminists argue that the death of the Enlightenment autonomous subject is the death of a patriarchal understanding of human subjectivity and agency and that other, more openly inclusive views of the self are possible. We are most indebted for this insight to Professor Lynda Lange in an unpublished paper, "Arguing for Democratic Feminism: Postmodern Doubts and Political Amnesia" (presented at the Institute for Christian Studies, March 26, 1992; Lange's paper was a sketch for her forthcoming book, *Claiming Democratic Feminism* [New York: Routledge]). Authors that Lange cites include Chris Weedon, *Feminist Practice and Poststructuralist Theory* (Oxford: Basil Blackwell, 1987); Iris Young, "The Ideal of Community and the Politics of Difference," in *Feminism/Postmodernism*, ed. Linda Nicholson (New York: Routledge, 1990); and Linda Alcoff, "Cultural Feminism Versus Postmodernism: The Identity Crisis in Feminist Theory," *Signs* (Spring 1988).

[7]Kenneth J. Gergen, *The Saturated Self: Dilemmas of Identity in Contemporary Life* (New York: Basic Books, 1991), p. 5.

[8]For a profound analysis of the roots of democracy in the Bible see Gabriel Sivan, *The Bible and Civilization* (New York: Quadrangle, 1973), pp. 143-89.

[9]Christopher Lasch, *The Minimal Self: Psychic Survival in Troubled Times* (New York: W. W. Norton, 1984), p. 137.

[10]Herman Dooyeweerd, *Roots of Western Culture*, trans. John Kraay, ed. Mark Vander Vennen and Bernard Zylstra (Toronto: Wedge, 1979), p. 150. Emphasis is Dooyeweerd's.

[11]For a profound Christian appraisal of the environmental crisis see *Earthkeeping in the 90's: Stewardship of Creation*, ed. Loren Wilkenson, rev. ed. (Grand Rapids, Mich.: Eerdmans, 1991).

See also Douglas John Hall, *The Steward: A Biblical Symbol Come of Age*, rev. ed. (Grand Rapids, Mich.: Eerdmans/New York: Friendship, 1990); James A. Nash, *Loving Nature: Ecological Integrity and Christian Responsibility* (Nashville: Abingdon, 1991); and H. Paul Santmire, *The Travail of Nature: The Ambiguous Ecological Promise of Christian Theology* (Philadelphia: Fortress, 1985).

[12]Douglas John Hall makes clear the connection between these two forms of mastery: "There can be no mastery of nature that does not finally disclose itself as the necessity of mastering human nature." See his *Imaging God: Dominion as Stewardship* (Grand Rapids, Mich.: Eerdmans/New York: Friendship, 1986), p. 165.

[13]Bob Goudzwaard, *Capitalism and Progress: A Diagnosis of Western Society*, trans. and ed. Josina Van Nuis Zylstra (Toronto: Wedge/Grand Rapids, Mich.: Eerdmans, 1979), p. 143. See also Jacques Ellul, *The Technological Society* (New York: Vintage, 1964), and *Propaganda* (New York: Knopf, 1971).

[14]Linda Hutcheon, *The Politics of Postmodernism* (London: Routledge, 1989), p. 7.

[15]Recognizing the heterogeneity of postmodern thought, Jane Flax can nonetheless make the claim that all postmodernists reject "any concept of self of subjectivity in which it is not understood as produced as an effect of discursive practices." See *Thinking Fragments: Psychoanalysis, Feminism and Postmodernism in the Contemporary West* (Berkeley: University of California Press, 1990), p. 188.

[16]Michel Foucault, *Language, Counter Memory, Practice* (Ithaca, N.Y.: Cornell University Press, 1977), p. 138.

[17]Gergen, *The Saturated Self*, p. 106; quoted in "The Critic as Host," in Harold Bloom et al., *Deconstruction and Criticism* (New Haven, Conn.: Yale University Press, 1979).

[18]Gergen, *The Saturated Self*, p. 107. Emphasis added. For Derrida's antilogocentric view of language see *Of Grammatology*, trans. Gayatri Chakravorty Spivak (Baltimore: Johns Hopkins University Press, 1977), and *Writing and Difference*, trans. A. Bass (Chicago: University of Chicago Press, 1978).

Richard Rorty draws a line from the late Heidegger to Derrida on the matter of language: "Heidegger and Derrida share a tendency to think of language as something *more* than just a set of tools. The later Heidegger persistently and Derrida occasionally treat Language as if it were a quasi agent, a brooding presence, something that stands over and against human beings." Indeed, the result is that Language becomes a "quasi-divinity," the latest substitute for God. See Richard Rorty, *Essays on Heidegger and Others* (Cambridge: Cambridge University Press, 1991), p. 3.

[19]Steven Best and Douglas Kellner, *Postmodern Theory: Critical Interrogations* (New York: Guilford, 1991), p. 284, commenting on Gilles Deleuze and Félix Guattari, *Anti-Oedipus* (Minneapolis: University of Minnesota Press, 1983), and *A Thousand Plateaus* (Minneapolis: University of Minnesota Press, 1987). Ihab Hassan speaks of postmodern literature as animated by a "revulsion against the western self" in *The Postmodern Turn: Essays in Postmodern Theory and Culture* (Columbus: Ohio State University Press, 1987), p. 5.

[20]For an insightful and comprehensive discussion of the notion of the self in modernity, see Charles Taylor, *Sources of the Self: The Making of the Modern Identity* (Princeton, N.J.: Princeton University Press, 1989).

[21]From the album *Us.* © 1992 Real World Music Ltd.

[22]From the song "Civilization and Its Discontents," on the album *Trouble with Normal.* © 1983

Golden Mountain Music Corp. We have explored the Christian relevance of Bruce Cockburn's artistry further in two other articles: "Dancing in the Dragon's Jaws: Imaging God at the End of the Twentieth Century," *The Crucible* 2, no. 3 (1992): 11-18, and "Theology at the Rim of a Broken Wheel: Bruce Cockburn and Christian Faith in a Postmodern World," *Grail* 9, no. 2 (1993): 15-39. See also Brian J. Walsh, "The Christian Worldview of Bruce Cockburn: Prophetic Art in a Dangerous Time," *Toronto Journal of Theology* 5 (Fall 1989): 170-87.

²³Gergen, *The Saturated Self,* p. 7.

²⁴Ibid., pp. 6-7.

²⁵Ibid., p. 7.

²⁶See Hutcheon, *The Politics of Postmodernism,* p. 109.

²⁷Gergen, *The Saturated Self,* p. 183.

²⁸Ibid., p. 184. The theme of role-playing in modern society (anticipating the postmodern) was developed in Erving Goffman's important book *The Presentation of Self in Everyday Life* (Garden City, N.Y.: Doubleday, 1959).

²⁹Gergen, *The Saturated Self,* p. 186.

³⁰Ibid., p. 189.

³¹Ibid., p. 193.

³²See Taylor's *Sources of the Self: The Making of the Modern Identity.* Christopher Lasch also speaks of the "technologies of the self" in *The Minimal Self,* p. 58.

³³A theme developed by Neil Postman in *Amusing Ourselves to Death* (New York: Penguin, 1986).

³⁴Cited by Quentin J. Schultze et al. in *Dancing in the Dark: Youth, Popular Culture and the Electronic Media* (Grand Rapids, Mich.: Eerdmans, 1991), p. 192. William Romanowski, one of the authors of this book, sums up the MTV gospel as "Come unto me, all you who are bored, insecure, and lonely, and I will give you identity, intimacy, and fun. My images are attractive, and my sounds are catchy" (p. 208). We would only add that that identity, intimacy and fun are fleeting and disposable. Dan Rubey identifies MTV with postmodern themes of carnival in "Voguing at the Carnival: Desire and Pleasure on MTV," *The South Atlantic Quarterly* 90, no. 4 (1991): 871-906.

³⁵Os Guinness says that among the defining features of postmodernism are "a rejection of an identifiable self for shifting sets of relationships, content for style, truth and meaning for impressions, beliefs for games, ethical rules for social role-playing, commitment for self consciousness and irony, vocation for strategies of manipulation, enduringness for disposability, originality for reproducibility and recycling, consistency and continuity for the spliced, blurred, the self-consciously created pastiche of forms and moods. Nothing epitomizes popular postmodernism better than MTV and the hand-held remote controls through which American adolescents nibble and dabble their way toward lostness, grazing at will in the flickering pastures of one greener channel after another" (*The American Hour: A Time of Reckoning and the Once and Future Role of Faith* [New York: Free Press, 1993], p. 129).

³⁶See Fredric Jameson, *Postmodernism: Or, The Cultural Logic of Late Capitalism* (Durham, N.C.: Duke University Press, 1991).

³⁷Roger Lundin, *The Culture of Interpretation: Christian Faith and the Postmodern World* (Grand Rapids, Mich.: Eerdmans, 1993), p. 249. Lundin goes on to say that "in the modern world the ideal of the self disinterestedly seeking truth has given way to a vision of the self as a unit of consumption seeking to slake its unquenchable thirsts" (p. 250).

³⁸The title of this section comes from Bruce Cockburn's song "Gavin's Woodpile" from the

album *In the Falling Dark.* © 1976 Golden Mountain Music Corp.

[39]Gergen, *The Saturated Self,* pp. 73-74. This is what Robert Jay Lifton terms the "protean self" in *The Future of Immortality* (New York: Basic Books, 1987). See also his earlier book *Boundaries* (New York: Vintage, 1969).

[40]Gergen, *The Saturated Self,* p. 174.

[41]Lasch, *The Minimal Self,* p. 32.

[42]See Walsh and Middleton, *The Transforming Vision,* p. 35.

[43]The Indigo Girls' song "Closer to Fine" is on their album *Indigo Girls.* © 1988 Godhap Music (BMI). All quotations in this paragraph are from this song.

[44]The image of being shipwrecked is rich with metaphoric potential. We think of Bruce Cockburn's evocative song "Ship-wrecked at the Stable Door" on the 1988 album *Big Circumstance.*

[45]Peter Berger, *The Sacred Canopy: Elements of a Sociological Theory of Religion* (Garden City, N.Y.: Anchor/Doubleday, 1969), p. 22.

[46]See Susan Littwin, *The Postponed Generation: Why American Youth Are Growing Up Later* (New York: Morrow, 1986).

[47]Lasch, *The Minimal Self,* p. 15.

[48]Ibid., p. 57.

[49]"The Future," from the album *The Future.* © 1992 Sony Music Entertainment Inc.

[50]Lasch, *The Minimal Self,* p. 38.

[51]Ibid.

[52]Lundin, *The Culture of Interpretation,* pp. 73-74.

[53]Ibid., p. 75.

[54]Albert Borgmann, *Crossing the Postmodern Divide* (Chicago: University of Chicago Press, 1992), p. 10.

[55]It is in response to this question that we see a revival of pragmatism in American philosophy: that which brings about the social good is true. The problem with this position is that it seems to beg the question of how we *decide* what will constitute the social good. For example, Richard Rorty argues that the best society we can have is "one which is content to call 'true' (or 'right' or 'just') whatever the outcome of undistorted communication happens to be, whatever view wins in a free and open encounter" (*Contingency, Irony and Solidarity* [Cambridge: Cambridge University Press, 1989], p. 67). But why should this encounter be free and open? Why should free and open communication be valued over restrained and closed communication? Rorty's only answer to this seems to be an appeal to the fact that the context in which he does philosophy is America. This amounts to little more than tribalism.

[56]See James Olthuis, "Undecidability and the Impossibility of Faith: Continuing the Discussion with Professor Caputo," *Christian Scholar's Review* 20, no. 2 (1990): 172. Lynda Lange makes a similar point: "Postmodern critique of universalism and 'totalizing discourse' reads as a critique of power and domination.... Yet as such it is often highly inconclusive. It challenges the traditional metaphysical justification of democracy and freedom in universal humanistic terms, but does this, it seems to me, by and large without providing much in its place that serves as a critique of the *wrongness* of domination. We are given a compelling analysis of how denial and silencing of 'difference' has been done, but little ethical reason why the practice should be given up!" ("Arguing for Democratic Feminism," p. 15).

Whenever ethical principles arise in postmodern books, they seem to come out of the air.

For example, in *The Politics of Postmodernism* Linda Hutcheon can allow the deconstructive ax to fall on all kinds of intellectual cultural conventions, until she comes to her last chapter and discusses the topic of feminism. At this point we reach a bedrock belief that is not to be argued with or denied. This criticism was raised by Philip Marchand in his review of the book in *The Toronto Star*, March 10, 1990, p. M3. A similar problem can be found in Daniel Liechty's book *Theology in a Postliberal Perspective* (London: SCM/Philadelphia: Trinity Press International, 1990). Liechty accepts the questioning of all transcendental categories of truth but then imposes, without argument, the values of creativity, transcendence and love.

⁵⁷Cited by Hutcheon, *The Politics of Postmodernism,* p. 47, from John Berger, *G* (New York: Pantheon, 1972), p. 75.

⁵⁸See David Harvey, *The Condition of Postmodernity: An Enquiry into the Origins of Cultural Change* (Oxford: Basil Blackwell, 1989), p. 116. Similar concerns are raised, from the perspective of critical theory, by Best and Kellner in *Postmodern Theory,* chaps. 7 and 8.

⁵⁹Michael Walzer speaks of home as a "dense moral culture" in *Interpretation and Social Criticism* (Cambridge, Mass.: Harvard University Press, 1987), pp. 15-16. We will return to the theme of home in chapter seven.

⁶⁰Gergen, *The Saturated Self,* p. 107.

⁶¹Ibid., p. 188.

⁶²Ibid., p. 195.

⁶³Ibid. Postmodern a/theologian Mark C. Taylor also employs the metaphor of masturbation to describe the self. "*Homo Linguisticus.* We make the game and the game makes us. Making it and being made. Playing the game we play with ourselves. Language is autoerotic—masturbation. *Homo linguisticus* is *homo* homo. Be careful not to get caught when you are playing hide-and-seek. Daddy will cut id off, or tell you to be silent. Wait until Abba is gone to play. Speech comes when 'Nobodaddy' is gone—He is dead when word(s) come" (*Deconstructing Theology,* AAR Studies in Religion 28 [New York: Crossroad/Chico, Calif.: Scholars Press, 1982], p. 114). The trouble with this description of the self (and its activity) is that it describes Taylor's own "a/theological" writings, nowhere more so than in this very text.

⁶⁴James Olthuis finds such a "cold heroism" in the postmodern theoretics of John Caputo. See "A Cold and Comfortless Hermeneutic or a Warm and Trembling Hermeneutic: A Conversation with John D. Caputo," *Christian Scholar's Review* 19, no. 4 (1990), esp. pp. 358-61. Olthuis's analysis focused on Caputo's important book *Radical Hermeneutics: Repetition, Deconstruction and the Hermeneutic Project* (Bloomington: Indiana University Press, 1987). In his more recent work, however, Caputo speaks of the giftlike life of "fools." This is a decided shift away from a postmodern heroism. See his *Against Ethics: Contributions to a Poetics of Obligation with Constant Reference to Deconstruction,* Studies in Continental Thought (Bloomington: Indiana University Press, 1993), esp. pp. 121-28.

⁶⁵John Dominic Crossan, *The Dark Interval: Toward a Theology of Story* (Niles, Ill.: Argus, 1975), p. 44.

⁶⁶In discussion of the thought of Jean Baudrillard, Best and Kellner say, "The postmodern world is devoid of meaning; it is a universe of nihilism where theories float in a void, *unanchored* in any secure harbour" (*Postmodern Theory,* p. 127). There is a sad irony here. William Barrett describes Hegel's appraisal of Descartes with these words: "Prior to Descartes philosophy has been sailing over the oceans, but now, with Descartes, the ship has come at last into harbor and discovered its native soil and subject matter: the conscious subject,

the I and its subjectivity" (*Death of the Soul: From Descartes to the Computer* [Garden City, N.Y.: Anchor/Doubleday, 1986], p. 16).

In the film *Pump Up the Volume* (directed by Allan Moyle and starring Christian Slater) teenage pirate-radio host "Happy Harry Hard On" sides with Baudrillard against Hegel. Using Leonard Cohen's song "Everybody Knows" as his theme, he figures that "everybody knows that the boat is leaking / everybody knows the captain lied" (from the album *I'm Your Man,* © 1988 CBS Records Inc.). The ship of modernity is sinking, and the supposedly safe harbor of the autonomous self has proven to be fraught with danger.

### Chapter 4: They Don't Tell Stories Like They Used To
[1]Aristotle *Poetics* 18.1-3.

[2]Michael Root, "The Narrative Structure of Soteriology," in *Why Narrative? Readings in Narrative Theology,* ed. Stanley Hauerwas and L. Gregory Jones (Grand Rapids, Mich.: Eerdmans, 1989), p. 269.

[3]Ibid.

[4]This means that in the biblical worldview *creation* is not simply equivalent to the setting of the story but takes on some of the attributes of a character, sharing in human brokenness and participating in God's redemption (see our discussion in chapter five).

[5]Note that we did resort to narrative in a section entitled "Redemptive History" in chap. 5 of Brian J. Walsh and J. Richard Middleton, *The Transforming Vision: Shaping a Christian World View* (Downers Grove, Ill.: InterVarsity Press, 1984). An important correction to our rather abstract use of the four worldview questions in *The Transforming Vision* is found in N. T. Wright, *The New Testament and the People of God* (London: SPCK/Minneapolis: Fortress, 1992), chap. 5. In his study of first-century Judaism and Christianity, Wright sometimes supplements our four worldview questions with what he regards as other distinct categories of worldview analysis, namely *story, symbol* and *praxis,* though he sometimes (inconsistently) treats the four worldview questions as essentially narrative in character, answerable in the telling of a story. We believe this latter approach to be the more fruitful.

[6]See Immanuel Kant, *Foundations for the Metaphysics of Morals.* For an English translation see *Immanuel Kant: Critique of Practical Reason and Other Writings in Moral Philosophy,* trans. and ed. L. W. Beck (Chicago: University of Chicago Press, 1949).

[7]David Burrell and Stanley Hauerwas, "From System to Story: An Alternative Pattern for Rationality in Ethics," in *Why Narrative?* ed. Hauerwas and Jones, p. 160.

[8]Stanley Hauerwas, *A Community of Character: Toward a Constructive Christian Social Ethic* (Notre Dame, Ind.: University of Notre Dame Press, 1981), pp. 98-99.

[9]Aristotle's account of ethics is found both in his *Nicomachean Ethics* and in his *Eudaimonean Ethics,* the former being the more acclaimed and influential work.

[10]Besides *A Community of Character,* see also Hauerwas's *The Peaceable Kingdom: A Primer in Christian Ethics* (Notre Dame, Ind.: University of Notre Dame Press, 1983).

[11]Alasdair MacIntyre, *After Virtue: A Study in Moral Theory,* 2nd ed. (Notre Dame, Ind.: University of Notre Dame Press, 1984). In the postscript to this second edition, MacIntyre responds to important criticisms of his work.

[12]See the analysis in ibid., chap. 2.

[13]Roger Lundin, *The Culture of Interpretation: Christian Faith and the Postmodern World* (Grand Rapids, Mich.: Eerdmans, 1993), p. 85.

[14]For a description of and engagement with that widespread moral disagreement, see Jeffrey Stout, *Ethics After Babel: The Languages of Morals and Their Discontents* (Boston: Beacon, 1979).

[15]See John D. Caputo, *Against Ethics: Contributions to a Poetics of Obligation with Constant Reference to Deconstruction* (Bloomington: Indiana University Press, 1993), p. 70, for the notion of a "tall tale."

[16]Alasdair MacIntyre, *Whose Justice? Which Rationality?* (Notre Dame, Ind.: University of Notre Dame Press, 1988), p. 393.

[17]According to MacIntyre, "Each particular conception of justice requires as its counterpart some particular conception of practical rationality and vice versa," and both justice and rationality are "closely related aspects of some larger, more or less well-articulated, overall view of human life and of its place in nature" (ibid., p. 289).

[18]Ibid., p. 391.

[19]MacIntyre, *After Virtue*, p. 216. Similarly, Stanley Hauerwas explains that "there is no other basis of moral convictions than the historic and narrative-related experience of a community" (*A Community of Character*, p. 99).

[20]MacIntyre explicitly calls his ethical proposals "pre-modern" in *After Virtue*, p. 205.

[21]For further discussion on the nature of narrative and its relevance for theology and ethics, see the anthology *Why Narrative?* ed. Hauerwas and Jones, as well as Anthony C. Thiselton, "Knowledge, Myth and Corporate Memory," in *Believing in the Church: The Corporate Nature of Faith* (London: SPCK, 1981), which is the report of the Doctrine Commission of the Church of England. The most comprehensive theoretical discussion of the nature of narrative is undoubtedly Paul Ricoeur's *Time and Narrative*, 3 vols., trans. Kathleen McLaughlin and David Pellauer (Chicago: University of Chicago Press, 1984-1988). An excellent summary of Ricoeur's contribution can be found in Anthony C. Thiselton, *New Horizons in Hermeneutics: The Theory and Practice of Transforming Biblical Reading* (Grand Rapids, Mich.: Zondervan, 1992), chap. 10, p. 2.

[22]N. T. Wright, "How Can the Bible Be Authoritative?" *Vox Evangelica* 21 (1991): 11.

[23]Ibid., p. 13.

[24]Thomas G. Long, *Preaching and the Literary Forms of the Bible* (Philadelphia: Fortress, 1989), p. 12.

[25]This is Kelsey's description of theologian Karl Barth's understanding of the Bible. See David Kelsey, *The Uses of Scripture in Recent Theology* (Philadelphia: Fortress, 1975), p. 48.

[26]For a classic definition of an "epic" as a large, loosely structured narrative containing many cycles of stories, see Aristotle *Poetics* 18.12-14, where he discusses the *Iliad* as an example.

[27]Wright, *The New Testament and the People of God*, p. 38.

[28]There are many further distinctions that could be made. For an analysis of different sorts of metanarratives, see Steven Best and Douglas Kellner, *Postmodern Theory: Critical Interrogations* (New York: Guilford, 1991), p. 172.

[29]MacIntyre, *After Virtue*, p. 216. The mythic foundations of all culture formation and conceptions of normativity is also addressed by Langdon Gilkey in *Society and the Sacred: Toward a Theology of Culture in Decline* (New York: Crossroad, 1981), esp. chaps. 4 and 5.

[30]Jean-François Lyotard, *The Postmodern Condition: A Report on Knowledge*, trans. Geoff Bennington and Brian Massumi (Minneapolis: University of Minnesota Press, 1984), p. xxiv. Lyotard's term is *grand récits*, which is translated in the text both as "metanarratives" and as "grand narratives."

[31]See Jane Flax, *Thinking Fragments: Psychoanalysis, Feminism and Postmodernity in the Contemporary West* (Berkeley: University of California Press, 1990), p. 33.

[32]Note that in Lyotard's analysis it is technically only modern scientific culture which has in fact produced metanarratives as second-order legitimating discourses (*The Postmodern Condition*, pp. xxiii, 27-37).

[33]See Linda Hutcheon, *The Politics of Postmodernism* (London: Routledge, 1989), p. 53. One of the most influential historiographers reflecting on the constructed character of historical narrative is Hayden V. White. See his *Metahistory: The Historical Imagination in Nineteenth Century Europe* (Baltimore: Johns Hopkins University Press, 1973) and *The Content of the Form: Narrative Discourse and Historical Representation* (Baltimore: Johns Hopkins University Press, 1987). We are indebted to a critical reading of White by Gay Marcille Frederick, "Hayden White on Historical Narrative: A Critique," M.Phil.F. thesis, Institute for Christian Studies, Toronto, 1992.

[34]Walter Truett Anderson, *Reality Isn't What It Used to Be: Theatrical Politics, Ready-to-Wear Religion, Global Myths, Primitive Chic and Other Wonders of the Postmodern World* (San Francisco: Harper & Row, 1990), p. 154.

[35]For example, Carol Gilligan analyzes Lawrence Kohlberg's purportedly universal stages of moral development from infancy to adulthood and concludes that Kohlberg's stages are not universal at all, but the expression of a particular group of people (white males) in a particular culture (Western) at a particular time (post-Enlightenment). See Gilligan's *In a Different Voice: Psychological Theory and Women's Development* (Cambridge, Mass.: Harvard University Press, 1982) and Kohlberg's *The Philosophy of Moral Development: Moral Stages and the Idea of Justice* (New York: Harper & Row, 1981). Albert Borgmann comments on the Gilligan critique of Kohlberg in *Crossing the Postmodern Divide* (Chicago: University of Chicago Press, 1992), pp. 53-54. J. Harry Fernhout offers a similar critique of Kohlberg, specifically addressing the question of particular faith commitments in moral development in "Moral Autonomy and Faith Commitment: Conflict or Integrality," Ph.D. dissertation, Ontario Institute for Studies in Education, Toronto, 1985.

[36]Cited by David Harvey in *The Condition of Postmodernity: An Enquiry into the Origins of Cultural Change* (Oxford: Basil Blackwell, 1989), p. 9, from Terry Eagleton, "Awakening from Modernity," *Times Literary Supplement*, February 20, 1987.

[37]Francis Fukuyama, "The End of History?" *The National Interest*, Summer 1989, pp. 3-18. Fukuyama later expanded this essay into a monograph entitled *The End of History and the Last Man* (New York: Free Press, 1992). Note that we briefly discussed Fukuyama's essay in chapter one, note 39.

[38]Brian Walsh has discussed and criticized the article at length in chapter 3 of *Subversive Christianity: Imaging God in a Dangerous Time* (1992; Medina, Wash.: Alta Vista College Press, 1994).

[39]Fukuyama is clear that this is a metanarrative, citing as his guides the nineteenth-century German philosopher G. W. F. Hegel (well known for his historical scheme of the evolution of world spirit) and the Hegelian scholar Alexander Kojéve. It is intriguing that Jean-François Lyotard cites Hegel's historical scheme of world spirit and the more individualist progress ideal of the autonomous ego as the two main versions of the modern metanarrative. See *The Postmodern Condition*, pp. 31-37.

[40]Fukuyama, "The End of History?" p. 9. Charles Taylor accuses Fukuyama of "glaring western

ethnocentrism" in "Balancing the Humours: Charles Taylor Talks to the Editors," *The Idler* 26 (November/December 1989): 21. William H. McNeill raises similar problems in his review of Fukuyama's *The End of History and the Last Man*, entitled "History Over, World Goes On," *The New York Times Book Review*, January 26, 1992, pp. 14-15.

⁴¹The oppressive function of the Babylonian metanarrative is evident especially when Neo-Babylonian kings assumed the part of Marduk, the head of the Babylonian pantheon, in the annual liturgical reenactment of the Enuma Elish at the Akitu festival every new year. In this reenactment, Marduk's primordial conquest of chaos was identified with the human king's political conquest of his enemies, thus legitimating Babylonian imperial supremacy. See Paul Ricoeur's insightful analysis of the Enuma Elish in *The Symbolism of Evil*, trans. Emerson Buchanan (Boston: Beacon, 1969), pt. 2, chap. 1. We will deal with the Enuma Elish in more detail in chapter six.

⁴²We have addressed the nature of Bruce Cockburn's artistry as both Christian and postmodern in "Theology at the Rim of a Broken Wheel: Bruce Cockburn and Christian Faith in a Postmodern World," *Grail* 9, no. 2 (1993): 15-39.

⁴³Bruce Cockburn, "Justice," from the album *Inner City Front*, © 1981 by Golden Mountain Music Corp.

⁴⁴See Hutcheon, *The Politics of Postmodernism*, p. 24, and Richard Rorty, *Essays on Heidegger and Others* (Cambridge: Cambridge University Press, 1991), p. 166.

⁴⁵Lyotard describes this as a return to paganism. See his "Lessons in Paganism," in *The Lyotard Reader*, ed. Andrew Benjamin (1977; London: Basil Blackwell, 1989).

⁴⁶Note our discussion in chapter three of MTV as a typically postmodern, nonnarrative form.

⁴⁷This description is quoted by MacIntyre in *Whose Justice? Which Rationality?* p. 368. Is the antitotalizing intent of the aphorism connected to the etymology, *apo* ("from"), *horizō* ("to set limits to")? Does an aphorism attempt to refuse the totalization of limits by, paradoxically, encapsulating openness within the aphoristic space? Isn't this simply blindness to the particularity of all language? Note that Robert Alter contends that it is the genre of prose narrative (such as typically found in the Old Testament) that is most genuinely open to the future. See *The Art of Biblical Narrative* (New York: Basic Books, 1981), chap. 2, especially pp. 25-27.

⁴⁸Hesiod, *Theogony*, trans. Norman O. Brown (Indianapolis: Bobbs-Merrill, 1953).

⁴⁹Norman O. Brown, *Life Against Death: The Psychoanalytic Meaning of History* (Middletown, Conn.: Wesleyan University Press, 1959).

⁵⁰Norman O. Brown, *Love's Body* (New York: Vintage Books, 1966).

⁵¹Note that Brown alludes on p. 234 to Nietzsche's comment about aphorisms in *Twilight of the Idols*, "Skirmishes of an Untimely Man," aphorism no. 51.

⁵²Norman O. Brown, *Closing Time* (New York: Random House, 1973).

⁵³For this insight into Brown's development we are indebted to Professor David Miller of Syracuse University. For a similar shift from sustained argument to aphoristic "lyrical discourses" or poetic meditations, compare John D. Caputo's earlier book *Radical Hermeneutics: Repetition, Deconstruction and the Hermeneutic Project* (Bloomington: Indiana University Press, 1987) with his later *Against Ethics* (1993).

⁵⁴The *Gospel of Thomas*, though noncanonical, is the best extant ancient text containing parallels for many canonical sayings of Jesus. It is the dominant view among American New Testament scholars that *Thomas* is at least as early as the canonical Gospels (first century)

and that it perhaps represented the "original" form of Christianity (a nonapocalyptic, that is, nonnarrative form), which was later transposed into a narrative framework by the Evangelists. For a summary of this position see the discussion on pp. 633-34 in Steven Davies, "The Christology and Protology of the *Gospel of Thomas,*" *Journal of Biblical Literature* 3, no. 4 (1992): 633-82. It is difficult to see, however, how N. T. Wright's cogent arguments for the derivative character (and late date) of *Thomas* could be effectively disputed, especially since Christianity began as a Jewish sect and first-century Jewish self-understanding was pervasively narrative in character. See Wright, *The New Testament and the People of God,* pp. 435-43.

[55]For a decidedly postmodern reading of Jesus, dependent upon the aphoristic *Gospel of Thomas* over against the narratively portrayed historical Jesus of the canonical Gospels, see John Dominic Crossan, *The Historical Jesus: The Life of a Mediterranean Jewish Peasant* (San Francisco: Harper San Francisco, 1992). A brilliant critique (nay, deconstruction!) of Crossan is found in N. T. Wright's article "On Taking the Text with Her Pleasure: A Post-Post-Modernist Response to J. Dominic Crossan, *The Historical Jesus: The Life of a Mediterranean Jewish Peasant,*" in *Theology* 96 (July/August 1993): 303-10.

[56]The affinity of Zen koans with the postmodern suspicion of reality claims may be seen in the ironic koan "If you find the Buddha on the road, kill him!"

[57]It is important that we not be understood here as making the claim that the aphoristic (or any nonnarrative) genre is illegitimate or inferior. The biblical book of Proverbs, for example, contains what are essentially groupings of aphoristic sayings, some in the short pithy category, others (like chaps. 1—9) constituting an extended lyrical meditation on wisdom and folly. The book of Proverbs, however, does not deny the validity of narrative. On the contrary, its placement in the Writings, the third grouping of books in the Hebrew Bible, assumes the narrative context provided by the first and second groupings of books, the Torah and the Prophets, which together tell the story of Israel.

[58]Rolf P. Knierim contrasts the vision of total warfare in Bosnia with his own experience of World War II: "And today one reads and sees (without personal experience) how among all involved parties in the former Yugoslavia, women are warriors more fierce in battle than men, and that for those parties this war is the only thing in their lives that matters at all, ethically, ethnically, religiously, beyond which no future is of interest. When one reads these things, one must ask who of us not directly involved in this or similar situations has any access to a mentality for which totally destructive war has become the ultimate value and reason for living or dying. Compared to this kind of experience, our WWII experiences are outdated." See Knierim, "On the Subject of War in the Old Testament and Biblical Theology," *Horizons in Biblical Theology* 16, no. 1 (1994): 2.

[59]Whereas the name of this militant faction comes from the Arabic for "to be hard, strict or severe," the cognate verb in Hebrew means "to do violence," and the Hebrew noun *ḥāmās* means "violence" or "bloodshed." It is because the earth was filled with *ḥāmās* that God sent the flood, according to Genesis 6:11-12.

[60]For an analysis of tribalism as an important postmodern trend, see Benjamin R. Barber, "Jihad vs. McWorld," *The Atlantic Monthly* 269, no. 3 (1992): 53-63.

[61]See African theologian John Pobee's insightful analysis of this phenomenon in "Images of the Enemy," *One World* 178 (August/September 1992): 15-17.

[62]Best and Kellner, *Postmodern Theory,* p. 171. See pp. 171-79 for an extended critique of Lyotard's "incredulity toward metanarratives."

[63]Thanks to Professor David Koyzis of Redeemer College, Ancaster, Ontario, for this insight.

[64]Anderson, *Reality Isn't What It Used to Be,* p. 183.

[65]The human need for coherent (nonviolent) metanarratives is argued, against Lyotard, by J. M. Bernstein in "Grand Narratives," chap. 7 in *On Paul Ricoeur: Narrative and Interpretation,* ed. David Wood (London: Routledge, 1991), pp. 102-23.

[66]Anderson, *Reality Isn't What It Used to Be,* pp. 182-83.

[67]For example, see David Harvey's discussion in *The Condition of Postmodernity,* chap. 18.

[68]The theme of the simulacrum (discussed in chapter two) is prevalent throughout this movie. There is, of course, a parallel between the replicants in *Blade Runner* and the character of Data in *Star Trek: The Next Generation.* However, while Data does experience the desire to become human, his attempts to ascend to that level are usually somewhat humorous, unlike the violent intensity of the replicants in *Blade Runner.*

[69]Quoted in Harvey, *The Condition of Postmodernity,* p. 313. It should be noted that a revised version of *Blade Runner* was released in 1992. One of the most notable changes was that the voice of Deckard that had originally functioned to tell the story over the film was dropped, leaving the viewer more room to determine the significance of the story. This would seem to make the film even more postmodern in its tone. The meaning(s) of the film is not imposed (by means of a voice-over) by the director but is left to the viewers to construct.

[70]In an analogous move, Best and Kellner critique Lyotard for "refusing to privilege any subjects or positions, or to offer a standpoint from which one can choose between opposing political positions. Thus he comes close to falling into a political relativism, which robs him of the possibility of making political discriminations and choosing between substantively different political positions" (*Postmodern Theory,* pp. 174-75).

[71]Jacques Derrida, "Plato's Pharmacy," chap. 1 in *Dissemination,* trans. Barbara Johnson (Chicago: University of Chicago Press, 1981), p. 70.

[72]Note that since *pharmakon* can be translated as either "poison" or "remedy," our third and fourth worldview questions, What's wrong? and What's the remedy? could be replaced, on an ironic Derridian reading, with the single question, What's the *pharmakon*? Perhaps this would be the more genuinely postmodern position, relativizing all answers to the third and fourth worldview questions.

### Chapter 5: The Biblical Metanarrative

[1]A more contracted version of the argument of this chapter can be found in our essay "Facing the Postmodern Scalpel: Can the Christian Faith Withstand Deconstruction?" in *Christian Apologetics in the Postmodern World,* ed. Timothy R. Phillips and Dennis L. Okholm (Downers Grove, Ill.: InterVarsity Press, 1995).

[2]In chapter eight we will explore a possible third antitotalizing dimension of Scripture, one that is more a formal characteristic than a central theme of the biblical story.

[3]The central ideas of this chapter have their origin in a seminal course in Old Testament theology taught by Werner Lemke at Colgate Rochester Divinity School in spring 1988.

[4]John H. Stek (in "Salvation, Justice and Liberation in the Old Testament," *Calvin Theological Journal* 13, no. 3 [1978]: 146) echoes our point in his comment that "the exodus is ground-zero as regards the historical perspective from which the primeval and patriarchal narratives [in Genesis] are related." Stek hastens to caution, however, that the exodus should not be abstracted from the overall canonical story of which it is a part. Although we ultimately agree

with this caution, we think it is heuristic first to focus on the exodus and then to put it in its larger metanarrative context.

[5]See Gerhard von Rad, "The Form-Critical Problem of the Hexateuch," in *The Problem of the Hexateuch and Other Essays* (London: SCM Press, 1984). Although von Rad classified these texts as creedal statements (in narrative form), this has been rightly challenged in recent years.

[6]Throughout this book we have departed from the NIV in using the name Yahweh (the name revealed to Moses in Ex 3:14-15) instead of the traditional rendering "the LORD." All other departures from the NIV (except this consistent change) will be noted.

[7]This particular psalm was probably sung in the second (postexilic) temple, since it originated in the exile, as we argue later in this chapter. For an analysis of the psalms of historical recital that addresses their critique of modernity, see Walter Brueggemann, *Abiding Astonishment: Psalms, Modernity and the Making of History* (Louisville, Ky.: Westminster/John Knox, 1991).

[8]See Michael Fishbane, *Biblical Interpretation in Ancient Israel* (Oxford: Clarendon, 1985), esp. chap. 1 on "Inner-Biblical Exegesis." On a similar phenomenon in the New Testament, see Richard B. Hayes, *Echoes of Scripture in the Letters of Paul* (New Haven, Conn.: Yale University Press, 1989).

[9]See Alasdair MacIntyre, *After Virtue: A Study in Moral Theory*, 2nd ed. (Notre Dame, Ind.: University of Notre Dame Press, 1984), p. 216.

[10]For excellent, accessible summaries of recent scholarship on the psalms of lament, see Walter Brueggemann, *The Message of the Psalms: A Theological Commentary* (Minneapolis: Augsburg, 1984), pp. 54-57, and Claus Westermann, *Praise and Lament in the Psalms*, trans. Keith R. Crim and Richard N. Soulen (Atlanta: John Knox, 1981), pp. 52-71.

[11]See, for example, *A Passover Haggadah: The New Union Haggadah*, ed. Herbert Bronstein, rev. ed. (New York: Central Conference of American Rabbis, 1975), pp. 48-49.

[12]For other statements of these two motivational clauses see Exodus 22:21; 22:27; Leviticus 19:34; Deuteronomy 5:15; 10:19; 15:15; 16:12; 24:17-22. Such statements amply testify to the paradigmatic nature of the exodus story for Israel's ethical life.

[13]Gottwald has argued in many places, but especially in his massive work *The Tribes of Yahweh: A Sociology of the Religion of Liberated Israel 1250-1050 B.C.E.* (Maryknoll, N.Y.: Orbis, 1979), that the distinctiveness of Yahweh vis-à-vis the gods of Egypt and Canaan is inextricably linked to the distinctiveness of Israel's egalitarian form of social organization. He describes the formation of Israel as "retribalization," a conscious sociopolitical rebellion against the oppressive hegemony of Egypt and the Canaanite city-states. Whether or not the details of Gottwald's historical and sociological reconstruction will stand the test of time, his central insight into the connection between Israel's God and their egalitarian form of life is clearly supported by the biblical data.

[14]Charles Taylor has addressed the centrality of this attitude toward suffering in our Western inheritance, although he traces it only as far back as the New Testament. See his *Sources of the Self: The Making of the Modern Identity* (Cambridge, Mass.: Harvard University Press, 1989), pp. 12-13.

[15]Walter Brueggemann, "A Shape for Old Testament Theology, II: Embrace of Pain," *Catholic Biblical Quarterly* 47, no. 3 (1985): 395-415.

[16]Walter Brueggemann, *The Prophetic Imagination* (Philadelphia: Fortress, 1978), esp. chap. 1 on the exodus and chaps. 3 and 4 on the prophets. On the suffering of God in the prophets,

see the seminal work by Abraham Joshua Heschel, *The Prophets* (New York: Harper & Row, 1962), as well as his earlier article "The Divine Pathos: The Basic Category of Prophetic Theology," *Judaism*, 1953, pp. 61-67. See also Terence E. Fretheim, *The Suffering of God: An Old Testament Perspective* (Philadelphia: Fortress, 1984).

[17]See Brueggemann, *The Prophetic Imagination*, chap. 2, and "A Shape for Old Testament Theology, I: Structure Legitimation," *Catholic Biblical Quarterly* 47, no. 1 (1985): 28-46.

[18]On "paganization," see George Mendenhall, "The Monarchy," *Interpretation* 29 (1975): 160.

[19]There is, however, a reinterpretation of the royal/imperial trajectory in Scripture such that royal terminology can be used to critique imperial totalizing claims. See our analysis in chapter six of humans created to be God's image and of Jesus as Messiah, both royal designations that serve as ideology critique. Helen A. Kenik has helpfully distinguished between the two sorts of royal trajectories in "Toward a Biblical Basis for Creation Theology," in *Western Spirituality: Historical Roots, Ecumenical Routes*, ed. Matthew Fox (Santa Fe, N.M.: Bear & Co., 1981), esp. p. 47.

[20]The vivid accounts of the opposition Jeremiah encountered (from priests, other prophets and the royal establishment) are recorded in Jeremiah 20, 26—28 and 37—38. See also the prophet-priest conflict recorded in Amos 7:10-17.

[21]To paraphrase a line from a Leonard Cohen song, they saw the future, baby, and it was murder.

[22]Our entire analysis of prophecy, exile and the shape of the canon is indebted to J. A. Sanders's major programmatic essays "Adaptable for Life: The Nature and Function of Canon" and "Hermeneutics of True and False Prophecy," in *From Sacred Story to Sacred Text: Canon as Paradigm* (Philadelphia: Fortress, 1987).

[23]Prophetic texts that speak of Israel's mission to the Gentiles include Isaiah 42:5-7 and 49:6, while texts that speak of the restoration of the nonhuman creation include Isaiah 55:12-13 and 65:17, 25. We will return to the theme of creationwide restoration in chapter seven.

[24]We have benefited tremendously from Lesslie Newbigin's insights in "The Logic of Election," chap. 7 of his *The Gospel in a Pluralist Society* (Grand Rapids, Mich.: Eerdmans/Geneva: WCC Publications, 1989).

[25]The Former Prophets (Joshua, Judges, Samuel and Kings) and the Latter Prophets (Isaiah, Jeremiah, Ezekiel and the Twelve) together form the Nevim (Prophets), the second major grouping of books in the Masoretic Text (MT) of the Hebrew Bible. The Septuagint, although grouping and ordering the books differently (an order followed by Christian Bibles), nevertheless agrees with the MT in beginning its next major section (the Historical Books) with Joshua.

[26]It is fascinating that Gerhard von Rad, arguably the greatest Old Testament scholar of the century, disregarded explicit canonical shape and regarded the Hexateuch (Genesis to Joshua), rather than the Pentateuch, as the basic textual unit of the Old Testament (see his "The Form-Critical Problem of the Hexateuch," in *The Problem of the Hexateuch and Other Essays*). But this is symptomatic of a generation of modern critical scholars who were prepared to foist their scholarly constructs on the Bible, assured that the canons of Enlightenment rationality were superior to the judgments of ancient biblical peoples. It was not until the postmodern crisis of Enlightenment canons of rationality and the dissolution of higher-critical hegemony in departments of biblical studies that scholars have begun to take seriously once again the biblical writings *qua canon*. On this shift see Walter Brueggemann, "Ca-

nonization and Contextualization," chap. 6 in *Interpretation and Obedience: From Faithful Reading to Faithful Living* (Minneapolis: Fortress, 1991).

[27]A partial listing of the various and diverse retellings of the story within the biblical text would include Deuteronomy 6:20-25; 26:1-11; Joshua 24:1-15; Judges 6:7-10; Nehemiah 9:1-38; Psalm 78; 105; 106; 136; Jeremiah 2:5-7; 32:16-38; Acts 7:1-54; 13:13-41; 1 Corinthians 15:1-11.

[28]Walter Brueggemann has analyzed the temptations of landedness in Israel's story with great nuance and profundity in *The Land* (Philadelphia: Fortress, 1976).

[29]Besides Jeremiah 32:17 and Nehemiah 9:5-6, creation is included as the start of the story in Psalm 136 (which we have previously discussed). Unlike the Jeremiah or Nehemiah texts, this psalm is not obviously exilic or postexilic, since it ends with the entrance into the Promised Land, while both Jeremiah 32 and Nehemiah 9 end with their contemporaneous exilic or postexilic situations. Nevertheless, the designation of Yahweh as "the God of heaven" in Psalm 136:26 is consistent with a late dating, since this phrase is used for God in Nehemiah (1:4, 5; 2:4, 20), Ezra (1:2; 5:11, 12; 6:9, 10; 7:12, 21, 23), Daniel (2:18, 19, 37, 44) and 2 Chronicles 36:23. Even those occurrences that are set before the exile speak to either pre-Israelite (Gen 24:3, 7) or non-Israelite (Jonah 1:9) situations, suggesting that the phrase designates Yahweh as the true God in contexts where Israel confronted other nations with their gods. There is even a striking similarity between Psalm 136:1 ("Give thanks to Yahweh, for he is good. *His love endures forever*") and Ezra 3:11 ("With praise and thanksgiving they sang to Yahweh: 'He is good; his love to Israel endures forever' "). For an important discussion of why it may have been inappropriate for Israel to emphasize creation prior to the exile, see Bernhard W. Anderson, *Creation Versus Chaos: The Reinterpretation of Mythical Symbolism in the Bible* (Philadelphia: Fortress, 1987), pp. 49-55.

[30]Besides Amos 1:2—2:3, the entirety of Nahum and Obadiah is directed against foreign nations, while Jonah tells the story of a prophet's mission to Nineveh, the Assyrian capital.

[31]On individual responsibility for sin see Ezekiel 18, and for its deep-seated character see Jeremiah 13:23 and 17:1, 9. Note that the story of the fall (Genesis 2—3)—which traces evil back to its source in human decision—is often cited and mentioned by Paul in the New Testament but is hardly alluded to in the Old Testament outside of Genesis 1—11. This suggests that this insight came relatively late in Israel's history.

[32]See Jeremiah 31:33; 32:40; Ezekiel 11:19-20; 18:31; 36:26-27.

[33]We are not arguing that this interpretation of election *originated* in the exile. Rather, the canonical placing of the creation story at the start of the metanarrative highlights what is already implicit, and often quite explicit, in the Bible. Its placing at the start of the metanarrative functioned, however, to correct self-serving, nationalistic readings of election which had arisen in Israel in the meantime. For an insightful creational analysis of election, see three works by Terence E. Fretheim: *Exodus* (Louisville, Ky.: John Knox, 1991), pp. 13-14; "The Reclamation of Creation: Redemption and Law in Exodus," *Interpretation* 45, no. 4 (1991): 358-59, 363-64; and "The Plagues as Ecological Signs of Historical Disaster," *Journal of Biblical Literature* 110, no. 3 (1991): 392. Fretheim goes on to argue that the creational reinterpretation of the exodus story does not just affect the meaning of election but compels us to see Egyptian oppression of the Hebrews as itself fundamentally anticreational. Pharaoh's imperial practice is judged evil because it contravenes God's original intent for shalom and justice among all peoples. The covenantal laws given at Sinai for Israel's common life

are thus seen as intended to shape an ethical community that embodied God's original, creational purposes for human life.

³⁴It is significant that Old Testament scholar Gerhard von Rad not only disregarded the canonical ending of Torah before land possession (see note 26) but also devalued the theme of creation in the Bible and regarded the placement of creation at the narrative beginning of the canon as theologically unimportant (see von Rad, "The Theological Problem of the Old Testament Doctrine of Creation," in *Creation in the Old Testament,* ed. Bernhard W. Anderson [Philadelphia: Fortress, 1984], p. 54). By misreading the shape of the canon, von Rad fundamentally misconstrued the point of the story, resulting in his assessment, "presumptuous as it may sound," that the Hexateuch (Genesis to Joshua) functioned ideologically to legitimate Israel's election and land possession (see von Rad, *Old Testament Theology,* vol. 1, *The Theology of Israel's Historical Traditions,* trans. D. M. G. Stalker [New York: Harper & Row, 1962], p. 138). Von Rad's misreading illustrates just how important it is to understand the shape of the canonical metanarrative.

³⁵The text of Psalm 146 which follows is the authors' adaptation of the NIV. Other biblical texts which connect these themes include the song of Hannah in 1 Samuel 2:1-10, the exilic pronouncements of Isaiah 40:21-31, and Psalm 22, a prayer of lament that combines the experience of marginality with acknowledgment of God as Creator (vv. 9-11) and as Lord of all nations (vv. 27-28). Not only did Jesus quote Psalm 22 on the cross (Mt 27:46), but the story of Jesus' death in Mark 15:22-37 contains numerous references and allusions to this psalm.

³⁶This is a pronounced tendency in some Reformed or Calvinist theology, with its central emphasis on God's sovereignty. An extreme contemporary example may be found in the Reconstruction movement, which seeks to restore America to an ideal Puritanlike theocracy. For the two most important articulations of this ideal see Rousas John Rushdoony, *Institutes of Biblical Law* (Nutley, N.J.: Craig, 1973), and Greg L. Bahnsen, *Theonomy in Christian Ethics* (Nutley, N.J.: Craig, 1977). For a good brief overview of the movement see Rodney Clapp, *The Reconstructionists,* rev. ed. (Downers Grove, Ill.: InterVarsity Press, 1990).

³⁷This may be seen as a tendency in some early liberation theology from Latin America. It is significant that Pedro Trigo, himself a Latin American liberation theologian, understands faith in God as Creator as an important antidote to both disempowerment and vengeful self-assertion. See Trigo, *Creation and History,* trans. Robert R. Barr (Maryknoll, N.Y.: Orbis, 1991), pt. 2, pp. 69-108.

³⁸Marcus J. Borg, *Jesus, a New Vision: Spirit, Culture and the Life of Discipleship* (San Francisco: Harper & Row, 1987), chap. 5; and Marcus J. Borg, *Conflict, Holiness and Politics in the Teaching of Jesus* (New York: Edwin Mellon, 1984), pp. 27-72. See also Chad Myers, *Binding the Strong Man: A Political Reading of Mark's Story of Jesus* (Maryknoll, N.Y.: Orbis, 1988), pp. 69-86.

³⁹For various lists of despised occupations in first-century Judaism, see Joachim Jeremias, *Jerusalem in the Time of Jesus* (Philadelphia: Fortress, 1969), pp. 303-12.

⁴⁰On holiness in the teaching of Jesus, see Borg, *Jesus, a New Vision,* pp. 129-42; and *Conflict, Holiness and Politics,* pp. 123-29, 133-34. It is intriguing that even Matthew's parallel to the Luke 6:36 text, "be perfect" (or possibly "mature"), does not use the language of holiness (Mt 5:48). In both cases the context makes it clear that the holiness, perfection or mercy in question consists in loving one's enemies, as God does.

⁴¹Walter Brueggemann has profoundly elucidated this dimension of Jesus' ministry in *The*

*Prophetic Imagination*, chaps. 5 and 6. See also Borg, *Jesus, a New Vision*, pp. 156-65.

⁴²N. T. Wright made the distinction between "creational covenantal monotheism" and "covenantal monotheism" in a series of public lectures on the Gospel of Mark at the Institute for Christian Studies in July 1988. See also Wright's *The New Testament and the People of God* (London: SPCK/Minneapolis: Fortress, 1992), pp. 246-52, and *The Climax of the Covenant* (Edinburgh: T & T Clark, 1991), pp. 108, 113-17, 137, 155. James Sanders proposed a similar reading of what Jesus was about in "The Bible, Anti-Semitism and the Monotheizing Process," a paper given at the 1992 annual meeting of the Society of Biblical Literature in San Francisco, California.

⁴³Although Jesus' ministry was, in the first instance, to the "lost sheep of the house of Israel," he foresaw the Gentile mission (as is evident in many of his parables, such as those of the vineyard and the banquet) and explicitly commissioned his disciples to bear the metanarrative (the gospel story) to the *gôyim*, making disciples of them (Mt 28:18-20).

⁴⁴See Wright, *The New Testament and the People of God*, p. 171.

⁴⁵Both Mark 11:18 and Luke 19:47 say that the chief priests and scribes were moved to plot against Jesus' life in response to the temple cleansing. Earlier in Mark (3:6; see the parallel in Mt 12:14) the Pharisees, together with the Herodians, plot against Jesus because of his healing on the sabbath, an act that anticipates the temple conflict. Matthew also portrays increased confrontational activity between Jesus and the authorities after the temple incident (Mt 21), culminating in the attempt to have him arrested (21:46). John's Gospel, however, sees things somewhat differently, placing a temple incident at the start of Jesus' career (Jn 2) and attributing the plots on his life to his miraculous raising of Lazarus from the dead (Jn 11).

⁴⁶See the servant songs in Isaiah 42:1-9; 49:1-9; 50:4-9; 52:13—53:12.

⁴⁷See Hans-Ruedi Weber, *Power: Focus for a Biblical Theology* (Geneva: WCC Publications, 1989), for an insightful analysis of Jesus as the convergence of a number of themes concerning power and justice in the Bible.

⁴⁸The same could be said of Jesus' appeal to Moses and the prophets in the conversation on the road to Emmaus (Lk 24). It was not a search for proof texts but an appeal to the very spirit and thrust of the biblical story when Jesus argued it was necessary that the Messiah should suffer these things (24:26-27).

⁴⁹This understanding of Israel's continuing bondage or exile after return to the land goes back to Ezra's prayer in Nehemiah 9:32, 36-37.

⁵⁰On the cosmic nature of redemption (a new heaven and earth) see our previous analysis of relevant biblical texts in *The Transforming Vision: Shaping a Christian World View* (Downers Grove, Ill.: InterVarsity Press, 1984), chap. 5. An important study which links this theme in the New Testament with the exodus is Sylvia C. Keesmaat, "Exodus and the Intertextual Transformation of Tradition in Romans 8.14-30," *Journal for the Study of the New Testament* 54 (1994): 29-56.

## Chapter 6: The Empowered Self

¹From "Sylvie and Bruno Concluded," vol. 2 of Carroll's heavy-handed moralistic tale *Sylvie and Bruno*. The text is, however, peppered with wonderful nonsense rhymes, including a series of verse-epigrams attributed to the Mad Gardener. See *The Complete Works of Lewis Carroll* (New York: Modern Library, 1936), p. 701.

²This chapter is dependent on the analysis in J. Richard Middleton, "The Liberating Image? Interpreting the *Imago Dei* in Context," *Christian Scholar's Review* 24, no. 1 (1994): 8-25, and also Middleton's Ph.D. dissertation at the Institute for Christian Studies, Toronto, entitled "The Liberating Image: A Socio-Ethical Reading of the *Imago Dei* in Genesis 1:26-27" (forthcoming).

³Christopher Lasch, *The Minimal Self: Psychic Survival in Troubled Times* (New York: W. W. Norton, 1984), p. 15.

⁴Ephesians 4:13-16 contrasts growing into the measure of Christ (which is the model of Christian maturity) with the immaturity of being "tossed back and forth by the waves, and blown here and there by every wind of teaching" (4:14). Is postmodernity, then, a regressive condition and the postmodern self essentially immature? If this is so, we suspect that modernity is equally immature, the adolescent posturing of a bully who seeks control of others to hide his own insecurity.

⁵A line from Bruce Cockburn's song "Gavin's Woodpile," from the album *In the Falling Dark,* © 1977 by Golden Mountain Music Corp.

⁶Although the exact dating of these texts is in dispute, see the major scholarly suggestions discussed in Donald Guthrie, *New Testament Introduction* (Downers Grove, Ill.: InterVarsity Press, 1970). These suggestions would place 1 Corinthians around A.D. 57 and Galatians (on one widely held theory) as early as A.D. 49, while Matthew would be 80-100, Luke around 75-85 and Mark, the earliest Gospel according to most scholars, possibly in the mid- to late 60s. For these discussions (in the above order) see Guthrie, pp. 441, 457-58, 46, 113 and 74.

⁷See chapter five for a fuller discussion of the significance of this point.

⁸Although various scholarly reconstructions of how the Bible (and the book of Genesis) came to be written have often been motivated by ideological biases against the possibility of revelation and the reality of the biblical God, our proposal is rooted in a commitment to the biblical God based on the historical revelation of Scripture. It is also, however, an attempt to understand *how* God's revelation occurred in the nitty-gritty of human history.

⁹Humans are not again referred to as the image of God until the intertestamental period, and the notion does not become widely used until the New Testament and subsequent Christian and rabbinic commentary on the Bible. This has led some biblical scholars to view the "image of God" notion as unimportant or peripheral to the Old Testament's overall understanding of what it means to be human. Our alternative to this view is to regard the actual term *image of God* as chronologically late, but as summarizing (in language appropriate to its time and context) the predominant view of humanity found throughout the rest of Scripture.

¹⁰There is a widespread tradition in Scripture of picturing pagan empires that opposed God's purposes as beasts, monsters, dragons or serpents, all associated with water, some with specific names such as Leviathan or Rahab. See, for example, Jeremiah 51:34, which pictures king Nebuchadnezzar of Babylon as a sea-serpent swallowing God's people, and Ezekiel 29:2-6 and 32:2-4, both of which describe the Egyptian Pharaoh as a great water-monster whom God will pull out of the Nile with fishhooks. Other references to historical empires as monsters or beasts from the sea include Isaiah 27:1 (Egypt or Assyria; cf. 27:12), Isaiah 51:9-11 (Egypt), Daniel 7:1-14 (four unnamed empires), and Psalm 74:12-17 and 89:5-14 (probably Egypt). Although this tradition is partially based in the Israelite experience of these empires as oppressive and terrifying, it is also an ironic reversal of a common ancient Near

Eastern mythology in which these very empires viewed their own enemies as beasts, monsters and dragons. See our analysis of the Enuma Elish later in this chapter.

[11]*Dancing in the Dragon's Jaws* is both the title of an album by Bruce Cockburn and a phrase from "Hills of Morning," a song on that album. © 1978 by Golden Mountain Music Corp.

[12]Israel's life in exile was precarious, at the mercy of the empire, just like that of Daniel, who refused to bow to pagan idols and prayed to Yahweh seven times a day in Babylon, only to find his friends ruthlessly thrown into a blazing furnace by one king and himself cast into a lion's den by another (Dan 3 and 6).

[13]The definitive study on kingship in the ancient Near East is Henri Frankfort, *Kingship and the Gods: A Study of Ancient Near Eastern Religion as the Integration of Society and Nature* (Chicago: University of Chicago Press, 1948). Also useful is Ivan Engell, *Studies in Divine Kingship in the Ancient Near East*, 2nd ed. (Oxford: Basil Blackwell, 1967), although Engell tends to exaggerate in claiming that ancient Near Eastern kings were quite literally deified.

[14]For references to ancient Near Eastern kings (and some priests) as the image of a particular god, see Phyllis A. Bird, " 'Male and Female He Created Them': Gen 1:27b in the Context of the Priestly Account of Creation," *Harvard Theological Review* 74, no. 2 (1981): 129-59; D. J. A. Clines, "The Image of God in Man," *Tyndale Bulletin* 19 (1968): 53-103; and Jeffrey H. Tigay, "The Image of God and the Flood: Some New Developments," in *Studies in Jewish Education and Judaica in Honor of Louis Newman*, ed. Alexander M. Shapiro and Burton I. Cohen (New York: KTAV, 1984), pp. 169-82.

[15]It is difficult for us to grasp the aura of godlike magnificence which was thought to rest on royal and cultic personages or the allure and attraction this would have had in ancient societies. Something of this magnificence and allure is powerfully communicated in the robust (and quite accurate) retelling of the ancient Gilgamesh Epic by Robert Silverberg in his historical novel *Gilgamesh the King* (Toronto: Bantam Books, 1985).

[16]See the detailed description of a ritual text for consecration of a cult statue in Thorkild Jacobsen, "The Graven Image," in *Ancient Israelite Religion: Essays in Honor of Frank Moore Cross*, ed. Patrick D. Miller Jr., Paul D. Hanson and S. Dean McBride (Philadelphia: Fortress, 1987), pp. 15-32. Jacobsen himself suggests the analogy of transubstantiation (p. 23).

[17]This was true primarily for contact with the major national deities of the land, those at the top of the divine hierarchy. Many people also participated in the worship of various "personal" gods and goddesses, access to whom was mediated by household shrines and images not under the direct supervision of the elites. For references in the Bible to such household gods, see Genesis 31:19, 30-32.

[18]For English translations of the Enuma Elish see E. A. Speiser, "Akkadian Myths and Epics," in *Ancient Near Eastern Texts Relating to the Old Testament*, ed. James B. Pritchard, 3rd ed. with supplement (Princeton, N.J.: Princeton University Press, 1969), pp. 60-72; Alexander Heidel, *The Babylonian Genesis: The Story of Creation*, 2nd ed. (Chicago: University of Chicago Press, 1951), chap. 1; and Stephanie Dalley, "The Epic of Creation," in *Myths from Mesopotamia: Creation, the Flood, Gilgamesh and Others* (Oxford: Oxford University Press, 1989), pp. 228-77.

[19]For an English translation of the ritual text used for the Babylonian new year festival (which lasted eleven days), see S. H. Hooke, *Babylonian and Assyrian Religion* (Oxford: Basil Blackwell, 1962), pp. 101-9. The text specifies that the entire Enuma Elish was to be recited before Marduk on the fourth day.

[20]For a commentary on the Enuma Elish that helpfully delineates the major characters and

the unfolding plot of the story and attempts to reconstruct the circumstances of its composition in ancient Babylon, see Thorkild Jacobsen, "Second Millennium Metaphors, World Origins and World Order: The Creation Epic," chap. 6 in *The Treasures of Darkness: A History of Mesopotamian Religion* (New Haven, Conn.: Yale University Press, 1976), pp. 165-91.

[21]Enuma Elish 6.5-8. Speiser's translation (see note 18).

[22]Ibid., 6.31-33.

[23]Humanity's creation out of the blood of a slain god (or gods) occurs also in the Sumerian myth Enki and Ninmah and in the short bilingual text known as KAR 4.

[24]The creation of humanity is recorded in Atrahasis 1.189-247. For English translations of the Atrahasis epic see W. G. Lambert and A. R. Millard, *Atra-Ḫasis: The Babylonian Story of the Flood* (Oxford: Oxford University Press, 1969); and Dalley, "Atrahasis," in *Myths from Mesopotamia*, pp. 1-38.

[25]Even the Atrahasis epic may, however, be interpreted as portraying the essentially rebellious nature of humanity if the word for *personality* or *intelligence* is translated as (devious) *plan* or *scheme* and is understood as the basis for later human disturbance of the gods, which led to the flood as punishment. Although this is not the dominant interpretation of the Atrahasis epic, it has been suggested by William Moran in "The Creation of Man in Atrahasis I 192-248," *Bulletin of the American Schools of Oriental Research* 200 (1970): 52.

[26]Speaking of Mesopotamian creation myths in general (whether they had a positive or negative appraisal of humanity), H. F. W. Saggs suggests that such myths were "not basically a comment on the nature of man [as an abstract theological doctrine] but an explanation of a particular social system, heavily dependent upon communal irrigation and agriculture, for which the gods' estates were primary foci of administration." See Saggs, *The Encounter with the Divine in Mesopotamia and Israel* (London: Athlone, 1978), p. 168. We do not have to accept Saggs's artificial distinction between theology and society to agree with his point. Indeed, we would argue that theology functions here ideologically to legitimate the social order.

[27]See Genesis 1:3, 6, 9, 11, 14, 20, 24, 26 for the series of divine pronouncements or decrees (known as *fiats*, from the Latin for "let there be") by which God demarcates the various regions or spaces of creation and brings into being the creatures that inhabit these realms.

[28]See, for example, Job 3:8; Psalm 74:14; Psalm 104:26; Isaiah 27:1.

[29]Most of our knowledge about Canaanite mythology comes from the so-called Baal cycle of myths discovered at Ras Shamra (ancient Ugarit) and written in Ugaritic, the closest ancient language to biblical Hebrew. In these myths Baal does battle sometimes with the waters (named *yām* or *nāhār*, which in both Ugaritic and Hebrew are the usual words for sea and river) and sometimes with a water-serpent named Lotan, which is the Ugaritic equivalent of Hebrew "Leviathan."

[30]For a fuller discussion of the world as God's good creation, see chapter seven.

[31]Our rendering of Genesis 1:26-28 here, and of Psalm 8 in the next paragraph, though based on the NIV, is our own.

[32]The phrase "little lower than God" is literally "little lower than *ᵉlōhîm*." Although *ᵉlōhîm* is the usual Hebrew word for "God," it is a plural noun and can also refer, depending on the context, to other "divine" or "heavenly" beings, such as (false) gods or angels. This is why the Septuagint of Psalm 8:5 renders the Hebrew *ᵉlōhîm* as Greek *angelloi*, which the NIV follows in its translation "the heavenly beings." Both translations, however, point to the same understanding of humans as God's royal representatives on earth. God is commonly

pictured in the Scriptures as a king seated upon a throne, holding court with various angelic creatures who are his royal emissaries and ministers in the world (Is 6 and Rev 4—5 are two vivid examples). Although the angelic attendants of this heavenly court are not explicitly mentioned in Genesis 1, their presence is suggested by the plural language of v. 26, "Let us make humanity in our image, in our likeness," language found also in the question God asks the seraphim at the call of Isaiah: "Whom shall I send? And who will go for us?" (Is 6:8). Whether, then, we have been created like God or like the angels (to whom God has also granted a royal status and task), both Psalm 8 and Genesis 1 describe humanity as God's appointed delegate and representative on earth.

[33]This generosity of God in creating may be seen also in his gracious invitation to the waters (Gen 1:20) and to the earth (Gen 1:11, 24) to participate in creation by bringing forth assorted creatures, and in his delegation of royal power not just to humans (Gen 1:26-28) but to the sun and moon as well (Gen 1:16).

[34]This is the suggestion of Phyllis Trible in *God and the Rhetoric of Sexuality* (Philadelphia: Fortress, 1980). See the entirety of chap. 4, "A Love Story Gone Awry," for a superb literary-theological analysis of the narrative of Genesis 2—3.

[35]By chapter 6 of Genesis, human beings have indeed multiplied and filled the earth as was part of their mandate in 1:28, but the nature of the rule they have exercised (the other part of their mandate) has resulted in the earth's becoming corrupted and filled with violence.

[36]See Paul Ricoeur, *The Symbolism of Evil*, trans. Emerson Buchanan (Boston: Beacon, 1969), pp. 194-98. Ricoeur's extensive analysis of the Enuma Elish occurs in pt. 2, chap. 1: "The Drama of Creation and the 'Ritual' Vision of the World."

[37]Ibid., pp. 182-83.

[38]In chapter seven we will contrast an ontology of primordial violence with an ontology of created goodness.

[39]Even when the image of the dragon is used to describe the devil as the embodiment of evil (as in Rev 12:3 and 9), the saints "overcome" the dragon not by violence but "by the blood of the Lamb and by the word of their testimony" (Rev 12:11). Likewise, Ephesians 6:10-18, which exhorts the church to take up the armor of God to do battle with the devil, counsels us, once armed, to *stand firm* and names *prayer* as the primary weapon of this warfare. Ultimately it is God (and not human beings) who defeats the power of evil (see Rev 20).

[40]On the ethical contrast between the *Chaoskampf* and biblical creation faith see J. Richard Middleton, "Is Creation Theological Inherently Conservative? A Dialogue with Walter Brueggemann," *Harvard Theological Review* 87, no. 3 (1994): 257-77. For Brueggemann's perceptive response, see pp. 279-89.

[41]There are eleven *tôlᵉdôt* headings in all, five introducing narratives (2:4; 6:9; 11:27; 25:19; 37:2) and the rest introducing genealogical lists (5:1; 10:1; 11:10; 25:12; 36:1, 9). For a while some scholars thought that these were markers *concluding*, rather than beginning, units of material (resulting in the translation "this has been the story of Terah," for example, at 11:27). But this could not be the case for at least two reasons. First, there is no such concluding marker at the end of the book of Genesis ("this has been the story of Joseph"). But second, and more important, very few of the *tôlᵉdôt* references (5:1 is an example) could be interpreted as conclusions, whereas reading them as headings or introductions makes sense of them all (including 5:1). To take one prominent example, "the *tôlᵉdôt* of Terah" does not make sense when read as a conclusion to the genealogy from Shem to Abram

(11:10-26) which precedes it, but makes perfect sense as introducing the story of Abraham (11:27—25:11) which follows, since Abraham is Terah's son (that is, the story of Abraham is what *developed out of* Terah). The same is true with the *ţôľᵈôţ* of Isaac (which introduces the story of his sons Jacob and Esau) and of Jacob (which introduces the story of his son Joseph).

⁴²Walter Brueggemann makes this insightful observation in his commentary *Genesis* (Atlanta: John Knox, 1982), p. 48.

⁴³Thanks to our student Shane Cudney for this vivid phrase.

⁴⁴We can make our own pun in English, noting that the towering aspirations of *Babel* have produced instead a chaotic *babble*. And interestingly, just as the ancient, exalted civilization of Babel/Babylon became in the Bible a name of derision, so in our time the term *modern* has largely moved from being a positive ideal of valorization to becoming the description of a failed, and often oppressive, human project.

⁴⁵For a fuller discussion of Egyptian bondage and the exodus, see our chapter five.

⁴⁶The significance of the Sinai covenant in the context of Israel's election and mission is that to accomplish the mediation of God's blessing Israel will have to develop a distinctive manner of social organization, a lifestyle alternative to that of imperial Egypt and Babylon, which will embody God's intent from the very beginning of the story. It is this alternative way of life that the Sinai covenant attempts to shape, with its combination of case laws (if someone does *x*, you shall do *y* as punishment or redress) and hortatory laws, which are not technically laws but ethical exhortations (such as the Ten Commandments and the injunctions concerning aliens, widows and orphans).

⁴⁷Note Helen A. Kenik's claim that the "central tenet" of creation theology is that "God wills that life be for others." See her essay "Toward a Biblical Basis for Creation Theology," in *Western Spirituality: Historical Roots, Ecumenical Routes*, ed. Matthew Fox (Santa Fe, N.M.: Bear & Co., 1981), p. 69. We would suggest that here creation theology and election theology coincide.

⁴⁸But Moses does more than confess his inadequacy for the task and claim he is not a good speaker; in a final act of desperation he pleads for God to send anyone else, but not him (Ex 4:13). Although he receives, like the prophets, assurance of God's presence and empowerment for his mission, his desperation prompts God to propose that his brother Aaron accompany him and speak for him: "It will be as if he were your mouth and as if you were God to him" (4:16). Not only does this description suggest the *imago Dei* theme (Aaron is Moses' authorized mediator), but its restatement in Exodus 7:1 explicitly characterizes Aaron as *Moses'* prophet. The royal-priestly vocation of humanity and the prophetic calling thus clearly overlap.

⁴⁹Solomon begins his reign in a manner reminiscent of Moses, the prophets and David, his father, with an acknowledgment of his inadequacy and dependence on Yahweh (1 Kings 3:7-9). But this humility soon evaporates, leaving us with the portrayal of a typical ancient Near Eastern king, amassing power and wealth for himself at the expense of his subjects. Indeed, Solomon becomes in the end a full-fledged idolater.

⁵⁰Note that Deuteronomy 17:18-20 specified that it was the primary duty of Israel's kings to study and meditate on God's Torah.

⁵¹For a particularly lucid and sensitive analysis of the monarchy in Israel, see Bruce C. Birch, "Royal Ideal and Royal Reality," chap. 6 in *Let Justice Roll Down: The Old Testament, Ethics*

*and Christian Life* (Louisville, Ky.: Westminster/John Knox, 1991), pp. 198-239.

[52]Ecclesiastes never actually claims Solomonic authorship in so many words. The writer describes himself as "son of David, king in Jerusalem" (1:1), which eliminates Saul, who preceded David, and David himself, but would fit any Davidic king from Solomon on. But the writer also describes himself as "king *over Israel* in Jerusalem" (1:12), which seems to eliminate the Davidic kings after Solomon, since upon Solomon's death the nation was split into two, and only Judah (no longer all Israel) was ruled from Jerusalem thereafter. The book's emphasis on wisdom (for which Solomon was renowned) further suggests that the author assumes the persona of Solomon.

[53]Although this is evident from the context (hence the NIV usually translates it as "worthless idols"), it is quite explicit in Jeremiah 8:19, where *hebel* is used interchangeably with *pesel*, the more usual word for idols, which is also found in the second commandment of the Decalogue: "You shall not make for yourself a *pesel* in the form of anything in heaven above or on the earth beneath or in the waters below" (Ex 20:4; Deut 5:6).

[54]Similar statements of this exchange of glory occur in Psalm 106, Hosea 4 and Romans 1. Psalm 106:20 describes Israel's very first act of idolatry, the golden calf episode of Exodus 32, as follows: "They exchanged their Glory for an image of a bull, which eats grass." Hosea 4:7 (which occurs, not so coincidentally, in a covenant lawsuit, as does Jer 2:11) describes Israel's persistent forsaking of Yahweh throughout their history. "The more the priests increased, the more they sinned against me; they exchanged their Glory for something disgraceful." And in Romans 1:23, the sin of all humanity is that they "exchanged the glory of the immortal God for an image made to look like mortal man and birds and animals and reptiles."

[55]Hence the famous essay of C. S. Lewis entitled "The Weight of Glory," chap. 2 in *Transposition and Other Addresses* (London: Geoffrey Bles, 1949), pp. 21-33. This essay has been republished many times in various anthologies of Lewis's writings.

[56]The metaphors of weight and lightness are often employed to describe the distinction between modernity and postmodernity. See Gary J. Percespe, "The Unbearable Lightness of Being Postmodern," *Christian Scholar's Review* 20, no. 2 (1990): 118-35. Milan Kundera's *The Unbearable Lightness of Being* (New York: Harper & Row, 1984) is often taken to be the paradigmatically postmodern novel. Kundera explains what he means by "lightness" in *The Art of the Novel*, trans. Linda Asher (New York: Grove, 1986). Referring to Descartes's view of man as the master and proprietor of nature, Kundera says, "Having brought off miracles in science and technology, this 'master and proprietor' is suddenly realizing that he owns nothing and is master neither of nature (it is vanishing, little by little, from the planet), nor of History (it has escaped him), nor of himself (he is led by the irrational forces of his soul). But if God is gone and man is no longer master; then who is master? The planet is moving through the void without a master. There it is, the unbearable lightness of being" (p. 41). For Kundera the only alternative is to have the weighty burden of a master, whether that be the totalitarian regime of Kundera's communist Czechoslovakia or some other totalizing vision of the world.

[57]Note that the *tôlᵉdôt* of Adam (Gen 5) traces the lineage not of Cain but of Seth, whom God granted in place of Abel (Gen 4:25) and to whom the *imago Dei* is transmitted (5:1-3).

[58]This is reflected in the NRSV translation of Hebrews 11:4.

[59]Note that the contrast between "futility" and "glory" is applied to the entire creation. Note

further that *mataiotēs*, the Greek word for "futility" in verse 20, and *doxa*, the Greek word for "glory" in verse 21, are the typical words used in the Septuagint to translate *hebel* and *kābôd*, respectively.

[60]See our discussion of the holiness ideology in chapter five.

[61]Authors' translation.

[62]The enthronement on a cross is an ironic theme in Mark's Gospel. It is signaled by Mark's description of the crucifixion of Jesus: "The written notice of the charge against him read: THE KING OF THE JEWS. They crucified two robbers with him, one on his right and one on his left" (Mk 15:26-27). This ironic portrayal is alluded to earlier in Mark, when two of the disciples demand places of privilege in the Messianic kingdom: "Let one of us sit at your right and the other at your left in your glory" (Mk 10:37). The irony is clear to the reader (if not to the disciples) when Jesus tells them that they don't know what they are asking (10:38) and that those places have already been assigned (10:40), alluding to the crucifixion scene. But the enthronement of the Messiah on a cross is also a Johannine theme, indicated by the ambiguity of Jesus' sayings about being "lifted up" (Jn 3:18; 8:28; 12:32-34) in connection with both his crucifixion and his glorification. Drawing perhaps on the lifting up of the suffering servant in Isaiah 52:13 (the same word, *hypsoō*, is used in both John and the Septuagint of that text), John portrays the death of Jesus as an exaltation, the inextricable beginning of his Messianic glorification, which finds its climax in the resurrection and ascension.

[63]Although the exact significance of this scroll (Rev 5:5, 7, 9) is shrouded in mystery and subject to great debate, in the context of the book of Revelation it seems to have something to do with the consummation of history and the enactment of God's purposes. It might well be taken to symbolize the unraveling of plot conflict in the story of the world.

[64]Biblical scholars have had a hard time understanding how a hymn describing Jesus' unique preexistent status (note the wording "in the form of God" and "equality with God") and his unique exaltation above every creature, resulting in universal acclamation and worship, could be used by Paul as an example for Christians to follow. Scholars therefore have been divided on whether the hymn teaches the deity of Christ *or* the imitation of Christ. See the extended discussion of this issue in N. T. Wright's *The Climax of the Covenant: Christ and the Law in Pauline Theology* (Edinburgh: T & T Clark/Minneapolis: Fortress, 1991), chap. 4. Wright makes the profound suggestion that Paul is teaching *both* the deity and the imitation of Christ by arguing that since it is God's characteristic modus operandi to use his divine power and prerogatives not for his own advancement, but compassionately on behalf of others, this ought to be the model for how we use our (human) power and prerogatives too.

[65]Cf. the parallel text in Luke 22:25-27, which occurs at the Last Supper in the context of Jesus' explanation of the significance of his death.

[66]See Matthew 28:19, Luke 24:47-48, John 20:21 and Acts 1:8. Note that whereas the exilic Israelites are called to be God's "witnesses" in Isaiah 32:10-12, Jesus calls the disciples his "witnesses" in Luke 24:48 and Acts 1:8.

[67]Authors' revision of the NIV. The renewal of the image of God in the church is alluded to in many New Testament texts, but it is mentioned explicitly in Romans 8:29, 1 Corinthians 15:49, 2 Corinthians 3:18, Ephesians 4:24, Colossians 3:10 and 1 John 3:2. See our earlier discussion of this theme in *The Transforming Vision*, chap. 5, esp. pp. 83-88.

[68]On the royal/judicial functioning of eschatological humanity, see also Luke 22:30, 1 Corin-

thians 6:2, 2 Timothy 2:12 and Revelation 20:4, 6.
[69]For our understanding of all of life as both divine gift and call, we are profoundly indebted to our colleague James H. Olthuis of the Institute for Christian Studies, Toronto. A convenient summary of Olthuis's views may be found in his "Be(com)ing: Humankind as Gift and Call," *Philosophia Reformata* 58, no. 2 (1993): 153-72 (see esp. pp. 170-72).
[70]From the song "Hills of Morning" by Bruce Cockburn, on the album *Dancing in the Dragon's Jaws,* © 1978 by Golden Mountain Music Corp. We have interacted extensively with the imagery of Christ as dancer in this song in "Dancing in the Dragon's Jaws: Imaging God at the End of the Twentieth Century," *The Crucible* 2, no. 3 (1992): 11-18.

### Chapter 7: Reality Isn't What It's Meant to Be
[1]Douglas Adams, *Mostly Harmless* (London: William Heinemann, 1992), pp. 83-84.
[2]Ibid., p. 89.
[3]Mark C. Taylor, *Erring: A Postmodern A/theology* (Chicago: University of Chicago Press, 1984), pp. 147, 150, 157, 156. We are indebted to James Olthuis for alerting us to these dimensions of Taylor's thought in his article "Crossing the Threshold: Sojourning Together in the Wild Spaces of Love . . . Glimpses of a Post/modern Theology," *Toronto Journal of Theology,* forthcoming.
[4]The problem of *roots* and the search for a place to call *home* was the theme of *Utne Reader* 39 (March/June 1990). See especially John Berger's article "You Can't Go Home: The Hidden Pain of 20th Century Life" (pp. 85-87).
[5]Peter Berger and Thomas Luckmann, *The Social Construction of Reality: A Treatise on the Sociology of Knowledge* (Garden City, N.Y.: Doubleday, 1966). Similar arguments were advanced with more theological and historical depth by Wolfhart Pannenberg, *Anthropology in Theological Perspective,* trans. M. J. O'Connell (Philadelphia: Westminster, 1985). For a critical appraisal of Pannenberg's anthropology see Brian J. Walsh, "A Critical Review of Wolfhart Pannenberg's *Anthropology in Theological Perspective,*" *Christian Scholar's Review* 15, no. 8 (1986): 247-59.
[6]See Peter Berger, Brigitte Berger and Hansfried Kellner, *The Homeless Mind: Modernization and Consciousness* (New York: Vintage, 1973).
[7]See Peter Berger, *The Sacred Canopy: Elements of a Sociological Theory of Religion* (Garden City, N.Y.: Doubleday/Anchor, 1969).
[8]Jean-François Lyotard, *The Postmodern Condition: A Report on Knowledge,* trans. Geoff Bennington and Brian Massumi (Minneapolis: University of Minnesota Press, 1984); Jacques Derrida, *Positions* (Chicago: University of Chicago Press, 1981); Michel Foucault, *Madness and Civilization* (New York: Vintage, 1973). Terry Eagleton says, "Post-modernism signals the death of such 'meta-narratives' whose secretly terroristic function was to ground and legitimate the illusion of a 'universal' human history." From "Awakening from Modernity," *Times Literary Supplement,* February 20, 1987; cited by David Harvey in *The Condition of Postmodernity: An Enquiry into the Origins of Cultural Change* (Oxford: Basil Blackwell, 1989), p. 9.
[9]For example, see Bill Devall and George Sessions, *Deep Ecology: Living As If Nature Mattered* (Salt Lake City: Peregrine Smith Books, 1985); Edward Goldsmith, *The Way: An Ecological Worldview* (London: Rider, 1992); Thomas Berry, *The Dream of the Earth* (San Francisco: Sierra Club Books, 1988); and Carolyn Merchant, *The Death of Nature: Women, Ecology and the Scientific Revolution* (San Francisco: Harper & Row, 1980).

[10]Christopher Lasch, *The Minimal Self: Psychic Survival in Troubled Times* (New York: W. W. Norton, 1984), p. 32.

[11]Walter Truett Anderson, *Reality Isn't What It Used to Be: Theatrical Politics, Ready-to-Wear Religion, Global Myths, Primitive Chic and Other Wonders of the Postmodern World* (San Francisco: Harper & Row, 1990), p. 183.

[12]Allan Bloom, *The Closing of the American Mind* (New York: Simon & Schuster, 1987), p. 25.

[13]As to who gets to speak for American values, we assume that this is a process that is carried out in the body politic of that nation. Insofar as the voices of many peoples in America have been silenced or ignored, then a democracy worthy of its name must insist that all the people, in all of their pluralistic diversity, must get to participate in the identification and revision of "American values."

[14]Albert Borgmann, *Crossing the Postmodern Divide* (Chicago: University of Chicago Press, 1992), p. 117. See also his article "Texts and Things" in *Lifeworld and Technology*, ed. Timothy Casey and Lester Embree (Washington, D.C.: University Press of America, 1990), pp. 93-116.

[15]Borgmann, *Crossing the Postmodern Divide*, pp. 118-19.

[16]Indeed we can find remnants of such an anthropocentrically aggressive attitude toward nonhuman nature in a writer as supposedly postmodernist (though he has abandoned the term) as Richard Rorty. In *Objectivity, Relativism and Truth* (Cambridge: Cambridge University Press, 1991), Rorty suggests that we need to change our metaphors of language use from those of "finding" to those of "making" (p. 189). He says that modernist language about hard facts, objectivity and representationalism is "masochistic," and he proposes instead that we employ metaphors of "linguistic behavior as tool-using, as grabbing hold of causal forces and making them do what we want" (p. 81). When he later describes our interpretive actions as "shoving items in the environment around" (p. 93) and claims that he wants to "ram home the point" that there is no God's-eye view or essential characterization of the world (p. 87), one might suspect that he has replaced representationalistic masochism with a constructivist sadism. At the very least this language is aggressive and violent. There is no sense of humility or respect for the givenness of the world in Rorty's intransigently anthropocentric worldview.

[17]We realize that *covenant* is a technical term in the Bible for God's validation of a relationship by an oath or a pledge after it has been threatened, as in the covenant with creation after the flood (Gen 9), the covenant with Abraham and Sarah after their barrenness (Gen 17) and the covenant with Israel after Egyptian bondage. (See John Stek, " 'Covenant' Overload in Reformed Theology," *Calvin Theological Journal* 29, no. 1 [1994]: 12-41.) There is, however, a long and important theological tradition of broadening the term somewhat to refer to the original relationship itself. Furthermore, in our present postfall context, a context threatened by human violence, God's relationship with creation is indeed covenantal, even in the narrower sense.

[18]Martin Buber, *I and Thou*, trans. Walter Kaufmann (New York: Charles Scribner's Sons, 1970), p. 69.

[19]Creation by the word (*creatio per verbum*) is a foundational biblical teaching. See Genesis 1; Psalm 33:6-9; 147:7-11, 15-20; 148:5-8; Hebrews 11:3; 2 Peter 3:5-8. And this creational word is identified with the Incarnate Word, Jesus Christ, in John 1:1-5; Colossians 1:15-20; Hebrews 1:1-3. We have discussed this and other dimensions of the biblical view of creation further in *The Transforming Vision: Shaping a Christian World View* (Downers Grove, Ill.: InterVarsity Press, 1984), chap. 3.

[20]We are indebted to John Stek of Calvin Theological Seminary for this reading of the rainbow in Genesis 9.

[21]On the covenantal relationship between God and creation see also Jeremiah 33:20-26 and Hosea 2:14-23.

[22]Walter Brueggemann, "Covenanting as Human Vocation," *Interpretation* 33, no. 2 (1979): 116.

[23]It is important that we are careful to maintain that God's love in creating the world is fundamentally a matter of gratuitous choice, not some kind of ontological necessity. For a critique of a contemporary theological articulation of the doctrine of creation that unwittingly reverts to such necessity see Brian Walsh's article "Theology of Hope and the Doctrine of Creation: An Appraisal of Jürgen Moltmann," *Evangelical Quarterly* 59, no. 1 (1987): 53-73.

For a classic articulation of the Christian understanding of creation see Langdon Gilkey, *Maker of Heaven and Earth* (1959; reprint, Lanham, Md.: University Press of America, 1986). Also instructive is Douglas John Hall, *Imaging God: Dominion as Stewardship* (Grand Rapids, Mich.: Eerdmans/New York: Friendship, 1986), pp. 132-37.

[24]See Walter Brueggemann, *Texts Under Negotiation: The Bible and Postmodern Imagination* (Minneapolis: Augsburg/Fortress, 1993), beginning at p. 29, and Pedro Trigo, *Creation and History*, trans. Robert R. Barr (Maryknoll, N.Y.: Orbis, 1991), p. 81.

[25]Thomas Berry, *The Dream of the Earth* (San Francisco: Sierra Club Books, 1988), pp. 16-17. Later in the book he says, "In relation to the earth, we have been autistic for centuries. Only now have we begun to listen with some attention and with a willingness to respond to the earth's demands that we cease our industrial assault, that we abandon our inner rage against the conditions of our earthly existence, that we renew our human participation in the grand liturgy of the universe" (p. 215). See also pp. 23, 35.

[26]For further discussion of these themes with specific reference to trees and forestry, see Brian J. Walsh, Marianne B. Karsh and Nik Ansell, "Trees, Forestry and the Responsiveness of Creation," *Cross Currents* 44, no. 2 (1994): 149-62.

[27]See Psalm 24:1-2; 95:1-5; 119:91.

[28]See Psalm 104:27-30; 136:25; 145:15, 16.

[29]See Psalm 19 and Romans 1:18-20. Calvin Seerveld speaks evocatively of the glossolalia of creation in *Rainbows for the Fallen World* (Toronto: Tuppance, 1980), pp. 10-17. See also Roland Murphy, "Wisdom and Creation," *Journal of Biblical Literature* 104, no. 1 (1984): 6.

[30]See Joshua 24:27.

[31]See Psalm 148; 150:6. For further reflection on these themes see Terence E. Fretheim, "Nature's Praise of God in the Psalms," *Ex Auditu* 3 (1987): 16-30.

[32]See Jeremiah 12:4; 14:2-6; 22:29; 23:10; Hosea 4:1-3. On themes of creational mourning and hope in Jeremiah see Brian Walsh, *Subversive Christianity: Imaging God in a Dangerous Time* (1992; Seattle: Alta Vista College Press, 1994), chap. 4.

[33]See Sylvia C. Keesmaat, "Exodus and the Intertextual Transformation of Tradition in Romans 8.14-30," *Journal for the Study of the New Testament* 54 (1994). Keesmaat develops these themes at greater length in "Paul's Use of the Exodus Tradition in Romans and Galatians," D.Phil. dissertation, Oxford University, 1994.

[34]Rorty, *Objectivism, Relativism and Truth*, pp. 5-6.

[35]In Martin Buber's terms, we need to open ourselves to an I-Thou relationship with the nonhuman. Speaking specifically of trees, Buber says, "But it can also happen, if will and

grace are joined, that as I contemplate the tree I am drawn into a relation, and the tree ceases to be an It" (*I and Thou*, p. 57). If we do open ourselves to creation in this way, then we must enter into a relationship of reciprocity characterized by "tenderness" (p. 79). Unfortunately, in both modernity and postmodernity such "will and grace" have, by and large, not been joined.

[36]On the nature of confessional language see Langdon Gilkey, *Naming the Whirlwind: The Renewal of God Language* (Indianapolis: Bobbs-Merrill, 1969), and James H. Olthuis et al., *A Hermeneutics of Ultimacy: Peril or Promise?* Christian Studies Today Series (Lanham, Md.: University Press of America, 1986).

[37]Walter Brueggemann contrasts a worldview focused on commodity with one focused on covenant: "Whereas commoditization presents the self as the sufficient and principal actor, covenant hosts the other as the focus of well being. . . . At the heart of the matter, the contrast of *commodity* and *covenant* hinges upon the reliability of the other" (*Texts Under Negotiation*, p. 54). In a biblical worldview the very reliability of the created other ultimately depends upon the reliability of the Creator who is known by his *ḥesed*.

John F. Kavanaugh makes a similar distinction between what he calls the "commodity form" and the "personal form" in *Following Christ in a Consumer Society: The Spirituality of Cultural Resistance* (Maryknoll, N.Y.: Orbis, 1981).

[38]Roger Lundin, *The Culture of Interpretation: Christian Faith and the Postmodern World* (Grand Rapids, Mich.: Eerdmans, 1993), p. 103. Lundin goes on to say, "This ingratitude, and its attendant resentment, are distinguishing attributes of much of contemporary literary and cultural theory." And he offers essayist and environmentalist Wendell Berry and poet Richard Wilbur as corrective voices that speak of the "grace of the given."

[39]John Milbank, *Theology and Social Theory: Beyond Secular Reason* (Oxford: Basil Blackwell, 1990), p. 4.

[40]Trigo, *Creation and History*, p. 80.

[41]Middleton has addressed this question in "Is Creation Theology Inherently Conservative? A Dialogue with Walter Brueggemann," *Harvard Theological Review* 87, no. 3 (1994): 257-77 (for Brueggemann's response see pp. 279-89). On the distinction between worldviews and myths that view evil and chaos to be primordial and the biblical worldview of primordial creational goodness, see Paul Ricoeur, *The Symbolism of Evil*, trans. E. Buchanan (Boston: Beacon, 1967); Paul Ricoeur, "The Hermeneutics of Symbols and Philosophical Reflection," in *Paul Ricoeur: An Anthology of His Work*, ed. C. Reagon and D. Stewart (Boston: Beacon, 1978); and Gilkey, *Maker of Heaven and Earth*, chap. 7.

[42]Trigo, *Creation and History*, p. 57. Later Trigo says, "In conclusion, we affirm the struggle [with real historical and institutional evil] because evil really exists, and it must be overcome. And we affirm it because good is deeper within us than we are within ourselves" (pp. 86-87).

[43]On the relationship of sovereignty and intimacy in creation see Bruce C. Birch, *Let Justice Roll Down: The Old Testament, Ethics and Christian Life* (Louisville, Ky.: Westminster/John Knox, 1991), chap. 3. On the contrast of the biblical account of creation with ancient Near Eastern accounts of struggles with primordial chaos see our discussion in chapter six; also Bernhard W. Anderson, *Creation Versus Chaos* (1967; Philadelphia: Fortress, 1987); and Gerhard F. Hasel, "The Polemic Nature of the Genesis Cosmology," *Evangelical Quarterly* 46 (1974): 81-102.

[44]Langdon Gilkey is right when he describes evil as "an intruder into a good creation and not

a necessary aspect of it" (*Maker of Heaven and Earth*, p. 185). Herman Bavinck described evil this way: "But although it exists, it has no right of existence; it should not exist, and therefore it shall not exist" (*The Philosophy of Revelation* [Grand Rapids, Mich.: Eerdmans, 1953], p. 308).

[45]This is John Milbank's term. See *Theology and Social Theory*, p. 279. Later, Milbank says, "By exposing the critical non-necessity of the reading of reality as conflictual . . . an alternative possibility of reading reality as of itself peaceful is gradually opened to view" (p. 296). Similarly, Walter Brueggemann, commenting on exilic texts, says, "Peacemaking is not only a vocation to which we are summoned but a cosmic commitment structured into reality that originates in the very heart of God" (*Interpretation and Obedience: From Faithful Reading to Faithful Living* [Minneapolis: Augsburg/Fortress, 1991], p. 208).

[46]Milbank, *Theology and Social Theory*, p. 5. Emphasis in original.

[47]We have addressed the problem of reductionism further in *The Transforming Vision*, chap. 12.

[48]Milbank contrasts the "oppositional difference" of Nietzschean philosophy with a Christian understanding of "affirmative difference" (*Theology and Social Theory*, p. 289).

[49]Brueggemann, *Texts Under Negotiation*, p. 51. Tom Sine also sees the power of a vision of new creation for a postmodern world. See his *Wild Hope* (Dallas: Word, 1991), chap. 9.

[50]See Jane Wagner, *The Search for Signs of Intelligent Life in the Universe* (New York: Harper & Row, 1985), p. 18.

[51]James Olthuis raises the question of whether we experience our life as "embedded" in the world or "entangled." See "An Ethics of Compassion: Ethics in a Post-Modernist Age," in *What Right Does Ethics Have? Public Philosophy in a Pluralistic Culture*, ed. Sander Griffioen (Amsterdam: Vrije Universiteit Press, 1990), p. 140. Whereas "embedded" affirms the goodness of our creatureliness, "entangled" draws attention to the ambiguity and brokenness of that creatureliness. Perhaps we could put the question this way: Are we embedded in our creational home or entangled in a deathly wilderness? We will see that it is precisely in the wilderness that God creates a creational home.

[52]See also Job 12:24; Psalm 107:40; Jeremiah 4:23.

[53]Walter Brueggemann, *The Land*, Overtures to Biblical Theology Series (Philadelphia: Fortress, 1977), pp. 34-35. See also his essays on land in *Interpretation and Obedience*, chaps. 11 and 12. Also instructive on the theme of land in the Bible are two books by Christopher J. H. Wright, *An Eye for an Eye: The Place of Old Testament Ethics Today* (Downers Grove, Ill.: InterVarsity Press, 1983); and his more technical *God's People in God's Land: Family, Land and Property in the Old Testament* (Grand Rapids, Mich.: Eerdmans/Exeter, U.K.: Paternoster, 1990).

[54]On reading the exodus story in terms of the forces of creation and anticreation see Terence Fretheim's commentary *Exodus*, Interpretation Series (Louisville, Ky.: John Knox, 1991). See also his article "The Plagues as Ecological Signs of Historical Disaster," *Journal of Biblical Literature* 110, no. 3 (1991): 385-96.

[55]See James H. Olthuis, "Be(com)ing: Humankind as Gift and Call," *Philosophia Reformata* 58 (1993): 153-72.

[56]See especially Deuteronomy 6 and 8.

[57]Brueggemann says, "The gifted land is covenanted land. It is not only nourishing space. It is also covenanted place" (*The Land*, p. 52).

[58]See the injunctions about the sabbatical year and the year of Jubilee in Leviticus 25.

[59]George Mendenhall, "The Monarchy," *Interpretation* 29 (1975): 160.

[60]Commenting on Jeremiah, Brueggemann says, "Israel had become numbed and dull, stupid (4.22), having lost the capacity to be embarrassed (8.12). In its alienated security it had settled for *nonreflective apathy*, surely the last achievement of *amnesia* in the land" (*The Land*, p. 111). Later he says that keeping land depends "on knowing that life is rooted in dialogue, of speaking and having to answer, of being surprised and precarious in the exchange which gives life" (p. 121).

[61]For a profound discussion of this theme, see Walter Brueggemann, *The Prophetic Imagination* (Philadelphia: Fortress, 1978).

[62]Brueggemann, *The Land*, pp. 125-26.

[63]"The Bible never denies that there is landlessness or that it is deathly. But it rejects every suggestion that landlessness is finally the will of God" (ibid., p. 127).

[64]Brueggemann makes this point in *Hopeful Imagination: Prophetic Voices in Exile* (Philadelphia: Fortress, 1986), chap. 5.

[65]In Romans 8:19-21 the nonhuman creation anxiously longs for the homecoming of the people of God because only in that event does creation experience its liberation.

[66]Brueggemann, *The Land*, p. 148.

[67]On the various movements of renewal in first-century Israel see N. T. Wright, *The New Testament and the People of God* (London: SPCK/Minneapolis: Fortress, 1992), chap. 7; Gerd Theissen, *The Shadow of the Galilean: The Quest of the Historical Jesus in Narrative Form*, trans. John Bowden (London: SCM Press, 1987); and Marcus Borg, *Jesus, a New Vision: Spirit, Culture and the Life of Discipleship* (San Francisco: Harper & Row, 1987).

[68]Brueggemann, *The Land*, p. 172.

[69]See Matthew 11:12.

[70]Parts of the following discussion of creation order have also been published in Brian Walsh's introductory chapter, "Setting the Table," in *An Ethos of Compassion and the Integrity of Creation*, ed. Robert VanderVennen (Lanham, Md.: University Press of America, forthcoming).

[71]Walter Brueggemann, "A Shape for Old Testament Theology, I: Structure Legitimation," *Catholic Biblical Quarterly* 47, no. 1 (1985): 40. This article and its sequel, "A Shape for Old Testament Theology, II: Embrace of Pain," *Catholic Biblical Quarterly* 47, no. 3 (1985), are foundational to the following discussion.

[72]Ibid., p. 41.

[73]See Walter Brueggemann, *Living Toward a Vision: Biblical Reflections on Shalom*, 2nd ed. (New York: United Church Press, 1982); and Nicholas Wolterstorff, *Until Justice and Peace Embrace* (Grand Rapids, Mich.: Eerdmans, 1984).

[74]See Psalm 68:28-31; 89:9-13; Isaiah 30:7; 51:9-11; Jeremiah 51:34-36, 42-44; Ezekiel 29:2-6, 32:2-4. For helpful biblical reflection on creation and chaos see Anderson, *Creation Versus Chaos*, and Trigo, *Creation and History*.

[75]See Brueggemann, *Living Toward a Vision*, p. 92.

[76]Brueggemann, "Shape for Old Testament Theology, I," p. 44. On pain and the church's mission see J. Richard Middleton, "Voices from the Ragged Edge: How the Psalms Can Help Us Process Pain," *Canadian Theological Society Newsletter* 41, no. 1 (1994): 4-7.

[77]Brueggemann, "Shape for Old Testament Theology, II," p. 399.

[78]Ibid., p. 402.

[79]Adams, *Mostly Harmless*, p. 84.

[80]Linda Hutcheon, *The Politics of Postmodernism* (London: Routledge, 1989), p. 34.

[81]As Langdon Gilkey puts it: "Naive realism assumes (1) that ontological entity and scientific explanation are isomorphic; (2) that this explanation uncovers the entire 'mystery' of the object, so that no other explanations are either necessary or possible; and (3) that any alternative explanations, or models of inquiry, are competing explanations on the same plane, unequivocally false, and thus cancelled out by the 'correct' explanation." See *Nature, Reality and the Sacred: The Nexus of Science and Religion*, Theology and the Sciences Series (Minneapolis: Fortress, 1993), pp. 50-51.

While one might be hard-pressed to find any philosopher of science or practicing scientist who holds to such a stark naive realism, we suspect that this remains the dominant view of scientific knowledge in the popular imagination.

[82]One of the first Christian philosophers to attend to the perspectival nature of all knowing was Herman Dooyeweerd. He argued that all knowing was rooted in the heart-centeredness of the knowing subject. Therefore, noetic access to the world is always mediated by the perspective of the knower. Furthermore, that perspective is characterized most fundamentally by the religious standpoint and worldview of the subject. See his *A New Critique of Theoretical Thought*, vol. 1, trans. David H. Freeman and William S. Young (Philadelphia: Presbyterian & Reformed, 1953), esp. the prolegomenon and chap. 2.

For an introduction to Dooyeweerd's thought see Brian Walsh and Jon Chaplin, "Dooyeweerd's Contribution to a Christian Philosophical Paradigm," *Crux* 19, no. 1 (1983): 8-22. An extended (and very accessible) discussion of a perspectival epistemology in the tradition of Dooyeweerd can be found in Roy Clouser's book *The Myth of Religious Neutrality: An Essay on the Hidden Role of Religious Belief in Theories* (Notre Dame, Ind.: University of Notre Dame Press, 1991). Also helpful are the essays edited by C. T. McIntire, *The Legacy of Herman Dooyeweerd: Reflections on Critical Philosophy in the Christian Tradition* (Lanham, Md.: University Press of America, 1985), especially the essay by Hendrik Hart, "Dooyeweerd's *Gegenstand* Theory of Theory."

[83]For example, see Gilkey, *Nature, Reality and the Sacred;* Wright, *The New Testament and the People of God;* Ian Barbour, *Issues in Science and Religion* (New York: Harper Torchbooks, 1971); and Ben Meyer, *Critical Realism and the New Testament,* Princeton Theological Monograph Series 17 (Allison Park, Penn.: Pickwick, 1989).

One can also detect this kind of critical realism at work in Mary Stewart Van Leeuwen, *The Person in Psychology: A Contemporary Christian Appraisal* (Leicester, U.K.: Inter-Varsity Press/Grand Rapids, Mich.: Eerdmans, 1985); Richard T. Wright, *Biology Through the Eyes of Faith* (New York: Harper & Row, 1989); Susan Gallagher and Roger Lundin, *Literature Through the Eyes of Faith* (New York: Harper & Row, 1989); and David Fraser and Tony Campolo, *Sociology Through the Eyes of Faith* (New York: Harper & Row, 1992).

[84]Wright, *The New Testament and the People of God,* p. 35. Emphases are Wright's.

[85]Gilkey, *Nature, Reality and the Sacred,* pp. 31-32 (emphasis added).

[86]Ibid., p. 214, n. 33.

[87]Jeffrey Stout describes epistemological realism (critical or otherwise) as "the hopeless attempt to make correspondence to undescribed reality serve as a criterion or explanation of truth (hopeless because criteria and explanations need to place reality under a description if they are to serve any purpose whatsoever)." Stout goes on to say that any correspondence theory that discerns truth in "the relation between our true beliefs and things as they are in

themselves, independent of our descriptions of them," is "a leading cause of mental cramps." See *Ethics After Babel: The Languages of Morals and Their Discontents* (Boston: Beacon, 1988), p. 298.

[88]Olthuis, "An Ethics of Compassion," p. 138.

[89]Wright, *The New Testament and the People of God*, p. 45.

[90]Similar themes are developed in Walsh, Karsh and Ansell, "Trees, Forestry and the Responsiveness of Creation."

[91]Trigo, *Creation and History*, p. 87. Emphasis added.

[92]John Milbank describes theology as a "master discourse" because "theology, alone, remains the discourse of non-mastery" (*Theology and Social Theory*, p. 6). While we may wonder why theology, of all the disciplines, has a special claim to the discourse of nonmastery (especially in light of the history of that discipline!), the sentiment of a discourse that demonstrates its mastery precisely by being a discourse of nonmastery concurs with our ideas about a stewardly knowing. But we would argue that all disciplines—indeed all knowing—must be in the mode of service, not mastery.

[93]Wright, *The New Testament and the People of God*, p. 64.

[94]Samuel Smith rightly argues that "God has created an open universe where beings made in God's image have the freedom to shape and reshape their understanding of human experience" ("Words of Hope: A Postmodern Faith," *Faculty Dialogue* 20 [Winter 1993-1994]: 142). Smith's articulation and defense of a Christian postmodern faith in this article resonates well with the position we have developed in this book. We would not embrace, however, a "relativist epistemology" any more than we would adopt "critical realism."

[95]Bruce Cockburn, "Broken Wheel," © Golden Mountain Music Corp., 1981. From the album *Inner City Front*. We have discussed Bruce Cockburn's art in general, and this song in particular, in "Theology at the Rim of a Broken Wheel: Bruce Cockburn and Christian Faith in a Postmodern World," *Grail* 9, no. 2 (1993): 15-39.

[96]Quoted by Stout, *Ethics After Babel*, pp. 1-2.

[97]See also 2 Corinthians 5:17; Ephesians 1:10; Colossians 1:15-20.

### Chapter 8: The Hope of Our Times

[1]We perceive such an abandonment in Mark C. Taylor, *Erring: A Postmodern A/theology* (Chicago: University of Chicago Press, 1984), and Mark S. McLeod, "Making God Dance: Postmodern Theorizing and the Christian College," *Christian Scholar's Review* 21, no. 3 (1992): 275-92. Less extreme, but in the same accommodationist mode, would be Daniel Liechty, *Theology in Postliberal Perspective* (London: SCM/Philadelphia: Trinity Press International, 1990).

[2]For a Christian philosopher's well-entrenched worldview see Ronald Nash, *Worldviews in Conflict* (Grand Rapids, Mich.: Zondervan, 1992). Brian Walsh has critiqued Nash's position in his review of this book in *Calvin Theological Journal* 28 (1993): 505-7.

[3]Jacques Derrida, "Plato's Pharmacy," chap. 1 in *Dissemination*, trans. Barbara Johnson (Chicago: University of Chicago Press, 1981). See our previous analysis of this notion in chap. four.

[4]See Paul Ricoeur, *The Symbolism of Evil*, trans. Emerson Buchanan (Boston: Beacon, 1969), pp. 351-52, 356. Ricoeur is referring to the postcritical appropriation of myths, biblical or otherwise. We are applying the term to our mode of receiving the biblical story after the

demise of modernity. For a similar notion see Walter Brueggemann's helpful analysis of psalms of "new orientation" in *The Message of the Psalms: A Theological Commentary* (Minneapolis: Augsburg, 1984), chap. 1. We have applied Ricoeur's notion of second naiveté and Brueggemann's notion of new orientation to an analysis of the Christian songwriter Bruce Cockburn in "Theology at the Rim of a Broken Wheel: Bruce Cockburn and Christian Faith in a Postmodern World," *Grail* 9, no. 2 (1993): 15-39.

[5] Walter Brueggemann, *The Prophetic Imagination* (Philadelphia: Fortress, 1978), p. 12.

[6] Whereas the former view is typical among evangelical theologians, the latter view was classically formulated by Paul Tillich in the introduction to *Systematic Theology*, vol. 1 (Chicago: University of Chicago Press, 1951), esp. pp. 3-8, 59-66. Correlation is also the basic methodology in Langdon Gilkey, *Message and Existence: An Introduction to Christian Theology* (New York: Seabury, 1979).

[7] We are indebted for this critique of the correlation model to Douglas Harink of the King's College, Edmonton, Alberta. In a panel discussion at the 1991 Canadian Evangelical Theological Association annual meeting on Clark Pinnock's book *Tracking the Maze: Finding Our Way Through Modern Theology from an Evangelical Perspective* (San Francisco: Harper & Row, 1990), Harink highlighted a significant discontinuity between part 3 of the book (consisting of Pinnock's innovative "postliberal" proposals on narrative theology) and the more traditional parts 1 and 2 (in which he utilized the notion of correlation to describe the theological task). Pinnock candidly acknowledged the validity of the observation, noting that part 3 was written some six months after parts 1 and 2 and reflected a shift in his thinking.

[8] Lesslie Newbigin, *The Gospel in a Pluralist Society* (Grand Rapids, Mich.: Eerdmans/Geneva: WCC Publications, 1989), pp. 97-102. Newbigin here utilizes the notion of "indwelling" from Michael Polanyi and the idea of "plausibility structure" from Peter Berger.

[9] Oscar Cullman makes a similar point, though perhaps too individualistically conceived, when he says: "Faith in the New Testament sense is the way by which the past phase of redemptive history becomes effectual for me. . . . [It] means to be convinced of the fact that this entire happening takes place *for me*" (Oscar Cullman, *Christ and Time*, trans. Floyd V. Wilson, rev. ed. [Philadelphia: Westminster, 1964], p. 219).

[10] Walter Brueggemann, *To Pluck Up, to Tear Down: A Commentary on the Book of Jeremiah 1—25* (Grand Rapids, Mich.: Eerdmans/Edinburgh: Handsel, 1987), p. 17 (his emphasis). Although the "text" Brueggemann is here referring to is the book of Jeremiah, his comments are applicable to the entire Bible.

[11] Alasdair MacIntyre, *Whose Justice? Which Rationality?* (Notre Dame, Ind.: University of Notre Dame Press, 1988), pp. 382-83.

[12] Walter Brueggemann, *Texts Under Negotiation: The Bible and Postmodern Imagination* (Minneapolis: Fortress, 1993), esp. chap. 3, but also pp. 18-25.

[13] Phyllis Trible, *Texts of Terror: Literary-Feminist Readings of Biblical Narratives* (Philadelphia: Fortress, 1984).

[14] Besides her careful handling of even the nuances of the texts she exegetes, obvious to anyone who reads her work, Trible's own story of faith is recounted in "The Pilgrim Bible on a Feminist Journey," *Perspectives* 6, no. 9 (1991): 16-19.

[15] Note that this is an earlier Tamar, distinct from the one discussed by Trible in her *Texts of Terror*.

[16] Bruce C. Birch asks, "Why is the upbeat Horatio Alger tale of Joseph interrupted by the story

of Tamar in Gen. 38? Is it to remind us of the ambiguities of righteousness, lest the Joseph story seem too glib?" (in *Let Justice Roll Down: The Old Testament, Ethics and Christian Life* [Louisville, Ky.: Westminster/John Knox, 1991], p. 64). Further specificity of the story's point is up to the reader to reflect on by attention to the actual text of the Tamar story against the background of Joseph's rise.

[17]Indeed, Trible illumines how attention to the larger narrative may compound the terror of the smaller story. Thus the story of the violence against the unnamed woman in Judges 19 serves to legitimate an extravagant amount of further violence, enacted as revenge. The tribe of Benjamin refuse to hand over the original perpetrators (who were from the city of Gibeah); this is used to justify the slaughter of 25,000 Benjaminite men in one day, plus every single woman, child and animal in the city of Gibeah and all the towns of Benjamin. Then, in order for the 600 male survivors of Benjamin to replenish the tribe, the very Israelites who have decimated Benjamin attack the town of Jabesh-Gilead and murder all its inhabitants except 400 young virgins, who are forcibly taken as mates for the Benjaminites. Then 200 other young women who had come out to dance in a yearly festival to Yahweh are abducted for the same purpose. Finally, the book of Judges makes the editorial comment that the reason for this tragic, unbridled violence (when "every man did what was right in his own eyes") is that "in those days there was no king in Israel"—a strange comment, Trible notes, since the sordid story of the house of David illustrates that when there was a king in Israel "royalty did what was right in its own eyes" (*Texts of Terror*, p. 84). Besides David's infamous murder of Uriah to cover his adultery, there is the rape of Tamar by David's son Amnon (one of Trible's texts of terror), along with the revenge killings that followed.

[18]Walter Brueggemann, *Abiding Astonishment: Psalms, Modernity and the Making of History* (Louisville, Ky.: Westminster/John Knox, 1991), p. 49.

[19]Ibid., p. 50.

[20]Trible indicates the significance of canonical shaping for reading texts of terror when she contrasts the seeming blindness to the excessive violence surrounding the murder and dismemberment of the unnamed concubine *within* the book of Judges with the stories that immediately follow the book. In the Masoretic text (the Hebrew Bible) we have the story of Hannah at the start of the book of Samuel, and in the Septuagint (the Greek Bible) we have the story of Ruth. In contrast to the unnamed woman who was horribly brutalized when grace and hospitality were called for, we have two stories of women who received and practiced exactly such grace and hospitality (see *Texts of Terror*, pp. 84-85).

[21]Brueggemann, *Abiding Astonishment*, p. 53. This antitotalizing function leads to Brueggemann's assessment of Scripture in its entirety as "profoundly evangelical, even in those parts of the text that are on first reading visibly antigospel" (*Texts Under Negotiation*, p. 70).

[22]Trible, *Texts of Terror*, pp. 28-29.

[23]Ibid., p. 57. Her emphasis.

[24]This is Trible's literal translation of Judges 19:30, against more traditional readings which obscure the feminine object of the first verb. See *Texts of Terror*, pp. 81-82, for her analysis.

[25]Ibid., p. 86.

[26]Jewish biblical scholar Will Herberg concurs: "Unless we receive this call and respond to it, the redemptive history that we apprehend is not redemptive. It does not really tell us who we are, where we stand, and what we may hope for; it does not really give meaning to existence" ("Biblical Faith as 'Heilgeschichte': The Meaning of Redemptive History in Hu-

man Existence," in *Faith Enacted as History: Essays in Biblical Theology,* ed. Bernhard W. Anderson [Philadelphia: Westminster, 1976], p. 41). Old Testament scholar Dale Patrick has recently elaborated a similar insight in his more technical description of the Bible as a performative text ("The Rhetoric of Revelation," *Horizons in Biblical Theology* 16, no. 1 [1994]: 20-40). Utilizing philosopher John Austin's speech-act theory, Patrick elucidates the "illocutionary" or "perlocutionary" character of Yahweh's self-disclosure to Moses in Exodus 3 (evident in the centrality of imperatives and promises in this self-disclosure), which renders this text (and by implication all of Scripture) formally incomplete, requiring the reader's response *outside the text* (obeying the imperatives and trusting the promises) to make sense of the text as it stands. Patrick's analysis of this performative dimension of the biblical text is helpfully complemented by the narrative analysis of Hanson and Wright which follows.

[27]See Paul D. Hanson's appendix, "Underlying Presuppositions and Method," in *The People Called: The Growth of Community in the Bible* (San Francisco: Harper & Row, 1986), pp. 519-46, and N. T. Wright's "How Can the Bible Be Authoritative?" *Vox Evangelica* 21 (1991): 7-32.

[28]Hanson, *The People Called,* pp. 537, 544.

[29]Ibid., p. 533. Emphasis his.

[30]Whereas Wright suggests a drama in five acts, we have separated his fifth act into two, thus distinguishing the age of the church from the final consummation. Wright's analysis, it seems to us, does not contain quite enough emphasis on the disjunction between the ages, the "not yet" character of the present. For other analyses of the main acts of the biblical drama, see the chapter divisions in Gabriel Fackre, *The Christian Story,* vol. 1, *A Narrative Interpretation of Basic Christian Doctrine,* rev. ed. (Grand Rapids, Mich.: Eerdmans, 1984), and Bernhard W. Anderson, *The Unfolding Drama of the Bible,* 3rd ed. (Philadelphia: Fortress, 1988). Although Fackre divides what we call Act V into two acts and Anderson divides our Act III into four, both agree with us in distinguishing the eschaton or culmination of the drama from the previous act.

[31]Wright, "How Can the Bible Be Authoritative?" p. 18. His emphasis.

[32]In a discussion on biblical authority, Frank Anthony Spina notes that "if the . . . theological story is only stable, it will atrophy by being reduced to propaganda or otiose ritualistic forms. If it is only adaptable, there will be no rootedness or *traditio* [that is, the content which is transmitted]" (Spina, "Revelation, Reformation, Re-creation: Canon and the Theological Foundation of the Christian University," *Christian Scholar's Review* 17, no. 4 [1989]: 326).

[33]Trible, *Texts of Terror,* p. 86.

[34]Ibid., p. 87.

[35]We affirm fully the classic statement on biblical inspiration in 2 Timothy 3:16: "All Scripture is God-breathed and is useful for teaching, rebuking, correcting and training in righteousness." Whereas many who affirm the doctrine of biblical inspiration don't know what to do about difficult texts and so end up *avoiding* them altogether, thus nullifying the point of the doctrine, our proposals concerning the authority of the biblical narrative allow us to put 2 Timothy 3:16 into practice by *attending* to offensive biblical texts in the context of the metanarrative's overall thrust.

[36]On the counterideological function of lament, see our previous discussion in chapter five and also J. Richard Middleton, "Voices from the Ragged Edge: How the Psalms Can Help Us Process Pain," *Canadian Theological Society Newsletter* 14, no. 1 (1994): 4-7. For a summary

of recent scholarship on the lament psalms, see Walter Brueggemann, *The Message of the Psalms: A Theological Commentary* (Minneapolis: Augsburg, 1984), pp. 54-57, and Claus Westermann, *Praise and Lament in the Psalms*, trans. Keith R. Crim and Richard N. Soulen (Atlanta: John Knox, 1981), pp. 52-71.

³⁷The text uses the word *šāmaʿ*, which is better translated as "to hear" than "to understand." See Walter Brueggemann, *Genesis* (Atlanta: John Knox, 1982), p. 103. The word *šāmaʿ* of course also conjures up the Jewish Shema, "Hear, O Israel," found in Deuteronomy 6:4, which calls Israel to worship of the one true God.

³⁸Michael Oakeshott, "The Tower of Babel," in *Rationalism in Politics* (London: Methuen, 1962), cited by Jeffrey Stout, *Ethics After Babel: The Languages of Morals and Their Discontents* (Boston: Beacon, 1988), p. 2.

³⁹Quoted in Stout, *Ethics After Babel*, p. 2.

⁴⁰For a comprehensive portrayal of the condition of first-century (or "second temple") Judaism see N. T. Wright, *The New Testament and the People of God* (London: SPCK/Minneapolis: Fortress, 1992).

⁴¹We have changed the NIV "servants" to "slaves" (either is a legitimate translation) to get at the original sense of the Joel 2 prophecy.

⁴²Walter Brueggemann, *The Prophetic Imagination* (Philadelphia: Fortress, 1978), p. 13.

⁴³See Bob Goudzwaard and Harry de Lange, *Beyond Poverty and Wealth: Toward an Economy of Care*, trans. and ed. Mark Vander Vennen (Grand Rapids, Mich.: Eerdmans, 1994/Toronto: University of Toronto Press, 1995).

⁴⁴See Brian Walsh, Marianne Karsh and Nik Ansell, "Trees, Forestry and the Responsiveness of Creation," *Cross Currents* 44, no. 2 (1994): 149-62.

⁴⁵See Calvin B. DeWitt, ed., *The Environment and the Christian: What Can We Learn from the New Testament?* (Grand Rapids, Mich.: Baker Book House, 1991).

⁴⁶See Stanley Hauerwas and William Willimon, *Resident Aliens: Life in the Christian Colony* (Nashville: Abingdon, 1989).

⁴⁷See Hanson, *The People Called*, esp. pp. 499-518.

⁴⁸We are indebted to the Canadian Christian political advocacy and research organization Citizens for Public Justice (229 College Street, Toronto, Ontario M5T 1R4) as a constant source of such an alternative political imagination.

⁴⁹Brian Walsh has discussed the matter of alternative imagination further in *Subversive Christianity* (1992; Seattle: Alta Vista College Press, 1994), esp. chap. 2, and we have addressed the issue in our "Dancing in the Dragon's Jaws: Imaging God at the End of the Twentieth Century," *The Crucible* 2, no. 3 (1992): 11-18. We have also attempted to foster such a biblical imagination in a book of meditations we authored together with Sylvia C. Keesmaat and Mark Vander Vennen: *The Advent of Justice: A Book of Meditations* (Toronto: Citizens for Public Justice, 1993; Sioux City, Iowa: Dordt College Press, 1994). On imagination, see also Walter Brueggemann, *The Prophetic Imagination*, and his *Hopeful Imagination* (Philadelphia: Fortress, 1986). On the role of dreaming in cultural transformation, see Thomas Berry, *The Dream of the Earth* (San Francisco: Sierra Club Books, 1988).

⁵⁰This dialogue is taken from the screenplay of *The Neverending Story*. The original novel was written by Michael Ende in German. For an English translation, see *The Neverending Story* (New York: Doubleday, 1983).

# Subject Index

Abel, *124, 126, 134-37,* 228
aboriginal people, *12, 76,* 197, 198
Abraham, *92, 98, 99-101,* 129, *135, 181, 186, 188, 189,* 227
absence, *94, 167*
abyss, *25, 36, 37*
Adam, *47, 136,* 228
AIDS, 26
America, *12, 24, 25, 30, 40,* 196, *201, 210,* 221; discovery of, *9, 10;* values of, *147,* 231
angst, 25
anomie, *36, 57, 78, 130, 161, 162, 187,* 201
anxiety, *25, 45, 57, 65, 145,* 155
aphorisms, *74,* 215
*archē/telos,* 70
architecture, *16*
Atrahasis, *116, 117,* 225
authority, *14, 49, 83, 119,* 140, 240
autonomy, *21, 22, 41, 48, 62, 108, 109, 118, 135, 147, 186-89, 199,* 201; *Homo autonomous, 20, 48, 50, 55;* autonomous language, *51;* autonomous subject, *20, 48-52, 56,* 109
Baal, *96, 120, 122,* 225
Babel (Tower of), *15, 16, 19, 27, 43, 44, 126, 127, 133, 164,* 170, *172, 187-90, 192, 199,* 227
baby boom, 25
Babylon, *44, 72, 111-19,* 127, *158, 159, 162, 179,* 199, 206, *214, 223-25,* 227; Israel's exile in, *96, 97, 111-18,* 120, *123, 137, 172*
Barabbas, *104*
Bible, *64, 68, 69, 87, 88, 94,* 123, *126, 129, 131, 134, 146,* 175, *176, 178, 183, 186, 194,* 199, *213, 219-21, 223,* 227, *233, 235, 238, 239;* authority of, *174, 182, 185;* canon of, *82, 88, 99,* 179,

*217, 219, 239;* (meta)narrative of, *181;* New Testament, *104-6, 223,* 238; Old Testament, *88, 93, 95, 99,* 220, 221; worldview of, *148, 148, 153, 157, 161, 164, 168, 169*
*Blade Runner, 78,* 216
blessing, *104, 114, 124, 127-30, 134, 135, 137, 139, 159,* 188
Book of the Covenant, *94*
Cain, *124, 127, 134,* 228
call, *64, 128-30, 139-41, 146, 148, 150, 156, 157, 160-71, 181, 184, 187,* 230, *234,* 239. See also gift
Canaan, *89, 91,* 218. See also land
canon, *13,* 198
capitalism, *55, 60, 72, 201,* 203
*Catch-22, 24, 25,* 201
categorical imperative, *65*
Central America, 9
certainty, *14, 30*
chaos, *37, 44, 72, 115, 118,* 125, *127, 134, 153, 162, 165,* 173, *214, 233,* 235
church, *69, 82, 107, 139-41,* 174, *175, 181-87, 190, 192-95,* 229, 240
cities, *15, 16*
Columbus (story), *9-12, 15,* 197, 198
comedy, *52, 54*
compassion, *82, 93, 107,* 136, *141, 165, 181, 187,* 191
El Conquistador, *9, 11, 48,* 55
consummation, *83, 139,* 154, *181, 229,* 240
control/mastery, *34, 124,* 135, *156, 158, 162, 168, 171,* 206; over humans, *34, 49;* over nature, *14, 17, 19-21, 41, 49, 54, 109,* 153; over destiny, *14*
covenant, *89, 92, 100, 101,* 128-*31, 135, 148, 149, 154,* 158, *160, 185, 188, 191, 194,* 231, *232, 234;* relationships *185, 188*
creation, *91, 100, 103, 106,* 120, *123, 134, 135, 140, 141,* 146-51, *154, 156, 171, 178, 181,* 185, *186, 192, 206, 212, 220,* 221, *225, 231-33,* 235; as good/gift, *152-56, 162, 163, 168,* 169; as home, *156-59,* 234; myth of, *115, 116,* 125; order of, *162-64;* story of, *47, 99*
creational covenental monothe-

ism, *103,* 222
crusades, 72
Crystal Palace, *18*
David, *105, 130, 131, 150,* 228, 239
death, *21, 22, 162, 185, 187,* 192
deconstruction/deconstructionism, *28, 33-37, 165,* 188, *203, 204;* deconstructive therapy, *36, 37, 45*
delegitimation. See legitimation
democracy, *9, 48, 71, 72,* 210, 231. See also liberalism
Diaspora, *94, 188-90*
difference, *35, 36, 83, 154,* 170, *180, 210, 211,* 234
disorientation, *36-38, 42, 46,* 112, *163, 165, 173, 176, 187,* 188
earth, *21, 29, 121-26, 150,* 164, *216, 226, 232* economics, *17, 19, 187, 190, 192, 194, 200,* 204
Eden, *198.* See also Garden (of Eden)
Egypt, *89-94, 105, 128, 156,* 162, *177, 217, 218, 220,* 227; bondage in, *88, 90, 94, 96, 129,* 175, *178, 185,* 227; plagues in, *90*
election, *98, 100-104, 117,* 118, *128-30, 139, 179,* 220; for service, *101*
Enlightenment, *13, 14, 43, 67,* 187, *200, 206, 207,* 219
Enuma Elish, *72, 115-18,* 122, *125, 214, 224,* 225
environment, *29, 37, 145,* 146, *155,* 207
epistemology, *30, 313, 70,* 147, *165-71, 202,* 236; as covenantal stewardship, *147, 167-71;* epistemological self-confidence, *19.* See also perspectivalism, rationality, realism, reason, truth ethics, *45, 57, 59, 65-71, 73, 93, 184, 191, 210, 212,* 213
eschatology, *134, 137, 139,* 181, 229
evil (brokenness/sin), *11, 20, 37, 63, 64, 76, 101, 116, 118,* 125, *137, 140, 153, 220, 226, 233,* 234
exile, *87, 96, 99, 105, 112,* 118, *122, 123, 155, 156, 159-61,* 173-*75, 187, 189, 218-20*
existentialism, 23
exodus, *88, 90, 92, 94-98,* 105, *106, 110, 178, 180, 217,* 220,

## Author Index